Francis Wey

Rome

Francis Wey

Rome

ISBN/EAN: 9783744784870

Printed in Europe, USA, Canada, Australia, Japan

Cover: Foto ©ninafisch / pixelio.de

More available books at **www.hansebooks.com**

ROME

By FRANCIS WEY

WITH
ABOUT TWO HUNDRED AND EIGHTY ILLUSTRATIONS

A New Edition

LONDON
J. S. VIRTUE AND COMPANY, LIMITED, 26, IVY LANE
PATERNOSTER ROW
1887

LONDON:
PRINTED BY J. S. VIRTUE AND CO., LIMITED,
CITY ROAD.

PREFACE.

TRULY Rome is a world: whatever has possessed greatness in the west—art, religion, history—has left its traces in this city. Pagan antiquity, the origin of Christianity and of Byzantine civilisation, the struggles and the transformation of the early middle age, the ecclesiastical supremacy of the thirteenth century, the Renaissance of the fifteenth and sixteenth—all these epochs had Rome for their centre; they covered it with their works, and they live again in it in a crowd of monuments. How many considerable States present us, in comparison with the reminiscences accumulated here, with nothing but fragments without significance! In such a collection each author has made his choice; it struck me that one ought, for once at least, to decide to see all and to study all.

Still, even in a special frame, completeness is rare. As day by day and slowly you pursue the pilgrimage of the wonders of Rome, at each step, in the reminiscences of the inhabitants, in the knowledge of the learned men of the country, in forgotten books, and most of all in personal discoveries, you come upon a series of facts which have not been collected before, and you gradually rectify a multitude of erroneous traditions as to the monuments and works of art. In the midst of the masterpieces that fill the churches and palaces, how many undetected gems! Among the famous ruins, all through the ancient dwellings of the populous quarters and deserted suburbs, how many remarkable footprints that have hitherto been little remarked! Even in the sanctuaries whose very names call to them the attention of all, how many explorations have been left only partly accomplished! Every one has spoken of the Vatican, but its multitudinous collections and the splendid halls raised to contain them have never been the object of a thoroughly complete description. To judge from the works I have consulted, half Rome still awaits its historian : I may hope, then, that long and laborious research will render some service.

If the share of personal research ought to be great, what account ought we not to make of the steps forward taken by erudition! Although surrounded with difficulties and dry details, which too often are the only points that strike the public, this science only aspires to awake the soul of the past ; a new touch, a livelier tint, brought to life again on the likeness of the vanished ages,—such is the last word of the most special monography. I took singular pleasure in this part of my task. There will be found in these pages the results of the most recent works on Roman antiquities, on primitive Christianity, on that strange life of the Renaissance, on the lives of painters and their works ; there will be found here not only the restoration, from the last excavations and from epigraphy, of certain regions, of many edifices of the city of consuls, Cæsars, pontiffs, but also the revelation of curiosities, of monuments hardly exhumed yesterday, such as the barrack of the Vigiles of the seventh cohort, the covered portions of underground Rome, the frescoes of the crypt of St. Clement, the imperial edifices of the Palatine, the admirable paintings of the house of Livia.

The external aspect of things occupies a considerable place in the emotions which make up a stay at Rome : all travellers have felt this ; but it seems to me that our time has new qualities for feeling and describing. The taste for precision, the eye for the beautiful and the interesting, while remaining faithful to reality, are carried very far in our time. Here still, to confine oneself to general impressions is to be incomplete ; we have to do for the sites of Rome and the Campagna, so different from all others, what works of art call for ; we have to be patient, curious, thoroughly penetrated with their poetry. How many pictures then offer themselves to our eyes! The artist finds richer and more varied galleries than those of museums and palaces, and they are no less vivid. The study of monuments and landscapes, that of men and manners, of past and present, mingle incessantly in this book, as they are confused also in the eyes of whoever lives in Rome : you refresh yourself with one after leaving the other ; and then the reader is accustomed to the indefinable charm of *the life of Rome*, and to those delights which you never forget after having once felt them.

Preface.

It had to be one of the cares of my work to seek the drawings which should furnish the best commentary on my descriptions. I am indebted to my publishers for leaving me full liberty, for not shrinking from either the number or the expensive perfection of the engravings; they animate and brighten many pages in which the tongue cannot say all: I could thus reproduce sites and a number of monuments not hitherto published. Eminent artists have given us their assistance, and some their useful advice; namely, Louis Français, Thérond, Catenacci, H. Clerget, C. Nanteuil, Anastasi, Jules Lefebvre, E. Bayard, A. de Neuville, Hector Leroux, Paquier, Viollet-le-Duc, Paul Baudry—artists who have given evidence of their tact in understanding and interpreting works of art and Italian nature.

Can I forget in this band him whom an heroic death has snatched from us? The best studies that Henri Regnault ever designed on wood are devoted to the illustration of this volume. His career, already marked out for glory, was fatally broken; he was only eight-and-twenty years old when he was killed in the defence of his country. Will people find in his rare pictures, as well as in the sketches collected here, the last relics of an artist so highly gifted, the variety of his imagination, his marvellous suppleness in dealing with all kinds of work, his skill in composing scenes and grouping figures?

What shall I say of the general idea of my book? You have no concern with Rome, unless you recognise two sentiments in yourself —the love of the beautiful and respect for what is great.

Rome is the museum of all ages. Above erudition, above scrupulous accuracy and the best conducted researches, what ought to rule here is the love of what Rome has loved; she has preserved her greatness in the world by the passion she declared for all the expressions of the beautiful. Many are the sects to-day in this religion of art, some simply didactic, others philosophical, historical, or even moral. The reader will see, after experience of them all, that we have not given ourselves slavishly to any of them, having recognised that the genius of the city and its artists was not dissipated in these chimeras, but that it followed surer instincts, which carried it on in the simple search after ideal beauty. When you come to Rome after an attentive study of the whole of Italy—and I had the good fortune to prelude by this necessary initiation,—you perceive that in this city the various schools of a country more fruitful in models than any other all sum themselves up, and that particular theories have here necessarily become general. I would fain have known how to explain all that has been exceptional and fertilising in their destiny; if I had only succeeded in part, this book would still contribute to the progress of the history of art.

As for reverence for all that is great, notwithstanding the criticisms that we might make and which escaped nobody, pontifical Rome, which I explored on the eve of an approaching revolution, would have commanded this in the most sceptical person. All of us, historians, artists, worshippers of traditions, had a difficulty in thinking of this city, fallen from its universal character, reduced to the condition of vulgar capitals, become a constitutional, military administrative centre; Rome seemed too deeply poetical for such a part. It was the reverses of France that brought about this occupation. We have not to seek what time will do with this conquest, but we could never find a way of regretting any of our illusions.

The Rome that I have depicted is the ancient metropolis, the religious metropolis, the native land of the arts, the sanctuary of incomparable memories, the home of a people who even to this hour are like no other. That city may look with indifferent eye upon our revolutions, upon our politics of a day: its glory, which has already defied so many ruins, will see new ones, but it has not to dread the fainting memory of men; so long as society stands, Rome will remain a holy city, or rather, as the admiration of the old world used to say with majestic simplicity, it will remain the *Urbs*—the City of Cities.

F. W.

CONTENTS.

CHAPTER I.

Broccoli.—The Fountain of Trevi.—The Corso.—St. Peter's.—The Pantheon of Agrippa.—The Trastevere.—St. Peter in Montorio.—Overlooking Rome . . . 1

CHAPTER II.

Forum Romanum.—The Temple of Concord.—Churches and Basilicas.—The Monuments.—St. Paul Extra Muros.—The Coliseum.—The Coliseum at Night . . 18

CHAPTER III.

Sights in the Streets.—The Barberini Gallery.—The Sciarra Gallery.—The Paintings. —The Cenci.—The Castle of St. Angelo.—The Cenci Tragedies.—Beatrice de' Cenci.—Execution of Beatrice de' Cenci.—The Castle Dungeons . . . 33

CHAPTER IV.

Roman Remedy for Grief.—St. Francesca Romana.—Temple of Antoninus and Faustina.—Basilica of Constantine.—The Arch of Septimius Severus.—The Arch of Titus 56

CHAPTER V.

The Baths of Caracalla.—The Basilica of St. Clement.—Antiquity of the Church.— Interior of St. Clement's.—Fourth Century Frescoes.—The Legend of St. Libertinus. —Ninth Century Frescoes.—Legend of St. Clement.—Tenth Century Frescoes.— Ninth Century Pilasters.—Romance of St. Alexius 69

CHAPTER VI.

The Church of St. Cecilia.—Santa Maria in Trastevere.—Tasso.—The Pescheria Region.—Palazzo del Governo Vecchio.—The Fishermen's Quarter.—Santa Maria in Cosmedin.—Rienzi's House 93

Contents.

CHAPTER VII.

Market of the Piazza Navona.—Church of St. Agnes Extra Muros.—The Catacombs. —The Early Christians.—Inscriptions in the Catacombs.—The Catacombs.— The Nomentano Bridge . . . 110

CHAPTER VIII.

Santa Maria della Navicella.—Playing at Mora.—San Stefano Rotondo.—The Two Dungeons.—The Tullianum.—Bronze of Marcus Aurelius.—The Statues.—The Hospital of St. Michael.—The San Spirito Infirmary 128

CHAPTER IX.

The Bambino.—Santa Maria in Ara Cœli.—The Quattro Capi Bridge.—The Island of the Tiber.—The Christian Festival.—The Farnesini Palace.—The Pamphili Gardens 149

CHAPTER X.

St. John of the Florentines.—The Library of the Philippines.—The Sette Sale.—The Baths of Trajan.—St. Martin Ai Monti.—The Pope's Pastoral Staff . 164

CHAPTER XI.

The Façade of St. Peter's.—The Building of St. Peter's.—The Nave of St. Peter's.— St. Peter's Chair.—The Pietà.—The Chapels.—The Sacristies.—The Cupola.— Inside the Bronze Ball.—The Obelisk of Caligula.—High Mass at St. Peter's.— The Procession.—The Benediction.—The Sacramental Prayers . . . 176

CHAPTER XII.

San Pietro in Vincoli.—Its Founder.—The Appian Way.—The Circus of Romulus . 204

CHAPTER XIII.

The Villa Madama.—Sant' Agostino.—The Tomb of Rossi.—The Murder of Rossi.— The Farnese Palace.—Old Book-stalls.—The Mattei Palace.—The Aventine . 212

CHAPTER XIV.

The Palatine Wall.—The Palatine Ruins.—The Empress Livia's House.—Its Decorations.—The Paintings.—The Palace of Tiberius.—The Connections.—The Galleries.—The Circus . . 229

CHAPTER XV.

The Alban Hills.—Rocca di Papa.—Tusculum 249

CHAPTER XVI.

Trajan's Column.—St. John Lateran.—The Monuments.—The Neighbourhood of St. John.—The Gregorian Museum.—Symbols . . . 257

CHAPTER XVII.

The Quirinal.—The Surroundings.—La Trinita dei Monti.—The Pincian Gardens . 271

CHAPTER XVIII.

The Villa Medici.—Inspiration from Rome . . . 281

CHAPTER XIX.

San Lorenzo.—The Pillars.—The Frescoes.—St. Pudentiana.—The Constantinian Mosaic.—Church of St. Cosmus.—Chapel of St. Prasseda.—The Crowning of the Virgin 287

CHAPTER XX.

The Carnival.—Clearing the Streets.—The Barbary Steeds.—The German Festival.—The Villa Albani 304

CHAPTER XXI.

The Pictures in the Borghese Palace.—Santa Maria del Popolo.—The Paintings.—The Statues.—Bernini's Works 314

CHAPTER XXII.

The Falls of Tivoli.—The Surroundings . . . 325

CHAPTER XXIII.

The Vatican.—The Gallery of Pictures.—The Transfiguration.—The Etruscan Museum 331

CHAPTER XXIV.

The Chiaramonti Museum.—The Statues.—The Braccio Nuovo.—The Sculpture.—The Nile Statue.—The Belvedere Torso.—The Laocoön.—The Hall of the Animals.—The Gallery of the Statues . 340

CHAPTER XXV.

Gallery of the Candelabra.—The Biga.—The Round Hall . 359

CHAPTER XXVI.

The Sixtine Chapel.—The Paintings.—The Ceiling.—The Creation of Man.—The Fall of Man.—The Frescoes.—Raphael's Poem of the Soul.—Raphael's Colour . . 367

LIST OF ILLUSTRATIONS.

	PAGE
FOUNTAIN OF THE TRITON	2
ARCH OF SEPTIMIUS SEVERUS	3
FOUNTAIN OF TREVI	5
COLUMN OF ANTONINUS	6
THE COLONNADES OF ST. PETER	9
"THE VALETS OF THE CARDINALS, VERY CEREMONIOUS UNDER ANTIQUATED LIVERIES." BY HENRI REGNAULT	10
THE PANTHEON OF AGRIPPA	11
TEMPLE OF ANTONINUS	13
FISH MARKET. BY HENRI REGNAULT	14
VIEW OF ST. PETER IN MONTORIO	16
ENTRY OF THE FORUM ROMANUM BY THE VIA SACRA; TEMPLE OF VENUS AT ROME; SANTA FRANCESCA ROMANA; ARCH OF TITUS; CAMPANILE OF THE CAPITOL, ETC.	19
TEMPLE OF VESPASIAN AND PORTICO OF THE TWELVE GODS	20
ENTABLATURE OF THE TEMPLE OF CONCORD	21
REMAINS OF THE TEMPLE OF CASTOR	22
COLUMN OF PHOCAS	23
PAVEMENT OF JULIAN BASILICA AND TABULARIUM	24
ST. PAUL EXTRA MUROS	25
UNDER THE GALLERIES OF THE COLISEUM	27
THE ARENA OF THE COLISEUM	29
GENERAL VIEW OF THE COLISEUM	31
A CORRIDOR OF THE COLISEUM	32
"THE SCHOLARS . . . WITH VOLUMINOUS SHOVEL-HATS." BY HENRI REGNAULT	34
ON THE PINCIAN. BY HENRI REGNAULT	35
THE AURORA OF GUIDO RENI IN THE ROSPIGLIOSI PALACE	36
LA FORNARINA OF THE BARBERINI PALACE, AT ROME	38
LA FORNARINA OF THE UFFIZI, AT FLORENCE	39
THE BEATRICE DE' CENCI. BY GUIDO RENI	40
THE VIOLINIST OF RAPHAEL (SCIARRA PALACE)	41
BRIDGE AND CASTLE OF ST. ANGELO	45
BANKS OF THE TIBER BETWEEN RIPETTA AND THE BRIDGE OF ST. ANGELO	47
CLOISTER OF ST. JOHN LATERAN	51
WOMAN AT THE BRIDGE OF ST. ANGELO. BY HENRI REGNAULT	55

	PAGE
GATE OF THE PALACE OF VENICE	57
PONTIFICAL PROCESSION AT THE FEAST OF THE MADONNA. BY HENRI REGNAULT	58
TEMPLE OF ANTONINUS AND FAUSTINA	60
THE ARCHES OF PEACE	61
INTERIOR OF THE BASILICA OF CONSTANTINE	62
TEMPLE OF NERVA, PANYANI POSTERN	63
FORUM TRANSITORIUM, OR FORUM OF NERVA	65
ARCH OF TITUS	66
BAS-RELIEF OF THE ARCH OF TITUS	67
BAS-RELIEF OF THE ARCH OF TITUS	68
CALDARIUM OF THE BATHS OF CARACALLA	70
ALTAR OF ST. CLEMENT'S	71
PULPIT OF THE EPISTLE AT ST. CLEMENT'S	73
STREET OF ST. JOHN LATERAN—SIDE ENTRY OF ST. CLEMENT'S	75
EXTERNAL PORTICO OF ST. CLEMENT'S	77
FRAGMENT OF A FRESCO OF THE FOURTH CENTURY	78
FRAGMENT OF A FRESCO OF THE FOURTH CENTURY	79
LEGEND OF ST. LIBERTINUS: FRESCOES OF THE EIGHTH CENTURY	80
ASSUMPTION OF THE VIRGIN: FRESCO OF THE TIME OF LEO IV.	82
BYZANTINE MADONNA: FRESCO OF THE NINTH CENTURY	83
LEGEND OF ST. CLEMENT: EPISODE OF SISINIUS (TENTH CENTURY)	85
MIRACLE AT THE TOMB OF ST. CLEMENT (TENTH CENTURY)	86
ST. BLASIUS PICKING A THORN FROM THE THROAT OF A CHILD: FRESCO ON A PILASTER (NINTH CENTURY)	88
DANIEL SPARED BY THE LIONS: PILASTER OF THE NINTH CENTURY	89
LEGEND OF ST. ALEXIUS: FRESCO OF THE TENTH CENTURY	91
THE PAULINE FOUNTAIN	93
THE STATUE OF ST. CECILIA. BY STEPHEN MADERNO	94
PORTICO OF SANTA CECILIA IN TRASTEVERE	95
YOUNG WOMAN OF THE TRASTEVERE	97
SANT' ONOFRIO	98
PORTRAIT AFTER THE MASK OF TASSO	99
PEDIMENT OF THE PORTICO OF OCTAVIA	101

List of Illustrations.

	PAGE
GATE OF ST. ANGELO IN PESCHERIA	102
COURTYARD IN THE PALAZZO DEL GOVERNO VECCHIO, VIA DELLA PESCHERIA	103
BARBER IN THE OPEN AIR. BY HENRI REGNAULT	104
A FISHERMAN ON THE WATCH BEFORE HIS GIRELLA. BY HENRI REGNAULT	105
FOUNTAIN OF BIZZACCHERI, AND TEMPLE OF THE SUN, OR VESTA	106
SANTA MARIA IN COSMEDIN	108
HOUSE OF RIENZI, AND TEMPLE OF FORTUNA VIRILIS	109
THE MARKET OF THE PIAZZA NAVONA. BY HENRI REGNAULT	111
"WHILE THE CONTADINI DRINK." BY HENRI REGNAULT	112
PIAZZA NAVONA AND CHURCH OF ST. AGNES	113
ST. AGNES: AFTER THE MOSAIC OF THE CHOIR (SEVENTH CENTURY)	114
ST. AGNES EXTRA MUROS ON THE VIA NOMENTANA	115
SUBTERRANEAN GALLERIES AND LOCULI OF THE CATACOMB OF ST. AGNES	117
SUBTERRANEAN ALTAR, TOMBS, AND CHAPEL IN THE CEMETERY OF ST. AGNES	118
VALERIANUS AND CÆCILIA. MOSAIC OF THE NINTH CENTURY AT ST. CÆCILIA	122
INSCRIPTION IN THE CATACOMBS	123
THE CHILDREN IN THE FURNACE; PRAYER; JONAH AND THE WHALE	124
PLAYING AT BOWLS. BY HENRI REGNAULT	125
PAINTINGS OF THE FIRST CENTURY ON A CHAPEL VAULT (CATACOMBS OF CALLISTUS)	126
PONTE NOMENTANO	127
STREET AND APSE OF ST. JOHN AND ST. PAUL	129
ARCH OF DOLABELLA AND GATE OF THE OLD CONVENT OF THE TRINITARIANS	130
ROMANS PLAYING AT MORA. BY HENRI REGNAULT	131
ENTRY OF THE CONVENT OF ST. JOHN AND ST. PAUL	132
SAN STEFANO ROTONDO	133
FRAGMENT OF RAPHAEL	134
MADAME VIGÉE-LEBRUN. BY HERSELF	135
ARCHES OF ST. JOHN AND ST. PAUL, AS SEEN WHEN DESCENDING FROM THE CŒLIAN	136
ONE OF THE TROPHIES, CALLED OF MARIUS, AT THE CAPITOL	137
STEPS OF THE SENATORIAL PALACE: TARPEIAN STAIRCASE	139
JUNIUS BRUTUS	140
PIAZZA OF THE CAPITOL GALLERY OF ANTIQUES	141
THE DYING GLADIATOR	141
FAUN, AFTER PRAXITELES	142
THE AMAZON	143
MESALINA	143
MARIUS	144
AGRIPPINA, DAUGHTER OF DRUSUS	144
ROMAN LADY, TAKEN FOR THE FIRST AGRIPPINA	145
THE HOSPITAL OF ST. MICHAEL	146

	PAGE
NEST OF HOUSES ON THE BANKS OF THE TIBER. BY HENRI REGNAULT	147
VIEW ON THE TIBER IN FRONT OF THE CLOACA MAXIMA	150
FRONTAGE OF SANTA MARIA IN ARA CŒLI	151
THE BAMBINO	152
INTERIOR OF THE CHURCH OF SANTA MARIA IN ARA CŒLI	153
HOLIDAY CARRIAGE OF THE HOLY FATHER—THE EQUIPAGE OF THE BAMBINO	154
PRINCIPAL DOOR OF THE ARA CŒLI	155
OGIVAL VAULTS IN ARA CŒLI	156
ISLAND OF THE TIBER, ST. BARTHOLOMEW, AND THE QUATTRO CAPI BRIDGE	157
UPPER GALLERY OF THE CLOISTER OF THE ARA CŒLI	158
LA PORTA SETTIMIANA IN THE TRASTEVERE	159
VIEW OF THE VILLA PAMPHILI-DORIA	160
GARDENS OF THE PAMPHILI VILLA	162
GARDENS OF THE PAMPHILI VILLA	163
ST. JOHN OF THE FLORENTINES.—TRASTEVERINE BANK.—SLOPE OF THE JANICULUM	165
THE FATHER-MANAGER OF THE PHILIPPINES. BY HENRI REGNAULT	167
PORTA MAGGIORE	168
INTERIOR OF THE MINERVA MEDICA	169
ARCH OF GALLIENUS	170
THE SETTE SALE	171
FAMILY OF BEGGARS	172
VIEW OF ST. PETER'S AND THE VATICAN	173
THE PIAZZA OF ST. PETER AT THE GREAT BENEDICTION	174
UNDER THE PORTICO OF ST. PETER'S (SIDE OF THE SACRISTY)	177
PLAN OF THE BASILICA OF ST. PETER'S	180
CURULE CHAIR, ATTRIBUTED TO THE APOSTLE PETER	183
TOMB OF INNOCENT VIII.	185
STATE CARRIAGE COMING FROM ST. PETER'S	186
ANGELS OF THE CUPOLA: AFTER MELOZZO DA FORLI	187
PASSAGE UNDER THE PORTICO OF ST. PETER'S	189
TRIBUNA AND CHAIR OF ST. PETER	191
OBELISK OF CALIGULA AND FOUNTAINS OF THE PIAZZA OF ST. PETER'S	193
FAN-BEARERS	194
OLD NOBLE GUARD. BY A. DE NEUVILLE	195
THE POPE'S OLD SWISS GUARD. BY A. DE NEUVILLE	196
THE POPE'S BEARERS. BY A. DE NEUVILLE	197
A BENEDICTION FROM THE LOGGIA BY POPE PIUS IX.	198
TIARA-BEARER. BY A. DE NEUVILLE	199
INTERIOR OF ST. PETER'S	200
NAVE OF ST. PETER'S	201
DISPLAY OF THE GRAND RELICS	202
A MACE-BEARER. BY A. DE NEUVILLE	203
THE MOSES OF MICHELANGELO	204
PIAZZA OF SAN PIETRO IN VINCOLI	205
VAULTED PASSAGE UNDER THE PALACE OF LUCREZIA BORGIA	206
WELL IN THE CLOISTER OF SAN PIETRO IN VINCOLI	207

List of Illustrations.

	PAGE
ARCH OF DRUSUS	208
THE APPIAN WAY	209
MAUSOLEUM OF CÆCILIA METELLA	210
CIRCUS OF ROMULUS MAXENTIUS	211
BETWEEN THE PONTE MOLLE AND THE MONTE MARIO	213
FOUNTAIN AT THE VILLA OF POPE JULIUS III. BY HENRI REGNAULT	214
CASINO OF JULIUS III.	215
ST. PETER AND ST. PAUL, BY THE BRIDGE OF ST. ANGELO	216
RAPHAEL'S FOUR SIBYLS	217
RIARIO PALACE (CANCELLERIA)	218
THE FARNESE PALACE	219
LOGGIA OF THE FARNESE, FROM THE BANK OF THE TIBER. BY HENRI REGNAULT	220
THE EXCAVATED HERCULES	221
THE SPADA POMPEIUS	222
BROKERS AND BOOKWORMS IN OPEN AIR. BY HENRI REGNAULT	223
FOUNTAIN OF THE TORTOISES	224
COURT OF THE MATTEI PALACE	225
TORCH OF ST. GEORGE IN VELABRO	226
IN THE PALACE OF CALIGULA	227
PORCH OF SANTA SABINO	228
EXHUMATION OF THE HOUSE OF LIVIA	230
RUINS ON THE PALATINE	231
REMAINS OF THE PUBLIC PALACE, AND LOGGIA OF THE FARNESE	232
REMAINS OF THE PUBLIC PALACE OF DOMITIAN	233
LIVIA'S HOUSE (LEFT WING)	237
PAINTINGS OF THE TABLINUM OF LIVIA	238
RESTORATION OF THE CLIVUS VICTORIÆ	240
VAULTED PASSAGE BETWEEN THE PALACE OF TIBERIUS AND THE PUBLIC PALACE	241
RUINS OF THE PALACES OF TIBERIUS	242
REMAINS OF THE LIBRARY OF THE PUBLIC PALACE	243
RUINS OF THE PALATINE, TOWARDS THE CIRCUS MAXIMUS	244
VIEW FROM THE PALATINE, TOWARDS THE CŒLIAN	245
OLD TOWER OF THE PALATINE, FACING THE CIRCUS MAXIMUS	246
STAIRCASE IN THE PALACE OF CALIGULA	247
ANCIENT PROCESSION TO THE LATERAN	248
ROAD TO CASTEL-GANDOLFO: LA GALLERIA	250
ARICCIA AND ITS VIADUCT	251
LAKE OF ALBANO AND PONTIFICAL VILLA (EVENING)	252
AT ROCCA DI PAPA. BY HENRI REGNAULT	253
YOUTHFUL SHEPHERDESS	254
OXEN OF THE ROMAN CAMPAGNA. BY HENRI REGNAULT	255
THE SALITA OF MARINO	256
THE PIAZZA OF ST. JOHN LATERAN	257
TRAJAN'S COLUMN AND ULPIAN BASILICA	258
WELL OF THE SIXTH CENTURY, IN THE CLOISTER OF ST. JOHN	261
SANTA CROCE IN GERUSALEMME	262
PORTICO OF ST. JOHN LATERAN	263
PENITENTS ASCENDING THE HOLY STAIRCASE	264
SOPHOCLES	266

	PAGE
CHRIST SYMBOLIZED IN ORPHEUS	267
"A GROUP SLUMBERING OVER A CRADLE"	269
VIA DELLA PILOTTA	272
FOUNTAIN OF THE PIAZZA MONTECAVALLO	273
ARRIVAL OF THE CARDINALS AT THE QUIRINAL PALACE. BY H. REGNAULT	274
LA BARCACCIA AND THE STEPS OF LA TRINITA DEI MONTI	276
HOUSE WHERE POUSSIN DIED	277
PERRON OF THE TRINITA	278
ON THE TERRACE OF THE PINCIAN	279
LA PASCUCCIA	280
THE EMBLEMS OF JUSTICE (RAPHAEL'S STANZE)	281
PORTICO OF THE VILLA MEDICI	282
VILLA MEDICI (GARDEN FRONT)	283
VIALE COPERTO, IN THE VILLA MEDICI	284
UNDER THE PORTICO	285
ON THE TERRACE OF THE MEDICI GARDENS	286
VIEW AT THE BACK OF THE CHOIR, SAN LORENZO	288
BASILICA AND CONVENT OF SAN LORENZO FUORI LE MURA	289
TRANSEPT AND CONFESSIONAL OF SAN LORENZO	290
PULPIT OF THE GOSPEL, AT SAN LORENZO	291
CLOISTER OF SAN LORENZO FUORI LE MURA	293
CONVENT OF ST. PUDENTIANA	294
ST. PRASSEDA AND ST. PUDENTIANA (CATACOMB OF PRISCILLA)	295
DOOR OF ST. PUDENTIANA	296
MOSAIC OF ST. PUDENTIANA	297
THE CHURCH OF ST. COSMUS AND ST. DAMIANUS	298
DOOR OF THE COLONNA CHAPEL, AT ST. PRASSEDA	300
SANTA MARIA MAGGIORE	301
INTERIOR OF ST. PRASSEDA	302
OFF TO THE CARNIVAL	304
PIAZZA DEL POPOLO	305
AWAITING THE ILLUMINATIONS. BY A. DE NEUVILLE	306
RACK OF THE BARBERI: THE START. BY H. REGNAULT	307
GERMAN MASQUERADING: THE MARCH PAST. BY H. REGNAULT	308
THE GERMAN FESTIVAL: ENTERING THE GROTTOES. BY H. REGNAULT	310
TERRACES AND PORTICO AT THE VILLA ALBANI	312
GARDENS OF THE VILLA ALBANI	313
NUPTIALS OF ALEXANDER AND ROXANA	315
PIAZZA AND PORTO DEL POPOLO; CHURCH OF SANTA MARIA	317
TOMB OF WILLIAM ROCCA (SACRISTY OF SANTA MARIA DEL POPOLO)	318
FLORENTINE STATUES, BAS-RELIEF OF THE PISANS (CORRIDOR OF THE SACRISTY)	319
BERNINI'S DAPHNE	321
FOUNTAIN IN THE BORGHESE GARDENS	322
THE BORGHESE VENUS	323
PORTICO OF OCTAVIA	324
RAVINE: TEMPLE OF HERCULES, CALLED OF THE SIBYL	326
A STREET AT TIVOLI	327
"SOME PECORARI LIKE CLEPHTS." BY HENRI REGNAULT	328

List of Illustrations.

	PAGE
Remains of the Villa Adriana	330
Vatican Library	332
The Throne-room at the Vatican	333
Porta Angelica—Pontifical Residence in the Vatican	335
The Chiaramonti Gallery	341
Sarcophagus of the Bacchantes	343
The Braccio Nuovo	344
Augustus (Braccio Nuovo)	346
Pio-Clementine Museum	348
The Nile (Braccio Nuovo)	349
Demosthenes (Braccio Nuovo)	350
Torso of the Belvedere	351
The Perseus of Canova	352
Hall of the Animals (Pio-Clementine Museum)	354
Antique Group (Hall of the Animals)	353
Menander (Pio-Clementine Gallery)	355
Gallery of the Candelabra	361

	PAGE
The Biga	362
Casino of Pius IX.	363
Exit from the Pontifical Garden	364
The Round Hall	365
The Ignudi (Vault of the Sixtine Chapel)	368
Julius II.	371
The Prophet Joel (Ceiling of the Sixtine)	372
Delphic Sibyl (Ceiling of the Sixtine)	373
The Creation of Man (from the Roof of the Sixtine)	375
The Creation of Woman (from the Roof of the Sixtine)	376
The Fall of Man (from the Roof of the Sixtine)	377
Poetry	378
Theology	379
The First Sin (La Segnatura)	381

ROME.

CHAPTER I.

Y first night in Rome was spent under a roof in the street of the Quattro Fontane, which, by the Felice and Sistini roads, comes out on the Pincian, the Tuileries garden of the city of Romulus.

On the following morning, I stole away from the house to venture alone into the labyrinth of streets.

On my right the straight and hilly street made with its high walls a distant frame for a conical belfry sketched against a grey and rainy sky. I did not know the situation of Santa Maria Maggiore. I was still furthur from suspecting that in these blurred swellings I saw the renowned Quirinal and Viminal hills. The road continued on the left in absolute monotony; before me in false square, in an ill-kept court, arose a vast building with a tolerably new look about it, and with a portico crowded with soldiers. The edifice struck me as handsome enough for a barrack; but recognising it as the famous palace of the Barberini, I thought it too much of a barrack for a palace.

On the Piazza Barberini, as you return towards the street, you come upon a fountain of sombre colour, but whose basin is in good proportion with the design that occupies the centre; four dolphins, whose gaping throats just touch the water, are solidly bound together, forming by their raised tails a base for the arms of the Barberini, and on this is placed, describing a semi-spiral and serving for an upper basin, a large shell, of which the overflow falls away in a shower of pearls. From the midst of this, solidly supported, there rises a vigorous Triton, who blows to the sky in a horn of shell form, from which spirts a thread of water, as shown in the illustration on the next page. This original and robust conception, which reminded me of

B

Pierre Puget, is the work of Bernini. I did not know it then, and in giving this piece of information I am anticipating: I beg the reader to allow me often to do this, and to complete these first impressions by the further results of my studies, so as thus to avoid returning to the same subject.

Turning my back to the piazza, I took a cross street, the Via del Tritone, which begins with shops for the sale of smoked and greasy meat, *trattorie* that the Germans must frequent, for you see in them a vast quantity of sausages and choppes of beer ; the common people, squatted or leaned against the wall all round the door, proud, idle, sober.

FOUNTAIN OF THE TRITON.

In this country, where fever is endemic, I do not know if sobriety be an instinct of self-preservation ; at any rate, it is exemplary in all classes, and in truth the quality of the articles of food decidedly encourages so estimable a disposition. Veal killed too young is bad and scarce ; mutton is stale and hard ; beef has little taste ; fowl is skinny and tough as leather. Game only is of superior quality, and, except partridge, it is common. Close and insufficiently kneaded, the bread is heavy; the wine, usually tolerable, is carelessly made : it should be excellent. Pastry, made with a mixture of oil and dripping, is repugnant enough to bring one's heart up.

Broccoli. 3

For that matter, the humbler folk care little about these culinary elements. This is how they sustain themselves: all the winter they

ARCH OF SEPTIMIUS SEVERUS.

prepare for the public at the street corners in large cauldrons, twice a day, those long, greenish cauliflowers called broccoli, and they are carried home on drainers from shop to shop. They eat also considerably of large lupins, round and yellow, cooked in water, without butter or dripping. On the broccoli they put salt and oil with vinegar. Add some olives, some dry figs, cervelas, parched and often rancid, and stalks of fennel; and for dessert, nuts, *pinocchi*, the seeds of the pine. In summer, fruits, especially water-melon and the green gourd with purple pulp, of so poor a flavour. Such is pretty nearly the substance of the diet of the people of Rome, if you add a few common pastes.

Some muddy streets, without footways; some mean, arched shops, with narrow doors, such as you see at La Châtre and Dinan; walls in which the peeling plaster has received a daubing of earth from the splashing of the gutter; now and then some church with shabby façade in the modern taste, set in among the houses; much animation and babbling among the people; all the women ragged, and with hair elaborately dressed, even those who have none, terrible to behold—this is what greets you at every corner. I there received, for the first time, the distinct impression of the odours or, more poetically speaking, the perfume of Rome; it is a local exhalation of cabbage or broccoli broth mixed with the raw smell of roots, sulphurous emanations to which one has to become accustomed, for the pavement and the black mud of the streets are impregnated with that essence, which has not become pure in becoming everlasting.

Gradually, as I advanced along a narrow street with the air of a kitchen-garden, in which the crowd was thickening, and where leaves of vegetables were all trampled under foot, I perceived a sort of indistinct murmur like that of the waves, which first accompanied and then overwhelmed the noises of the throng, and all at once, at the corner of the street, I was dazzled by sheets of water, which, from a pell-mell of rocks, dominated by a building covered with statues, tumbled foaming and sparkling on every side, to be engulfed in cavernous holes. I was in front of the fountain of Trevi.

It is a showy example of ostentatious decoration as understood by the school of Bernini. In the midst of rock-work and shell, Neptune emerges with his steed from the basement of a palace to which this enormous construction is fixed. The pretty and graceful bas-reliefs describe the discovery of the Acqua Vergine by a youthful maiden in the neighbourhood of Tusculum. From the upper basins, from the hollow of rocks in which intertwine climbing plants carved on rough stone, streams, of whose size one has no idea, spout forth on every side; a cataract or river .... in the guise of the stage! The waters, for that matter, are the most limpid and pure; their salutary

FOUNTAIN OF TREVI.

virtues are reputed to cure twelve disorders. The torrent breaks forth with the tumult of a mountain cascade.

On the brink of the lower basin, on an evening when the moon makes this agitated sheet sparkle like the steel links in a hauberk, you sometimes see a young maiden bend over the water, while a lover eyes her pensively. She has drawn in a new glass, which she will break as soon as used, some water to offer with a smile of hope to the friend, who leaves her for a journey. It is a popular tradition, that if you have drunk from this spring, you cannot remain absent from Rome for ever; destiny will bring you back. For some this ceremony is a simple form of vow; praised be they who have full faith in the presage of the fountain! The Germans expect to make it favourable by bribery; when they have quaffed the philtre of return, they throw a half-penny into the basin.

COLUMN OF ANTONINUS.

Must we judge the fountain of Trevi in the name of the principles of a severe art? No. It is what one might call rococo triumphant, but endowed with a size, an exuberance, which are the apology and the attraction of this kind. If we could perceive from the distance this tower of water with its majestic scaffolding, its impression would be thoroughly victorious. We understand, after all, that the dry and poverty-stricken imitation of such a style, as it is to be seen in France, and especially in Prussia, is the most obsolete of all the forms of artistic decline.

By accident I came out into the Corso. Another deception: this famous road, which serves as a turf for equestrians, is narrow and full of shops, like our St. Martin's Lane, which it recalls still further by its mean footpaths. A number of small shops where wares of no great value are retailed; a palace here and there to relieve the rows of houses. In passing by the side of the great Colonna piazza, I measured with my eyes the tall Doric shaft of white marble which adorns the centre, vaguely provoked that the column of Trajan left so slight an impression. Far abroad as I was, a man becomes thoughtless; it was only the Antonine pillar, and I never even thought of it.

It was under Sixtus V. that, in restoring the half-buried pedestal of this monument, raised in honour of Marcus Aurelius after his victories over the Germans, they mistook its real purpose, and attributed to Antoninus Pius a structure that only dates from his successor. The old inscription, with several bas-reliefs, was brought under Gregory XVI. to the middle of the Giardino della Pina, so called because in the centre of one of the façades with which Bramante surrounded this great space surrounded with quincunxes, there figures between two iron peacocks a large bronze pineapple—funereal emblems taken from the Pantheon of Agrippa, and not, as has been said, from Adrian's Mole. The vast square where the pillar of the Antonines rises is monumental, surrounded as it is with the Ferraioli and Chigi palaces, the last raised by the nephews of Alexander VII., as well as the Piombino palace, which on the Corso fronts the building of the Grand' Garde, carried on a long peristyle whose pillars came from the excavations of the ancient city of Veii.

Leaving the Corso, I met an old friend, an abbé, who took me by the arm, and said, "Come, my good friend, I shall take you straight to St. Peter's." So to St. Peter's we went.

From the end of the Santa Lucia bridge to the bridge of St. Angelo, you follow an interminable row of streets, whose appearance is wretched, and even reaches downright repulsiveness, as one approaches the Via di Tordinone. This ugliness at last amuses you. Besides, as I look about, I listened to the abbé with all my ears; with him this polypus of streets became full of life. At the point where two lanes divide, he showed me the Albergo dell' Orso where Montaigne once lodged. Nothing has been changed there;

nothing does change in Rome : waggoners and market people put up their carts under this gateway, even then ancient, where the Bordelais gentleman dismounted with his suite.

It is a symbolical protest against the vanities of the stage to have condemned Apollo, patron of the opera at Rome, to take up his abode in a kind of ignoble closet, which, seen from without from the extremity of the street, under its robe of brown plaster and bare of all ornament, has at once the equivocal physiognomy of an ill place, and the ghastly look of a sinner in the livery of public penitence. The high blank wall which descends steeply to the river, flanked with little huts and wooden corridors, is like the enclosure of a tannery.

I was blunted by too many iconographic reminiscences, but, with the satisfaction of a vision realised, I recognised the bridge of St. Angelo and Adrian's Mole. My companion laid himself out to distract my attention; he named a hundred objects, and flashed in my eyes a hundred souvenirs. I was surprised by the breadth of the Tiber and the extent of the buildings of the San-Spirito Hospital.

At last, at the end of the Borgo Nuovo, from the bottom of the Piazza Rusticucci, we discerned the façade of St. Peter, colossal collet of the ring described by the colonnades of Bernini.

This was the great deception of the day. The vain majesty which renders this gigantic work empty and dumb struck me spontaneously with a crudity that was almost choking.

From the bottom of the place the columns of Bernini connected themselves easily with the façade, on each side of which they are seen to mark nearly a right angle. But when, as I went forward, I saw them fold in a circle behind me, and thus form with the portal a sort of scorpion with a double tail, it all seemed to me an abuse of the permission to pile stone on stone for the mere amusement of the eye. The real vastness of the work might have had the power of impressing me : nothing of the kind ; the immensity of the proportions escaped me. The commonplace of the style extinguished whatever interest the whole ought to have inspired.

Looking to the ground, I found the open space well paved ; the obelisk of Sixtus V. interested me, especially on account of Fontana ; the three-story arcades where the Loggie are, glazed as they are at the present day, affected me like an enormous cage, and nothing, in truth—I confess it to my shame—nothing within me would have stirred, unless the abbé, showing me behind the other buildings a small, low roof on a corner of bare wall had not said, "'Tis the roof of the Sistine Chapel."

THE COLONNADES OF ST. PETER.

To enter that sanctuary was not to be thought of in a moment of such dismay. I even refused to enter the church.

In the open space I had noticed a carriage pass by, which only pulled up at the foot of the great steps. I thought the vehicle and its horses ridiculously small. There got down from it two or three ants.

"THE VALETS OF THE CARDINALS. . . . VERY CEREMONIOUS UNDER ANTIQUATED LIVERIES." BY HENRI REGNAULT.

. . . When we came in front of the portico, the abbé gently said to me, " Place yourself quite close — closer ; there, measure with your arms the diameter of these columns and their flutings."

Their size was indeed formidable ; statues might have been niched in the flutings ! " Come away," I cried, overwhelmed. My guide was a trifle discouraged: I was no less so at responding so ill to his instructions. " I have no longer," I said, "any occasion to seek the origin of the French decline of the last two centuries ; from Louis XIII. to Thermidor ; all is there, down to the endive wreaths of the Panthéon Ste. Geneviève."

" The basilica of St. Peter's," said my friend, "offers one particularity; at the first approach its faults all stare you in the face, and its aspect surprises nobody ; but the more you visit it, the more unforeseen revelations you find there ; and there comes a moment when surprise, gradually developed, becomes prodigious—the single example of an energetic impression like amazement and marvelling admiration springing up by degrees. As soon as you can appreciate St. Peter's, you will have taken a great step."

But in what sense ? thought I, with inward disquiet.

I had time to reflect on it ; for the abbé left me alone for half-an-hour, to execute in passing a commission at the house of an Eminent Excellency who received that day.

We mounted to a story as high as the third in London houses, and I waited for my companion in the antechamber, where loitered, in an indolence quite in harmony with my own discouragement, groups of

THE PANTHEON OF AGRIPPA.

valets, very important and in very poor feather. A few poor wretches crouched on benches ; the valets of the cardinals affected a diplomatic style, being extremely ceremonious under antiquated and rich liveries, too large, too narrow, or too long for those whom they clothed. Pretentious disclosures of domestic distress, these cast-off things must have passed into the possession of half-a-score of dignitaries, and held as many lackeys as a sentry-box shelters sentinels.

My mentor next brought me by a meshwork of alleys to the Pantheon of Agrippa, which he made me enter without any preparation. The portico, though added afterwards, appeared to me in all the bold and original solidity of its Roman character, with more clearness than impressiveness. I had visited the Greek temples at Præstum. Still I regarded with interest a monument raised at the dawn of the age of Augustus. I went out, I turned round it, and looked at it from the bottom of the piazza; I returned to it again, never wearied of examining an example so precious of the art of building at the end of the Republic.

Perhaps earlier than Agrippa who finished it, and primitively dedicated (Pliny tells us) to Jupiter the Avenger, the Pantheon, whose dome offers a very model of building, is, as has been said, fronted by a portico or peristyle or sort of *hors d'œuvre*, which rests on sixteen enormous monolithic columns of oriental granite, crowned by the finest capitals that Rome has bequeathed to us. These columns, eight in front, are doubled by a second row; engaged pilasters form a third against the building itself. Here, mark another singularity, which produces an illusion as to the depth of the portico. Instead of being arranged in line on parallels forming a right angle with the steps, these columns radiate gradually, in such a way that from the middle of the piazza, where those of the first row that support the pediment ought to conceal those of the second and the third row, we see them on the contrary in échelons, because their slightly oblique position produces an imaginary perspective, whose result is to throw the distances back.

This piazza of the Pantheon, cleared by Eugenius IV. of the ruins, which included the basalt lions, a bronze head of M. Agrippa, a chariot, a porphyry sarcophagus in which Clement XII. made his bed, this little piazza, inherited by the hucksters with their petty trade, was once a wild and mysterious spot, the valley of the She-Goat; swamps bristling with reeds, surrounded with underwood, in the midst of which the second prodigy of the genesis of Rome was accomplished—the disappearance of Romulus.

It was at the end of the seventeenth century that the *douane de terre* was installed in the remains of a temple of the second century, dedicated, to all appearance, to Antoninus Pius. The old building was vaulted, and, seen from the inside, the back part of the architrave and the base of the vault seem like a rock raised in the air, and resting on a wall. We must know that Borromini, who restored two centuries ago the frieze and the entablature, connected the whole with a coating of stucco, which produces the illusion. The Corinthian engaged columns in the modern building have branches of olive among the acanthus of the capital, but the delicacy of these capitals is far from equalling the purity of the Pantheon. Fires have cracked the shafts, torn like the trunks of trees that the lightning has blasted. In the court, among the bales, boxes, carts, a whole population of clerks and draymen is busy; incongruous spectacle of that dead ruin, which encloses and shows in its bosom a house full of life.

It seems that we had arrived in the Trastevere without any understanding either why or where I was so swiftly carried along. I noticed three streets by reason of the monotony of their names: the Lungara, the Lungarina, the Lungaretta. In the midst of this rapid flight one recollection struck me, and remained with me. Close to the Borgo, by the ancient Septimian gate, at the corner of the Via Santa Dorotea, in the old rag-stone wall of a dirty building, is the outline of the stopped arch of an arcade of shops. It is flanked

TEMPLE OF ANTONINUS.

by a granite column, over which rises an Ionic pilaster, the whole enframed in the wall. "An old bakery," said the abbé, "before which Raphael passed many a time; it was there that the Fonarina lived."

As we began to ascend, and as the grass became more abundant in the streets as the houses grew less frequent, I asked whither we were going, and was told that we were climbing the Janiculum, the Monte d'Oro where Janus had his town of Antipolis in front of that of Saturn; where, according to Titus Livius, the tomb of Numa was found; where the citadel of Ancus Martius rose; where, according to the Christian legend, the Apostle Peter was crucified.

Along the street I had already remarked that snuff-boxes are a usage as hospitable as universal, and that in this respect Rome still lingered in the habits of the age of Fontenelle, when both sexes carried about a snuff-box and a walking-stick. The Romans have dropped the stick; it would need an effort to carry one. The monks of the Montorio took and offered about two pinches a minute; it is the base of conversation. The abbé, who insisted on hindering me from looking behind me, was eager to inform me that in all classes, young and old, handsome and ugly, bourgeois, peasants, monks and soldiers, everybody crams his nostrils most zealously. "You will see at the Sistine Chapel, where the whole sacred college figures, how funny this labour of nasal alimentation is. A veteran snuff-taker, Pius IX., constantly uses a genuine Capucin's handkerchief, a bit of cretonne of red and blue check, such as we hardly ever see at home except among the Scottish farmers. This poor rag jars with the gold and purple of the heir of the emperors of Rome; don't you think that such a sample from the wardrobe of the sovereign-pontiff reveals the conventual simplicity of the monk framed in the splendours of the church?"

At the moment we were going to cross the threshold of the church, the abbé, plucking me by the arm, resumed: "Let me tell you, before going in, that Baccio Pintelli of Florence, who died in 1480, rebuilt, at the expense of Ferdinand IV. of Spain, the church of St. Peter in Montorio for monks of the Order of St. Francis, to whom it had been ceded."

We cannot, however, help admiring there one of the good works of Sebastian del Piombo—the *Flagellation of Christ*. The work is supposed to have been executed after a cartoon of Michael Angelo; its style is lofty without being either violent or harsh; the painting, of a very deep quality, would be more easily appreciated if the small chapel which gives it shelter were less sombre. It is on the master altar of St. Peter in Montorio that, before the Italian campaigns, Raphael's Transfiguration was to be found—a famous work of a painter whom it represents when handed over to the ambitions of his third manner: then this famous canvas was sent to the Louvre,

whence it was restored in 1854. Since then it remains at the Vatican.
I should have noticed at St. Peter's the sepulchral chapel of the Del

FISH-MARKET. BY HENRI REGNAULT.

Monte family, by Ammanato, who has carved some fine figures,
among others that of Justice, which offers the little-known singularity of having been taken from the same model as the renowned

statue of G. della Porte at the tomb of St. Paul in the Vatican basilica.

Let us mention a small round temple, surrounded by sixteen grey marble columns, and surmounted by a cupola. Ferdinand and Isabella had it erected by Bramante at the very spot where St. Peter is said to have been crucified. A gift of alms will procure you a present of a pinch or even a packet of the dust of the place. I scandalized my companion by considering this little object as a fine *example* of those correct styles that the Joseph Prud'hommes of art have consecrated. Nothing is worse adapted for a great commemoration, or so ill becomes a spot where Nero had set up the cross of the first of the popes, as this prototype of the belvederes which, in the English gardens under Lewis XVI., prepared resting-places at the top of the grass-plots for the Aspasias of the Directory.

VIEW OF ST. PETER IN MONTORIO.

To describe what meets one on this terrace, from which Montaigne three centuries ago threw his eye over a noble winter prospect (26th January), one would have to introduce into the description the abridgment of Roman history. Rome is only a foreground of the picture; for the view extends towards the north over the plains reaching as far as the Apennines, whence once rushed down Equi,

Overlooking Rome.

Sabini, Hernici. Towards the south-east at the foot of the Alban mountains it embraces those plains of the old Latium which open out by the country of the Rutuli on the swamps of the Volsci. The sun, ready to set behind us in the Tyrrhene Sea, inflamed with its crepuscular purple the domes, towers, and pinnacles, the façades of palaces and ruins, as well as the volcanic mounds scattered at the foot of the chains and over the plateaux; a few peaks silvered with early snow crowned the violet Apennines with a pyramid of rose-colour, where brighter lines marked here and there a hamlet perched high. Between these two extreme points, the blue-tinged mountains, the city glowing and ruddy in the midst of the bronze zone of its Byzantine walls, lay stretched before us a mixture of verdure and russet outlines, the country crossed by aqueducts covered with ancient villas, and pierced by long roads of old renown, marked out and lined with tombs. The yellow Tiber, *flavus*, as Horace called it, winds at your feet like a track of sand; going up towards the horizon, it melts, on one side in the azure of the sky, on the other in the fires of the setting sun.

While the abbé continued to point out to me each monument, each site, from Mount Soracte to Tivoli, from the tomb of Adrian to the mole of Cæcilia Metella, I fancied I saw again what he introduced to me. To the right especially, beyond St. Paul and the Ardean road, to the culminating point of the hill of Jupiter, from Alba Longa and the distances of the Appian Way to the old Latin gate, memorable spots occur in such numbers, on a theatre so noble, that one looks forth, as in a dream where one traversed the air with wings, over all the legend of the ages closing in its sanctuary—the Forum Romanum, whose ruins, rising to the left of the Coliseum, at this moment glittered in a burning light. Framing panoplies of ruins and little domes and terraced gardens, the famous hills, the Cœlian, the Palatine, the Capitoline, marked the enclosure of the dale of Romulus and the swamps of the Velabrum. How many mighty names, how many mighty things in this little space! How many kingdoms in miniature destroyed by wars of giants!

CHAPTER II.

WHEN we remember what this bit of narrow valley was, the interests of the world that have been debated there, the voices that have resounded there, the dramas that have been there unfolded; when we think that from the almost fabulous time of the alliance of the Sabines with the hordes of Romulus down to the last Augustuli, this spot was the very brain of the immense Roman Empire, we hardly dare to tread its soil, so profoundly is one seized with a religious impression. The entire history of a people, of the most renowned of all peoples, worked itself out on this scene, soul and sanctuary of Rome.

We know where the Forum was, but its exact boundaries leave room for a host of uncertainties, and have given rise to numerous controversies. A portion only of the place has been exposed by excavations. The truth as to the whole is still half buried under four-and-twenty feet of ruins heaped up in the eleventh century by the vandalism of Robert Guiscard, who, to avenge the Popes, destroyed their capital, the marvel of the old world. It would have been necessary, therefore, only the coffer of St. Peter is not rich enough, to continue on this long space, divided by two distinct levels, the excavations begun under Paul III., pushed on with more activity when Rome, violently usurped, made part of the French Empire, and since then under the reigns of Leo XII. and Gregory XVI.

The Temple of Saturn is separated from that of Vespasian by a branch of the Via Sacra, which was called the *Clivus Capitolinus*, or slope of the Capitol. Leaving this to follow a sort of alley encumbered with broken marbles, you reach the Schola Xantha. Here are the lodges (*tabernæ*), to the number of six, which served as bureaux for the scribes, the archivists, the *præcones* of the curule ædiles. These vaulted shops have still their threshold; they continue

ENTRY OF THE FORUM ROMANUM BY THE VIA SACRA.—TEMPLE OF VENUS AT ROME.—STA. FRANCESCA ROMANA. ARCH OF TITUS. CAMPANILE OF THE CAPITOL, ETC.

below and in front of the portico of the Twelve Gods as far as the foot of the Tabularium. Pius IX. had them cleared out and restored in 1857.

Let us now cross, parallel to the Tabularium, the base of the Capitoline *intermontium*, by directing our course on the side of the Tullian prison and the Gemoniæ, which have given way to the slope of the Ara Cœli. We shall come across, between the arch of Septimius Severus and the corner of the portico erected in 676 of Rome by Lutatius Catulus, in front of the building where they kept the tables of bronze (the archives of the Republic), the remains of the renowned Temple of Concord, erected, it is said, by Tiberius. On this point no uncertainty; votive inscriptions confirm with reference to the site and aspect of this edifice the indications of Plutarch, Dion Cassius, and Festus. The entry of the temple, one of the stirring historic spots of Ancient Rome, is still marked by the holes in which the hinges of the gates turned. The monument was enormous, nearly square; they descended from its vast portico by steps of marble, of which numerous fragments still remain in their place.

TEMPLE OF VESPASIAN AND PORTICO OF THE TWELVE GODS.

Turned to the Forum, close to the Gemoniæ, standing back at the foot of the Capitol, the portico of the Temple of Concord served as a meeting-place; the senate assembled there on great occasions, where it was necessary to address the people congregated before the rostra. The place of the speaker, therefore, must have been placed between the steps of the temple and the popular comitia of the Forum.

Now the tribune, at first placed near the Temple of Castor and Pollux, long confounded with the Græcostasis, where from the time of Pyrrhus foreign ambassadors were quartered, the tribune for orations was afterwards transferred between the comitium, of which these steps are still to be recognised, and the foot of the many steps of the Temple of Concord, almost in the angle of Severus's arch. There still remain of it massive constructions of peperino or volcanic rock ten yards long. I have measured them. Close by is the office of the scribes who preserved the speeches, officials who, from Tullius Tiro downwards, Cicero's freedman, may be compared to our shorthand writers.

ENTABLATURE OF THE TEMPLE OF CONCORD.

These signs are written unmistakably, and the essential portions still subsist. I shall be forgiven, then, if I abstain from dissertations on the subject. I should fear to chill the impressions which this spot stirs. Nor will I expatiate on the monography of the Temple of Concord; facings of the *cella* in antique yellow, African marbles that introduced all the animation of natural polychromy, ...

extinguished pleasures of which one is reduced to a mere list of memories. To establish the antiquity of the work, I will remind the reader that one superb entablature and some highly decorated bases of columns preserved in the Capitol are in work and design closely recalled by some square bases and other fragments found in Nero's palace under the baths of Titus.

It was at the entry of the Forum that the Piso lived whom Agrippina accused of having poisoned Germanicus, and it was there where he was mysteriously assassinated; Tacitus insinuates that it was at the instigation of Tiberius, who might have been compromised by his complicity. What wondrous events on a scene as narrow as that of a play-house, from the days since Brutus showed there the dagger of Lucretia, and Virginius bought in the shops to the north of the Forum, whose site is still marked, the knife which, to reach the decemvirs, was to pass through his daughter's heart, down to the memorable occasion when the curia was burnt before the body of Cæsar! To animate all, to justify all, to bring back the great spectres of history that they may introduce the emotions of their presence, it is enough to seat oneself on a column, and fit reminiscences to that fallen ornament.

REMAINS OF THE TEMPLE OF CASTOR.

At the very foot of the Palatine, at the bottom and on the lower sides of the Forum, as well as along the Via Sacra, was a row of shops of which one strikes the remains at the first stroke of the pickaxe; there are still collected here shopkeepers' signs engraved on squares of marble. I have beheld one, belonging to one of the jewellers who succeeded one another there, from the time when Papirius Cursor distributed the bucklers of chased gold and the magnificent arms of the Samnites, so that being displayed in front of the shops those trophies might furnish a magnificent decoration to the Forum. The custom was afterwards observed by the ædiles.

Into whatever place you step, you come upon memorials; on whatever side you turn, the eye is interested by monuments. A little on this side of the column of Phocas, right of the Via Sacra, the damp ground covers the fountain of Juturna where Curtius sacrificed himself. Exactly here stood

COLUMN OF PHOCAS.

the *milliarium aureum*, and on this pavement Galba was massacred by his furious legionaries, who carried off the bald head of the emperor supporting it through the mouth. Lift your eyes beyond the Forum, turning your back to the Palatine; the walls, the brackets, the stucco of the Emilian basilica lose themselves under the portal of St. Adrian. Near the gaol of Tullius is St. Luke, formerly St. Martine; between St. Luke and St. Cosmo here is San Lorenzo in

Miranda, which grasps in its arms the temple of Antoninus and Faustina. As we cross the open space transversely going towards the arch

PAVEMENT OF JULIAN BASILICA AND TABULARIUM.

of Septimus Severus, we follow the road along which Vitellius was dragged down to the narrow staircase of the Gemoniæ by which criminals passed out from the Mamertine prison.

The Forum with its frame of buildings, from the heights of the Capitol to the basilica of Constantine, was assuredly within small

ST. PAUL EXTRA MUROS.

compass the most imposing spot in the universe; no wonder the restoration of this city of monuments, perched one above another under the sides of the three hills is the privileged historic romance of all architects! It is certain that this multitude of temples, basilicas, porticoes, piled up and placed one above another, and stretching against the blue sky their white and rose profiles, that these forests of columns of all shades, standing in rows from the Julian basilica to the Temple of Jupiter Capitolinus, and letting the oblique sun-rays play between their ruddy shafts, that these deep vaults, this net-work of aisles and shining architraves against the chiaro-oscuro of the galleries, must indeed have dazzled barbarian and Gaul as they drew near the Olympus of the conquering divinities.

Such as it became, this necropolis is still, I repeat; for one still feels it, until one is overwhelmed beneath the thought, to be the most considerable spot on the globe. After losing oneself in forgetfulness there until night, like a scholar on his first pilgrimage, one turns away with a blue veronica between the pages of one's album and a tiny bit of marble in one's pocket.

Still, a son of the north, something of an archæologist and always an arguer, will have some trouble in preventing himself from regretting, as he makes his way into St. Paul's, that the piety of the faithful towards sacred traditions should have led them to restore what a catastrophe had laid in ruins. The new church is splendid; the most costly materials are piled up; it costs Christendom millions; so much expense and effort only succeeds in mournfully recalling the basilica founded by Constantine on the tomb of St. Paul, rebuilt with great splendour from 386 to 392 by the Emperors Valentinian, Theodosius, Arcadius, and Honorius, preserved for fifteen centuries, and burnt in 1823, by some clumsy plumbers.

When the Ostian basilica was destroyed Pius VII. was dying; they contrived to hide the disaster from his knowledge. It was then Leo XII. who ordered the reconstruction of St. Paul on the same dimensions, copying the dead basilica from memory. The whole world joined in the work. Schismatical Russia offered the gift of an altar of malachite; Mahomet brought as tribute to the sanctuaries of Christ four columns of oriental alabaster, presented by the Sultan; gold, silver, and jewels flowed in from every side. Hence the porticoes of veined Greek marble, the pilasters taken from the quartz of the Simplon, the walls of Carrara, framed with gems of varied hues; the entablature of Paros with its violet frieze; the enormous capitals, so lavish in size, so delicate in execution. Wondrous spectacle, at first sight especially, that vast monument so ancient and so new, unique in our bourgeois age, of a colossal reliquary executed as if it were a miniature, and revealed in all its dazzling freshness.

UNDER THE GALLERIES OF THE COLISEUM.

But you do not lose yourself there, as in the old edifices of Ravenna, in a dream of wondering and confiding admiration. The moment you pass to analysis, the poverty of existing artists is disclosed in such a degree, that to restore to this noble shrine something of its soul and the veneration that it ought to inspire, you apply yourself to the search for the smallest vestiges of the primitive basilica that may have escaped from the disaster of 1823. This examination is repaid by a few consolations.

Notwithstanding all its imperfections, St. Paul will continue to be reckoned among the important monuments of Rome; its richness and splendour, and certain details still preserved, make the building still interesting. But if the church did not exist, it would yet be necessary to go there to visit the cloister, one of the two finest works in that kind that the thirteenth century has bequeathed to us. The other is the cloister of St. John Lateran, which this recalls very closely.

Farther on you leave to the left the artificial mound of Monte-Testaccio, formed in long years by the pile of earthenware vessels, in which the peasants placed most of their wares that they brought to the great market of Rome, and whose fragments they threw away in this common place of deposit established behind the Emporium, from which they have recently cleared away the débris. Most of the wares they unloaded there, even dried vegetables, were carried in vessels of clay, and not as in our time in tilted carts, in baskets, sacks, or chests. These worthless vessels once emptied were tossed away, and this explains what was for long the enigmatical existence of the enormous *cumulus*. You then come to the Marmorata, a store of the marbles of Greece and Italy; they have just exhumed, for the purpose of making use of them, blocks that have been unloaded there these fifteen centuries, and known ever since the time of Sixtus V., a fact that facilitated a discovery that has in these later times made much noise. Hence we pass to the foot of the convent of Sta. Sabina, whose bells sound on the Aventine, whose church has seen St. Dominic and Father Lacordaire; famous names that open and close the annals of the order of preaching friars. In front beyond the Tiber is the hospital of St. Michael, where they have a school of arts and trades for orphans. Finally, at the extremity of this escarped face of the Aventine, covered with shrubs and brambles, you gradually see the city encircle the stream behind the remains of the Pons Sublicius which Anchus Martius placed on wooden joists, as its name indicates, and which was rebuilt by the censor Æmilius Lepidus in the reign of the second of the Cæsars. This was the bridge that Horatius Cocles defended; it is from this primitive monument, whose construction, preservation, and maintenance was confided to the college of priests, that our word pontiff comes.

THE ARENA OF THE COLISEUM.

The magnificence of the Coliseum has been so well appreciated, that the popes have at great expense restored and consolidated the Flavian amphitheatre; they are proud of a solicitude with which all

Rome associates itself. We may conceive the fine effect produced some years ago by one of the French bishops, when preaching in the pulpit of the Coliseum, he ventured to exclaim, "What, ruins of abomination, relics of impurity, you still stand! O shame, that Christians should endure the sight of these infamous walls! They do not scatter the stones of this Babel, heaped up by the impious pride of the enemies of the faith! . . . ." Here were eloquent emotions to convince a Genseric or an Attila; but the prelates of Rome have a less primitive zeal. Whence it follows that in condemning, by this appeal for the destruction of the Coliseum, so many pontiffs who had been the religious preservers of its antique splendours, Monseigneur just a little compromised his country. "At the bottom of your hearts," an official remarked to me on this subject, "you are the descendants of the Gauls who devastated Italy."

The quantity of shrubs, of pellitory, of saxifrage, that the Coliseum nurtures is even less surprising than the rarity of the species. Whether it is that this vast mass raised high in the air intercepts wandering germs on their passage, or that the nature of the artificial soil or the composition of the cements that bind the stones have been favourable to exotic growths, it is the case that the botanists have drawn up a considerable herbarium of Colisean objects that are to be found in no other place under the Roman sky. This mountain of the Flavii has its own flora, like Hymettus or Hybla.

It is not, however, in the first moments that you give your attention to these details that are so close to you. By an instinct which is an aspiration after the infinite, the eye first of all darts to the farthest point of the horizon that the soul would fain pass. Above the escarped edges of this crater, you discover at the points of the four cardinal winds, not landscapes, not a city, not a simple bird's-eye view, but the unnumbered illustrations of the greatest book of history. This spectacle you regard with the sensations of dream peopled by apparitions.

Silence, which often makes its impression without the spirit being conscious of it, perhaps increased the illusion of the mirage, and for that reason a noise that was suddenly made conveyed to us the sensation of being roughly awakened. From the bottom of this crucible for fusing stars in, confusedly issued strains of church music; our eyes attracted to the bottom of the abyss distinguished a microscopic procession of penitents masked by their sheets, taper in hand and banner at the head, who, followed by countrymen and shepherds, chanted the office of *Via Crucis* before the fourteen chapels

GENERAL VIEW OF THE COLISEUM.

which are arranged round the arena. From these depths up to the purple of the west, where the solar ball was sinking, we measured strange distances, gradations of light and colour more marvellous than ever.

And without being able to speak, we gazed; as the night fell we still gazed.

A CORRIDOR OF THE COLISEUM.

CHAPTER III.

AT Rome the multiplicity of journeys and visits, the absence of omnibuses, the scarcity of cabs, all combine to keep you on the trot more than half the day from street to street. But you take this duty with patience, because the streets change in physiognomy according to the quarter, and because on pavement there overflows a tide of common people, simple in their manners, and bringing with them into full day, besides their porringers and chafing-dish, their household habits, sometimes the practice of their trade, without being disturbed by prohibitive regulations.

In the long monastic streets where the grass grows—on the road for instance from Santa Maria Maggiore to the Lateran—amusing processions move without noise along with the few and discreet passers-by. The scholars of seminaries and colleges, originally from the five parts of the globe, dressed up like little abbés in all colours according to their nations, with voluminous shovel-hats on thin bodies and childish faces, furnish a diverting sight. The Germans wear red cassocks, the English violet; the white frock of the little Americans contrasts with the browned heads of young negroes and red-skins brightened by the Indian sun.

On the Pincian every morning appointments are made for talking politics between heteroclite and discreet persons whom you would take for retired clerks or merchants, were it not for their clerical dress, which savours of the ancient *régime* and suggests the old comedy rather than the church. A yellowish umbrella under the arm, a snuff-box in the hand, these prelates have the air of honest shopkeepers of old days.

In consequence of some maternal vow one used to see Carmelites, Franciscans, Carthusians, from eight to ten months old at their nurse's breast; this is what still happens in the Kingdom of Naples Down to Leo XII. and Gregory XVI., who put an end to another abuse, the clerks of solicitors and notaries, as well as a host of officials belonging to the administration, arrogated to themselves the privilege of wearing the cassock, while they kept the life and behaviour of the young men of the day. Hence for foreigners many an occasion for scandal, they attributing to the clergy the follies and misdeeds of the lawyers' clerks. The cassock is there what with us the administrative frock and military uniform are—the dress of those who are something in the State.

"THE SCHOLARS .... WITH VOLUMINOUS SHOVEL-HATS." BY HENRI REGNAULT.

Many monks and nuns and a certain quantity of soldiers are what contribute to give variety to the look of the streets, setting off somewhat the raggedness of the Trastevere or of the Suburra. Popular costumes no longer exist at Rome, but there still come a few from the country. The country districts send up to the great city, besides models for painters, families who in order to utilise some necessary journey of the head of the tribe will accompany him in full force in their fine costume, equipped with some gewgaws to sell, some couplets to sing, or a curiosity to exhibit. The principal business concluded, or the market closed, the good folks stay where they have got out, at the piazza Montanara, in the quarter of the Regola, in the environs of the Farnese Palace, towards the Ponte Sisto, or at the corner of the Quattro Capi bridge, waiting for the hour of return to the mountains, and munching morsels of bread. Seated on a curb-stone, or arranged in a group on the angular heap and the parapets, a rural household will be seen there all installed as if in their quarters, the youngsters sporting round the maternal skirts, and the contadina suckling the youngest while she waits her lord.

These are the sights of the street; they offer a diversion as one hurries from a church, or from one gallery to another.

Warned against the classic seductions of Guido no less than against those of Domenico Zampieri, I still felt as I looked in the original on the ceiling of the Aurora,

ON THE PINCIAN. BY HENRI REGNAULT.

too chilled by the graver of Morghen, the sensation that is produced by a work poetically treated and indebted for a happy effect to a choice of colour full of freedom and delight. Preceded by a Genius who bears in the air the torch of day, Apollo on his car advances in flame through the sky to commence his day. He is followed by Flora and surrounded by the Hours, who dance around. These have been nourished without any economy, and are perhaps a little too plump; would to heaven that in these full and jubilant visages one could recognise the poor and wretched. At the bottom of the picture, in the distances of earth, the sea and its shores, still bluish, are not warmed by the freshness of the dawn. The composition is harmonious, the painting bright and tranquil; the draperies are studied, and the poses graceful. It is the attractive masterpiece of an artist usually cold, and of whom we shall find among the Barberini collection the best, or at any rate the most agreeable, portrait.

As to the First Fault, by Domenichino, it is a sketch of Breughel de Velours enlarged by a Roman from Bologna who knows his rank; the graces of the subject humanise the magisterial cleverness of the painter. Adam plucking the apple, Eve who receives it stooping, are attractive figures; the menagerie distributed in an Eden inspired

THE AURORA OF GUIDO RENI IN THE ROSPIGLIOSI PALACE.

from the Roman Campagna gives animation to a scene of rich fancy. Built for Scipio Borghese, the Rospigliosi Palace was formerly acquired by Mazarin. After the death of the cardinal minister they stationed the French Embassy there, which only left it in 1704. Let us go down again to the street of the Quattro Fontane.

The vast Barberini Palace, at which three generations of architects worked, Charles Maderno, Borromini, and Bernini, is thrown in false square on hilly gardens whose lofty trees have seen pass beneath them all the race of the nephews of Urban VIII.

As soon as one had mounted the staircase on the right or the staircase on the left—the one of Borromini, imitated from Bramante, who took a model from St. Nicolo of Pisa, the other of Bernini—one had crossed a frontier; Rome showed herself on the spot by the peculiar note of her patrician dwelling-places. The great hall to which you approach by two staircases of honour, has for ceiling an immense production of Peter of Cortona, the Triumph of Glory, *capo d'opera* as far as knowledge and skill, a swarming conception which escapes from all the conditions of verisimilitude that have hitherto been respected in ceilings. On the walls an ancient picture of Roman Masquerade, infinitely curious; in the neighbouring rooms family portraits and ancient busts. In the form of credence or console a Madame Barberini of old days, travestied as Diana in repose, sleeps her last sleep over an enormous and ancient sarcophagus. Restored mausoleums in this way become here furniture for an antechamber or a dining-room.

As for the gallery, which is situated in a low entresol, one of its attractions is that it offers the original and indisputable portrait of a woman beloved by Raphael, whom tradition has made a female baker. Rome possesses five or six copies of it; they are inferior to the authenticated example of the Villa Barberini. They show that the adorable brunette of the Tribuna of the Uffizi at Florence is not that friend of the painter whose real name was Margaret and who is called La Fornarina, and I regret it for his sake, for the lady of the Uffizi is handsomer than the lady at Rome. The latter, as she is represented by the portrait of the Barberini, is the relief of an artist wearied of the ideal and of ethereal creations. She is a substantial, hearty woman in full bloom, whose nose drinks the wind with full aspiration, accompanying little greedy eyes, and a mouth softened by laughter. The jet-black locks are harmonized with the skin by browned tones of a burning warmth; she has over her the sketch of a diaphonous robe. The signature of the master, or of the slave, is on a narrow circlet attached in the shape of a bracelet round the biceps of the left arm. One perceives that she was very finely made; the hands are pretty, but we discern there as well as on the arms vexatious repaintings. The piece in its smoky tone is cleverly restored; still the model has less delicacy than frankness.

For anybody who knows the two portraits, that of Rome and that of Florence, two women who have not the most distant likeness, the once-celebrated work of Quatremère de Quincy on the works of Raphael loses much of its value. He expatiates gravely on the question whether it is the Fornarina of the Pitti Palace, *or its reproduction* in the Barberini Palace, which is the true original. He can only have seen one of the two pictures.

Around this picture there are others of which one ought only to speak in order to warn good souls against the pretensions of the Notice. The Holy Family of Andrea del Sarto, that one of his pupils would have painted with a less awkward servility of imitation; apocryphal Madonnas of Bellini, of Francia, of that Antonio Razzi who is calumniated in more forms than one; a Jesus among the Doctors, a bit of Teutonic barbarism, impudently attributed to Albert Dürer; a cardinal's portrait which would compromise the name of Titian if the draperies were less dull; a so-called portrait of Masaccio, in which they have only copied his cap: here are equivocal works denoting the oblivion of tradition in a country so rich in subjects of study.

A curious picture of this gallery, a portion detached from that of the Sciarra Palace, is the Death of Germanicus, by Poussin; a canvas of a fine colour, of a dramatic sentiment, full of simplicity; and with this master candour is hardly common. Probably, when he executed it, the artist had not yet impregnated his spirit with the monuments of antiquity. A reminiscence of the etiquette of courts governs the arrangement of the Death of Germanicus: before these Romans we think of the warriors of Lebrun; we involuntarily look for Lauzun and the Marshal de la Feuillade by the pillow of the son of Drusus. Robbed of his manner, away from his system, Poussin becomes less professorial and more pleasing.

It is here also that we find the original of an extremely sweet portrait of a young girl, a hundred times reproduced by engraving in all sizes—the Beatrice de' Cenci of Guido, a face fascinating and

LA FORNARINA OF THE BARBERINI PALACE, AT ROME.

suffering, with a head-dress of white draperies heavily arranged—a melancholy, interesting figure, though a little too set.

Michael Angelo of Caravagio painted, in an effect of shadow after the manner of Rembrandt, with a head-dress still more massive, the mother of this heroine; finally, a third picture, the best and the least remarked, the portrait of a ripe beauty with an elegant sweep of outline and a physiognomy expressive of calm cruelty, transmits to us, they say, the features of the mother-in-law of Beatrice, the Lucrezia Petroni : this work is by Scipio of Gaëta. Not here, but a little later, we shall attempt to retrace that horrible tale; these fine portraits, especially the first, being suspected of being apocryphal.

In fact, although at the death of Beatrice, Reni was already four-and-twenty, it is doubtful whether he arrived at Rome before the death of Clement VIII. Moreover, the portrait of the Cenci has less the air of a study executed from nature than of a head composed with the help of an earlier portrait. Guido may have executed afterwards an idealized likeness of the famous heroine. However this may be, to personify so romantic a victim no face could have been chosen more touching in expression or more sure to move pity.

LA FORNARINA OF THE UFFIZI, AT FLORENCE.

From the street of the Quattro Fontane to the Corso the distance is not great; it is still less from the Barberini Gallery to the Sciarra Gallery, a collection which is the *tribuna* or sanctuary of the other. The casket presents in fact among some pebbles of the Rhine certain precious stones of fine water. The two figures called Vanity and Modesty justify by their perfection the mistake of those who have so often attributed to Leonardo the works of Bernardino Luini, that affectionate artist so loyal to the glorification of his master, like all who heard and loved that famous man. Between the Circe of Garofalo, a landscape where the companions of Ulysses are in the very struggle of being transformed into beasts, and the St. Sebastian of Perugino, Albert Dürer in the Death of the Virgin makes us pardon the country of his birth by force of skill and simplicity. He is rarely seen to gain this triumph.

Poussin has in this palace some curious canvases: the St. Erasmus, whose bowels executioners are tearing out, a ghastly subject handled with vigour so as to be occupied in mosaic, a picture with more energy and truth than his representation of St. Peter; the St. Matthew writing, a very fine piece which has not become too dark; the views of the banks of the Tiber, and of the Acqua Acetosa, rendered by a master who loves the sites and the district.

But among smaller marvels are certain tiny landscapes of Claude of Lorraine; one in particular, which, from the sides of the green crater into which heaven has poured the lake of Albano, represents on the horizon the crest of Castel Gandolfo. Another of these compositions, of a more costly finish, was painted on a plate of silver, a piece of far-fetched luxury to little purpose, which nobody can perceive, and that I should not know of but for the Princess Barberini having since then revealed it to me in a Paris salon. The weight of a silver mounting scarcely adds to the value of the jewels of the master, Claude.

THE BEATRICE DE CENCI, BY GUIDO RENI.

Rome Triumphant, and the Death of St. John the Baptist, are the two most important pieces of Valentino. This last painting has an effect in relief of great power; the Herodiad is a magnificent piece. From this picture to that of Michael Angelo of Caravagio, realist in a time when people did not yet possess works so ill compounded, the interval is easily traversed; it will strike a simple spectator vividly, and may possibly stop in passing the connoisseur, and even the moralist, who usually only understands the vicious sides of the arts. Two sharpers agree to pluck a pigeon; one posted behind the stripling marks on his fingers for his accomplice the number of points. The first is an old rascal, seamed, stamped, and branded by vice and infamy in every line of his face; the other, the accomplice who plays, pale, stooping, prematurely degraded, confronts with his debased adolescence the candid youth of his victim. From his doublet he withdraws a card, assuring himself by an oblique and false glance of the success of his knavery.

I have reserved to the last the Young Man with the Bow, or Violinist of Raphael. It is here we find this so justly renowned picture, dated 1518 and signed. Everybody recalls that delicate and feminine face, with its black cap so gracefully adjusted and posed over a broad collar of fur.

THE VIOLINIST OF RAPHAEL (SCIARRA PALACE).

These two palaces, whose galleries are not too undigested, gave me a fancy for collections formed by families of the country, the intelligent luxuries of the Roman princes. Some deceptions, however, awaited me at the Corso, in the Doria Palace, whose salons, richly decorated in the time of Innocent X. with those daubings that our architects of the great reign imitated, exhibit among several masterpieces mediocre copies and apocryphal pieces in great number. The catalogues not being published, it may be convenient to point out the best pictures, and to mark among the golden ears parasitic blights, such as some Murillos, several Andrea del Sartos and Francias, that those masters never saw. Poussin, Van Dyck, Titian especially, are frequently compromised by cold imitators; they give for the original of the last painter a weak enough copy of his Magdalen of the Pitti Palace.

Wandering here and there, you come upon a fine Descent from the Cross in the style of the primitive painters of the north, attributed presumptuously to Hemling; and a good portrait of a man, attributed to Giorgione. On the right hand of the great gallery let us notice a pretty little Reader, by Lucas of Leyden, and let us unmask a copy of the Aldobrandine Nuptials, attributed very gratuitously to Poussin. In the centre of the bay you will be scandalized by portraits usurping the names of Raphael, Rembrandt, Rubens, Van Dyck. Those who have named these paltry things have not even had respect to the chronological indications furnished by the dress, for the way in which the pictures are assigned involves the most amusing blunders. Thus a rather villainous copy of a picture of three faces in the Pitti Palace, which represents three Italians without beard, is thus described, "Calvin, Luther, and Catherine, by Giorgione." Giorgio Barbarelli, who died in 1511, cannot have painted the portrait of the wife of Luther, still less that of Calvin, who was born in 1509. They attribute to Leonardo da Vinci a copy of the Jane of Aragon that the books of the Louvre properly give to Raphael. In the Doria Palace the face offers some variations, and especially in the background, where a bright green curtain recalls Andrea di Solaria. This charming head of the granddaughter of Ferdinand I., who married the Constable Colonna, is known at Rome under the pseudonym of Queen Jane of Naples. What more common than such blunders! At Paris did they not take the Lucrezia Crivelli for La Belle Férronnière? This good and old copy of Madame Colonna has a false air of the school of Leonardo; but the original, that we have had in our possession since the reign of Francis I., has not the very marked characteristics of a portrait of Raphael. So recourse has been had to the usual expedient of throwing on to Giulio Romano the execution of the body and the accessories.

The painting by Claude, called "The Mill," contains all the poetry of the Roman Campagna. A river of some breadth, its basin cut off by a sluice, descends facing the spectator from the Alban hills which bound plains strewn with the ruin of aqueducts; at the back to the right is a small town inspired by that picturesque Etruria of which the old painter dreamed before the ruins of the Latin towns; on the other bank turns, at a corner of a rustic manufactory, a water-mill, whose wheel shines like silver; it contrasts with the small Temple of Vesta perceived at the foot of a hilly indentation; the whole is toned in vast foregrounds of verdure plunged by enormous trees into thick translucent shadow, in which idyllic figures glance to and fro in dancing and rustic games. The vigour, the intensity, the movement of this foreground, prolonged in far perspective, produce a delicate and variegated light which fascinates our eyes and attracts them to the sky, to the Monte Gennaro, the snows of the Apennines, and the remote hills which fall away in the Campagna. Before a diversity of detail like this we have a difficulty in understanding such limpid tranquillity of effect and impression. There is nothing staring ; as in nature, you have to get accustomed and recognise the whole site little by little.

After my visit to the Barberini Palace the features of the Beatrice de' Cenci remained in my memory, and I had vague dreams of seeking out the palace once inhabited by the actors in one of the most sombre tragedies of the past time. I was still ignorant of the situation of the house, when one day wandering about the city I took it into my head that chance had brought me to the quarter of the Cenci.

The aspect of the house is scarcely less appropriate to the melodrama which has made the old name of the Cenci so familiar. It is in the corner of a small choked and uneven piazza that the old entry to the palace hides itself under a truncated tower, the palace on this side only revealing a straight outline. Iron cross bars impress on the façade a character of mystery and duress; one of the gates, arched and carved, is surmounted by an antique mask of a Medusa of a dreary and tearful expression. In the other corner of the piazza, shut in and lugubrious as the court of an old dungeon, Francesco Cenci—he who was assassinated—had raised towards 1575, to the honour of St. Thomas, a small oratory on the wall, of which an inscription perpetuates this reminiscence. They have also fitted into the walls adjoining two small cippi, or funeral altars, bearing the name of one Marcus Cintius. They were for the Cenci stone charters, for their boast was that they had descended from this Cintius, as the Muti descended from Mutius Scævola. They would have been more happily inspired in claiming kinship with Lucius Cincius Alimentus, who, 153 before our era, being prætor in Sicily, was made prisoner by Hannibal, of whom he wrote a history, quoted by Macrobius, and praised by Livy. But the ignorance of the feudal barons was as great as their vanity, as is frequently proclaimed by their pretensions of this sort. The Santa Croce boasted of being of the line of Valerius Publicola : hence the name of Santa Maria de Publicolis given to the church where they have their burying-places, among which, besides fine monumental stones of the fourteenth century, one ought to mention a magnificent Florentine mausoleum.

The continuation of the Cenci Palace, in the inside of which there is nothing any longer to recall the contemporaries of Clement VIII., reaches to another larger and lower square in front of the synagogue.

The principal existing entry is surmounted with the inscription, CENCI BOLOGNETTI; but the heirs of the name do not live in the palace.

It was in the Castle of St. Angelo, that Roman version of the Tower of Nesle, and in face of the mole of Adrian, that the terrible adventure of their ancestors came to its end. You can by making some turns approach this strange-outlined monument by alleys that isolate and set off the massive and imposing prison-house.

In spite of the original head-dress with which the popes from the time of Boniface IX. crowned it, the tower-shaped burying-place of the Antonines, which is not less than six hundred feet in circumference, still keeps an equivocal and sinister expression, especially when viewed from the river, or from the poor districts of which I have spoken. Transformed in the middle ages into a prison and into a fortress; disguised afterwards as the residence of a prince, then as a barrack, the mole of Adrian, of which the Orsini in the fourteenth century made a lair for themselves, has never been able to strip itself of the physiognomy of its original destination; before the postern one still expects to see a coffin go in and an executioner come out.

These sepulchral dungeons were then in use. Without speaking of those of the Appian Way, let us remember that on the other bank at Ripetta there rose, and still stands in part, the model of the Castle of St. Angelo, the mole built by Augustus for the Cæsars of his family. It is well to say a few words about it, if only to prove the uselessness of troubling oneself about it.

It is a thick, large, squat tower, engaged in buildings; its masonry was almost entirely of reticulated work. The Colonna fortified and quartered themselves there in the middle age; but since then, mockery of fate, they have arranged a small daily spectacle in that vast *columbarium*, where, with the exception of Nero, most of the Cæsars down to Adrian reposed.

What a monstrous melodrama, the history of the Castle of St. Angelo! It only wore a rather smiling look in the days when it received the dead. Procopius paints it for us at that first epoch; the immense rotunda, terminating in different elevations, with the imperial colossus on the summit, had its sides covered with Parian marble; the circumference had pilasters surmounted with a ring of Greek statues; the whole on a basement, decorated with festoons, and tablets with funeral inscriptions, and colossal equestrian groups in gilt bronze at the four corners. Round the monument was an iron grating surmounted by peacocks, also in gilt.

The Castle of St. Angelo. 45

In 537 this fine structure was still intact; but Vitiges having attacked it, they broke the statues, in order to hurl the pieces on the

BRIDGE AND CASTLE OF ST. ANGELO.

assailants. During the three centuries which followed, the mole of Adrian, connected from the time of Honorius, perhaps, with the defences of the city, served as a fortress. It was to entrench himself that the patrician Crescentius, who wished (974) to restore the Roman republic, made himself master of it. He even kept it tolerably long, as the monument took from him the name of Castel Crescenzio. But, invited by one of the anti-popes of that anarchic period, the Emperor Otto having invaded Rome and massacred Crescentius with his principal partisans at a banquet, the tomb of Adrian was discovered and dismantled.

Half a century before, this spot had been the theatre of a tragedy which followed strange saturnalia. An incongruous relic of antique profligacy and of the monstrosities of the lower empire, drawing a mischievous power from feudal institutions, Theodora, a Roman lady, illustrious for her rank and her beauty, quartered herself from the year 908 in the Castle of St. Angelo, from which she exercised over Rome a complete tyranny, sustained against German influence by an Italian party, which counted among its chiefs Adalbert II., Count of Tuscany, the father of this Messalina. Theodora caused several pontiffs to be deposed, and nominated eight popes successively. She had a daughter as beautiful and as powerful as herself, and of still worse perversity. Marozia, so she was called, reigned likewise in the Castle of St. Angelo, where she caused the election of Sergius III. and Anastasius III. and John X., a creature of Theodora, who had had him nominated to the bishopric of Ravenna. Early the widow of a Marquis of Tusculum, and married to Guy, Prince of Tuscany, Marozia speedily had John X. suffocated in the Castle of St. Angelo; then united by a third marriage to Hugo of Provence, brother of her second husband, after having successively exhibited on the pontifical throne Leo. VI. and Stephen VIII., she gave the tira to John XI., one of her youngest sons. She had only too many children, for one of them imprisoned in this same dungeon both his mother and his brother, the Pope, and there destroyed them. Such at that time, under the brutal pressure of feudal anarchy, had the chair of St. Peter become.

The Castle of St. Angelo, from the seventh to the ninth century, is found connected with all the outrages and all the factions that desolated Rome; and, down to the end of the fourteenth, its destiny was not very different. It was then that Boniface IX., a Neapolitan by origin, crowned the dungeon, to make it still stronger, with the works which make it at once less gloomy and more striking. Alexander VI. completed the restoration, and, by a passage con-

The Castle of St. Angelo. 47

structed in the wall of the Leonine city, he brought the Castle of St.

BANKS OF THE TIBER BETWEEN RIPETTA AND THE BRIDGE OF ST. ANGELO.

Angelo into communication with the Vatican. This idea was profitable

(1527) to Clement VII., when he was obliged, in order to escape the unbridled hordes of the Constable de Bourbon, to seek an inviolable asylum in the thick walls of the Castle of St. Angelo.

Before entering, let us recall the manner in which it acquired the name that time has consecrated.

In the year 590, as St. Gregory the Great, recently called to the pontificate by the people and the bishops, was bewailing the misfortunes of his flock that a plague was then decimating, he ordered a general procession to the tomb of St. Peter to seek the removal of this scourge. The procession was headed by Pope Gregory himself, who walked with naked feet. As it crossed the Tiber on the Ælian Bridge, built by Adrian, a bridge which still stands and confronts his mausoleum, suddenly above the mole Gregory saw, starting from the clouds and appearing to him as symbol of hope, the radiant Archangel St. Michael. Thus it was not by any means, as the guide-books have it, on account of the bronze statue placed on the top by Benedict XIV. that the mole became the Castel Sant' Angelo. The first book would have proved that they had called it so for a thousand years.

Every country possesses among its judicial annals some never-to-be-forgotten drama of which legend takes possession. The middle age had among ourselves the adventure of Gabrielle de Vergy, that of Aubri de Montdidier; later, the assassination of the Marquise de Ganges and the poisonings of Madame Brinvilliers supplied stories for an evening. In Italy, and at Rome especially, these atrocities have never been rare; the great school is there. But nothing equals the interest, and nothing has counterbalanced the renown of Beatrice de' Cinci.

The family was extremely rich, and in possession of a sombre kind of celebrity of remote date; for it boasted of counting in its ancestral stock Crescentius, that consul of whom we have just spoken, and who took up his quarters in the Castle of St. Angelo, where we see the prison of his descendants. It was one of the Cenci who, being stationed on Christmas night in the same dungeon by Henry IV., while Gregory VII. was celebrating the first mass, seized him at the altar and dragged him by the hair out of the sanctuary to throw him into a cell. These examples had perhaps contributed to maintain a violent spirit in the family, of which the most odious shoot is, towards the end of the sixteenth century, that Francesco Cenci who had inflicted on three of his sons the most abominable and unspeakable outrages; who had the second and the third assassinated; who overwhelmed his daughter and his second wife with ill-usage; and who, twice convicted of the most infamous crimes, escaped the penalties by bribing his judges.

Taking pity on the eldest among the children, as well as on the eldest of the two sisters, the Pope had rescued the sons from a degrading yoke and married the daughter, at the same time compelling Francesco to give her dower. Afterwards, the youngest children of the monster, Beatrice and Bernardino, as well as Lucrezia Petroni, their stepmother, losing courage to go on bearing the usage that lay so heavy on them, addressed to Clement VIII. one of the most touching memorials, imploring his pity and protection. Their supplication miscarried and remained unanswered, to the despair of Lucrezia and of Beatrice, who abhorred in her father the dishonour of the family and the murderer of her two brothers.

At last, one night when Francesco Cenci was at the quarters of the Colonna, at the castle of Rocca di Petrella in the kingdom of Naples, he was assassinated there by unknown hands and in the most singular manner. During his sleep, two enormous nails were driven into his eyes with a hammer, a feat which implied the co-operation of two accomplices at least. This took place the 15th of September, 1598. Lucrezia was speedily suspected. On the first inquiries, Guerra, a very handsome monsignore who passed for the chosen friend of the young Beatrice, took to flight, after procuring the murder of one of the two assassins whose track had been discovered and who was called Olimpio. The other, named Marcio, arrested and put to the torture, declared that he as well as his slain comrade had been hired by Jacopo, Lucrezia, and Beatrice de' Cenci, seconded by Guerra, who, having put their victim to sleep with a narcotic draught, then introduced the two *bravi* into his room, where Lucrezia had placed in their hands the nails that were to be the instruments of vengeance. After that they had given them a thousand crowns of gold.

At the first rumour of these inquiries, the female De' Cenci returned tranquilly with the two sons to Rome to their palace, where the Pope placed sentinels to hold them in arrest. Marcio was transferred to the pontifical prisons, where he repeated his declarations; but, being confronted with Beatrice, he was so crushed by the reproaches, the denials, and the ascendancy of that marvellous beauty, that he retracted all, and persisted thenceforth in his denial even in the midst of the tortures which at last killed him.

It was at this moment that there began in this extraordinary trial the strange turns brought by unforeseen circumstances. The whole of Rome was absorbed with the event, and offered all its vows for two beautiful, young, oppressed women. The recantation of Marcio was then all the better received by the judges, as Beatrice had endured the torture with superhuman courage, while she protested her innocence.

But while the issue was going in this direction, the police arrested for some offence a ruffian, who was recognised as the assassin of Olimpio, the second murderer of the count. The witness thus suddenly raised up confirmed the first deposition of Marcio. This story charged the two women, as well as Jacopo and Guerra. The whole family of the Cenci was thrown into the Castle of St. Angelo where the proceedings were resumed and slowly persevered in.

This anguish of the torture Beatrice de' Cenci confronted for nearly a year without a word of confession. Such was the interest excited by her courage that even the judges were subjugated by so many attractions of youth and eloquence. It was necessary to withdraw the cause from them and to entrust it to more callous persons. Her elder brother and her mother-in-law, their constancy worn out, then confessed; the young Bernardino, a stranger to the whole affair and who knew nothing of it, confessed all that they wished, in order to escape from that Gehenna. Later on his innocence was demonstrated. Why should one not regard as acquitted all the wretches condemned on their own testimony thus extracted by torment? But it was in vain that they opposed to the young heiress of the Cenci the crushing evidence of her family; she persisted in the enthusiastic declaration of her innocence. No threat, no torment, vanquished her; and her tenacity suspended the doom of the accused.

The winter passed in this way; Beatrice was compared to Lucretia, to Virginia, to Clelia, Roman women of the heroic time, whose firmness she recalled while she surpassed their charms. One day, in order to apply some new torture, they had to begin by cutting off all her hair; they were fair locks, the most silken, the longest, the most marvellous in colour ever seen. Beatrice grew pale; she was vehemently stirred, and, repelling the executioner, she cried out, ' Touch not my head; let me die without mutilation !'

Sad wage for so much bravery! She destroyed herself to save her tresses; and by a full confession confirmed all the depositions.

They were all four condemned to die, a decree against which Beatrice protested by a fierce access of indignation that found an echo in every soul. In the city, in the palaces, even in the cloisters, they talked of nothing else. If the valour of this noble soul had won for

CLOISTER OF ST. JOHN LATERAN.

her so much sympathy, judge of the effect wrought on a population of artists and poets by this unforeseen weakness, childlike and truly touching, by which the young maiden and the woman had betrayed the heroine! It was an effect of delirium, of adoration; and Clement VIII. was inclined to yield to the current of feeling, when, by a second stroke of fate, one Massini poisoned his father. Other crimes of this kind already weighed heavily on the nobles; the Pope resolved on making an example, and he confirmed the judgment on the four prisoners. Such a sentence, undoubtedly unjust so far as it touched the young Bernardino, and of doubtful equity, as we must confess, with reference to the others, revolted the whole city. Cardinals and religious corporations, magistrates and citizens, threw themselves at the knees of the Pontiff, urgently seeking revision of judgment. Clement VIII., yielding to this request, supplied the Cenci with skilful champions, Nicolo de' Angeli and Farinacci, and he ordered the case to be argued in his presence.

Officially appointed to plead before the Holy Father, the two advocates displayed irresistible eloquence; recalling the abominations of Francesco Cenci twice snatched from justice, and the probable murder of his two sons, Farinacci argued that such a monster must have created a host of foes and stirred up against him more than one avenger. He had the art of convincing and softening to such a degree, that the Pope left the hearing profoundly moved. Everybody then was in expectation of mercy when, third fatal accident! while the case was yet pending, a young Marquis of Santa Croce assassinated his mother. Did the Pope believe himself warned by heaven and exhorted to harshness? In any case, from this moment he remained inflexible; and having pardoned Bernardino, whose innocence was notorious, he gave the order for hastening the execution, forcing the youthful son of the Cenci to look on at the butchery of his family. The judicial agony of these unhappy souls had lasted a year.

They were to be slain on the 8th of September, 1599, but it was the festival of the Holy Virgin. It was Beatrice who thought of this, and who, that the day of the Madonna might not be stained with blood, implored the respite of a few hours—an act of piety which rendered her fate still more touching.

On the morning of the 9th, the Pope Aldobrandini, to be far away from the scene of punishment, quitted Rome; he passed before the Castle of St. Angelo, over the bridge that was soon to be trodden by the condemned. A pontiff with erudition, the son of an illustrious man of letters, Clement VIII. was not inaccessible to pity; he only went as far as a convent that was near the walls, so that being warned by three discharges of cannon of the fatal moment, he might absolve the poor folk who were going to die. When the booming resounded through the air, the Pope raised himself; he went through the form of plenary absolution and then fell back almost swooning.

If he had seen what was passing the same hour in the section of the piazza of the bridge of St. Angelo, lying between the quay and the opening of the streets Paolo and del Banco di San Spirito, what would he then have done, what thought then of his justice!

For the punishment of these three victims, there had been organized there, under the name of *mannaja*, a sort of mechanism with a knife whose clumsy play perhaps retarded for two centuries the great political machine of 1793. The heat was suffocating; the sun poured down on the crowd held in by horsemen; the carriages were crowded together up to the very edge of the scaffold; the three open spaces were densely thronged; from the streets, from the piazza, from windows, from roofs, everybody could see advancing across the bridge in front of the huge and massive dungeon of the Antonines, the sinister procession. The condemned ascended the scaffold, which was placed on the piece of ground before the statues of St. Peter and St. Paul. Soon this crowd, which had been already stirred to the heart by the youth and beauty of Beatrice de' Cenci, saw with horror Lucrezia, who was large and corpulent, struggling for shame, held down and uncovered under the hands of the executioner, while the knife hacked her throat.

The shrieks of the wretched woman were answered by cries of horror from the depths of the crowd. Whilst the rage of the people directs itself to the scaffold, and the horses of the soldiers rear against the carriages, which are thrown in their turn on the women and children crushed in the shock, the executioners, dripping with blood, stricken with confusion, hasten to cut off the head of Beatrice; and as Giacomo de' Cenci, mastering with his voice the tumult that surrounded him, denounces the sentence which makes their young brother a witness of the appalling scene, bitter shrieks answer him— the shrieks of Bernardino, torn by convulsions, and who was hurried away at the moment when he saw one of the executioners raise a mass of iron over Giacomo and strike him down like an ox.

His body was cut into four quarters in the presence of the crowd; those of the women remained exposed until nightfall on the bridge of St. Angelo, and after that Beatrice de' Cenci, being claimed by a religious company, was buried behind the altar of St. Peter in Montorio, at the foot of the Transfiguration of Raphael.

By her will, the reading of which raised to its height the compassion that always surrounded the heroine, she disposed of a part of her property in dowering and marrying fifty young girls. But nearly all the appanages of the Cenci were confiscated, an incident of condemnations which never helped to make them less frequent; it was the result of this acquisition that a few years after, by the wish of Paul X., the domains of the Cenci were given to his nephews. In this way one estate of the condemned became the Villa Borghese, a spoliation which rendered this terrible tragedy yet more unpopular.

It was under the impression of this tragic legend that I entered the Castle of St. Angelo.

Along the circular passage, which by a gentle inclination slopes spirally to the foundations of the tower, throw a cannon-ball; it disappears in the shadow, and continuing to roll on the arena and awaking a multitude of echoes, conveys to the ear with the prolonged sound of thunder the perspectives of the distance. In the heart of the dungeon a vault of extreme height, with niches hollowed out to receive Colossi, marks the old Columbarium of the Antonines. The solid structure of this Roman catacomb, smoky with the torches which with their tongues of resinous fire half reveal its lines, gives it a character all the more mysterious and solemn, inasmuch as sounds are swallowed up there just as light is. The useless splendour of mosaics and facings of Parian marble had been lavished in this densely black chamber; the corridors found from a few pyramidal loop-holes a memory of the light.

The modern prisons, that is to say of the last three centuries, have been arranged in upper stories; they consist of cells, small obscure rooms surrounding an oblong court: here for the grandiose ferocity of absolute will and arbitrary power is substituted the mean ugliness of a wretched social institution. You will have shown to you the dungeons of the Cenci, and many others; you will be invited to shudder over prisons . . . which are the repository of the archives. It is in pleasant rooms decorated by the school of Raphael that you must seek the chamber in which, by order of Pius IV., was strangled Cardinal Caraffa, nephew of the previous Pope, the same day on which his brother the Prince Paliano had his head cut off; the room in which an old rancour was gratified against the nephew of Paul IV. is designated quite naturally Chamber of Justice. Zuccheri, who has drawn

The Castle Dungeons. 55

there the Virtues in fresco, has endowed the virtue of justice with graces that are perhaps slightly deceptive. On the doors, on the walls of these apartments, adorned by care of Cardinal Crispo and recently occupied by a French commandant, pupils of Giovanni d' Udine or Perino del Vaga traced elegant arabesques by way of frame for divers pieces of local history. Now in this country the annals of this city are another name for Roman history.

WOMAN AT THE BRIDGE OF ST. ANGELO. BY HENRI REGNAULT.

CHAPTER IV.

WHEN a prince or a princess of Rome dies, they clothe the dead in robes of ceremony and lay them out on a state-bed under the canopy of the throne, where the body remains exposed in the midst of a constellation of tapers for the sensibility of the populace. You will not be edified, as in our countries, by the tender assiduity of relations or by their affectionate urgency round the dying. At Rome, and throughout nearly all Italy, when a sick person is at the extremity, the family flee from the house: a husband, a beloved wife, a father, a grandfather, dies abandoned; the last gaze meets only hired faces. This custom, which speaks clearly as to the real religion of the people of Rome, has for its origin the rather pagan dread of being bewitched; they imagine that the dying have the evil-eye. They do not accompany the train of friends to the cemetery; the procession—a procession of state (more decent at Rome than in Tuscany, where in an evening, carried along by the light of torches, the dead hasten so swiftly)—is only recruited from among the religious orders. It is joined by the servants, the carriages of the defunct, his horses if he has any, and his dogs, very likely, if their inclination carries them thither.

Nothing is lighter than the temperaments of demonstrative and violent passion. When the Romans are struck by an affliction, they hasten to apply alteratives and drench the stomach. One day as I accompanied a friend to a *trattoria*, where the host and hostess with two marriageable daughters were sitting together, my companion inquired the reason why on the preceding evening the house was closed. "Alas!" replied the father, "they were carrying our son to his grave; we are deeply afflicted!"

Whilst my friend brought forward the usual formulas of condolence, there comes up an apothecary with four bottles, which he places in a row upon the table, and while the father, the mother, and the two daughters, each seize one, the landlady says to us, in a pathetic tone, "One may well take *rimedio* for such deep grief!"

They shake them off, these deep griefs, with a good deal of courage. I remember that on the eve of the funeral of the father of a family, I saw the widow and the two daughters all dressed up to go out. "Poor things!" said the mother; "they have wept so much that they need some distraction. For me, I only do it on their account...."

She was taking them to the play!

* * * *

The Venetian Palace, in the neighbourhood of St. Mark, is a purely Florentine building and of a fine epoch. The church, a monument of the same stock, has been made young again after the Roman manner. One and the other were built in 1468, not by Julian de Maiano, as Vasari says, but, as is proved from a contemporary chronicle quoted by Muratori, by one Francesco di Borgo San Sepolcro. Mino da Fiesole executed, they say, nearly all the sculptures; it is permitted us to doubt that.

GATE OF THE PALACE OF VENICE.

Pope Paul II., who was called Barbo and came originally from Venice, reconstructed the church that Gregory IV. had already built over again in 833, and that had been founded in 336 by the Pope St. Mark in honour of the Evangelist his patron. Paul II. could not be content without having a fine church freshly decorated in the

58 *Rome.*

neighbourhood of a palace in which he lived, and where there dwelt

PONTIFICAL PROCESSION AT THE FEAST OF THE MADONNA. BY HENRI REGNAULT.

more or less after him nineteen pontiffs; it was to this natural desire that the oratory of Gregory IV. was sacrificed, of which, however, they respected the tribuna on account of its ninth-century mosaic, which has for predella the symbolical lamb with its twelve sheep, but which is otherwise meanly rude. The porch of this temple is graceful, and its grace is exquisite.

A sermon had attracted a number of women to the church; it was charming to see them leaning against some pillar, the head covered by the hood, the eyes lifted and attentive, like the holy women of an old painting. We know that it is forbidden to the sex to enter the naves bareheaded at Rome, where women of every age go out without a head-dress even in winter. To attend a mass or a *funzione*, they make a hood out of their shawls or a muffler with their handkerchiefs. This prescription dates from the primitive church; I believe even St. Paul says something on the subject. The Barbo Palace had cost the friends of antiquity dear; to raise its walls they have used materials chipped away in the Coliseum, which was turned into a quarry.

As it is necessary to take a little rest, on arriving at the Piazza of Trajan, I entered St. Marie de Lorette, the little octangular church of which Antonio of San Gallo ornamented the cupola with such a beautiful lantern, and I paid a visit to the St. Susannah of Francis Duquesnoy, one of the exquisite statues produced by the seventeenth century.

The masterpiece of the estimable Duquesnoy recalled to me that at the left of the Sacred Way the little church of St. Francesca Romana contains the work of a French artist. So I went there by the avenue of stupid little trees, ill nourished by a heap of rubbish which ought to be cleared away, and which, without giving me much shade from the burning sun of this evening, intercepted the frame of the Forum. It is not to vaunt the carvings designed by Bernini on the tomb of Francesca, a Roman lady of the fifteenth century who, under the title of Oblates, founded beguines at Rome, that I shall mention this little church; nor to point out the tomb of Gregory XI., who re-established the pontifical see at Rome after seventy-two years of exile. I shall content myself with commending some interesting objects that people do not usually seek, and of which the guides say nothing. There is, to begin with, behind the master-altar, a mosaic of the tenth century, which represents the Virgin surrounded by four saints, separated from one another by arches and columns. In a transept on the left are two pictures attributed to Perugino: one is of the school of Francia, and the other might very well be the work of a rare master—Gerino da Pistoja.

TEMPLE OF ANTONINUS AND FAUSTINA.

The church of Antoninus and Faustina, with its travertine *cella*, crowned with the frieze on which griffins sport, separated by candelabra and vases, was formerly a pagan temple whose columns,

Temple of Antoninus and Faustina. 61

the greatest monoliths of cipollino that are known, have for diadems an entablature of enormous blocks of Carrara. The columns of the

THE ARCHES OF PEACE.

hexastyle, are not less than forty-three feet; they are under the ground in our time by about five yards: under the emperor you ascended twenty-one steps to reach the temple.

At a little distance we come in front of three high and broad apses in which the eye seeks as if on the threshold of three caverns

INTERIOR OF THE BASILICA OF CONSTANTINE.

to pierce the darkness, and which the vulgar call the Arches of Peace. The remains of the building, whose plan is not at the first glance intelligible, are so massive and thick, that we should be mistaken as to their elevation if the people of the neighbourhood, who have worn a short cut under these naves, did not give you so many

TEMPLE OF NERVA, PANTANI POSTERN.

opportunities of comparing with the size of the blocks, as well as of the scattered foundations of the fallen portion, the lilliputian proportions of a passer-by.

The vaults are more than sixty feet in arch; the marble cornices measure an immense cubic contents, and their weight must be tremendous.

From all time these ruins and the mystery that belongs to them have filled the popular imagination. Some authors since the fifteenth century have fancied that they recognised a Temple of Peace erected by Vespasian: an inscription from the Capitol found in the neighbourhood gave rise to this supposition, but it is no longer tenable. The character of the architecture, the plan, which is that of a basilica, the testimony of the annalists, the marks stamped on the bricks employed in the construction—everything denotes that it is later, and must be attributed to Maxentius, the competitor of Constantine.

In these quarters it seems that the ancient city prolongs itself indefinitely. At the bottom of a street a little before the basilica you see in a row, captive in a trench, the columns of the Temple of Nerva, supported by a wall which bars the way, and is pierced by an enormous arch, by which there was a communication with the Forum, that bore several names. They called it Transitorium, because it was necessary to cross it to ascend the three hills that command it; Forum of Nerva, because Trajan had dedicated it to his father; and Forum Palladium, because the Colonnacce, the remains, according to some, of a temple to Minerva erected there by Domitian, bear on their fluted shafts, that are two-thirds underground, a figure of Pallas crowning the fine entablature of an attica. The frieze has bas-reliefs of charming execution, but much damaged. Below these marbles, these reliefs, this foliage of acanthus and laurel, a baker has his stall and his oven.

Near this are the triumphal arches which have served for models to so many votive buildings. Like the custom of triumphs, these vaulted arches are of Roman origin; the oldest was raised in the year 634, two years after the death of Caius Gracchus, in honour of a Fabius who had beaten the Allobroges. The three most splendid types of this construction are found very little apart from one another, by the side of the way along which the triumphs passed.

What a marvel is the smallest of the three! It is that of Septimius Severus, which marks the old level of the Forum at the foot of the steps of the Temple of Concord. (See p. 3.) It was surmounted by a car with six horses, in which the emperor was seen seated between his two sons. On the front of the structure a long and fine inscription describes the dedication of it, a memorial doubly

FORUM TRANSITORIUM, OR FORUM OF NERVA.

interesting since Caracalla, having assassinated Geta his brother, had his name and all that concerned him erased.

What I had previously explored, and with an impatient curiosity, was the Arch of Titus, entirely bared of the *castrum* with which in

ARCH OF TITUS.

the middle ages the Frangipani had overloaded it. What a glorious

The Arch of Titus.

effect is produced from three or four different points of view by this noble arch, with a single gateway, robust in its ensemble, exquisite in detail, and which, seen from afar, has for its principal decoration the fine letters of its inscription!

On the other face they have described in a summary the capture of Jerusalem and the submission of Judæa. Seventeen hundred years and more have gone by since Domitian dedicated this triumphal arch to his brother and to their father Vespasian. *Divo Tito* proves that the work was completed after the death of Titus.

On the bas-relief placed in front the spoils of the subjugated nations

BAS-RELIEF OF THE ARCH OF TITUS.

are conveyed on litters, borne by legionaries wreathed with laurel. We recognise the table of shew-bread, which was of solid gold, the trumpets of the jubilee, and the golden candlestick with the seven branches from Solomon's Temple so often repeated on this monument, which alone has transmitted its form to us. After the tables of the law marched barefooted in a black robe the chief of the Israelites, Limon, son of Gioras. In point of execution, in point of delicacy, and in point of design, these bas-reliefs, alas, too much damaged, are to be classed among the most perfect that antiquity has left in Italy. They demonstrate the veracity of Josephus, and Josephus attests the fidelity of the sculptors.

The Arch of Constantine produces the liveliest impression; we admire without having analyzed any part of it. Perhaps it wants solidity, but in front it fascinates by its grandeur, by the harmony of its proportions, by the fine ordering of its chief parts. It is the finest of the three, exclaim nearly all travellers; only scarcely any of them have examined its details sufficiently to remember it. This is its single defect, the abuse of richness. It only tends towards degeneracy by the fixed resolution it shows to accumulate wonders. What it contains in exquisite figures, in charming groups, in bas-reliefs that form pictures composed with a master's hand, it is impossible to enumerate.

BAS-RELIEF OF THE ARCH OF TITUS.

CHAPTER V.

ONE of the most considerable monuments in the world is the Baths of Antoninus Caracalla, which are situated at the extremity of the Circus Maximus, between the back of the Aventine and that of the Cœlian, in one of those stripped suburbs where fields and gardens flourish over the graves of an ancient quarter. Contained in a valley, measuring their height with the elevation of the hills, these baths are the finest ruins in Rome.

We should have a false idea of these establishments if we were to take things literally, and see in them only a place of luxurious and very perfect baths. Assuredly the stoves occupied a notable place in them, since, according to Olympiodorus, the baths of Caracalla could supply warm baths for sixteen hundred persons at a time; but that was only a pretext of a monument, the porticos of which, according to Lampridius, were only erected between Heliogabalus and Alexander Severus. Besides the baths of different temperatures, the chambers heated by steam, and the basins and fountains, there were found in the thermæ scent-shops, stalls for articles of fashion, buffets for refreshments, kitchens and refectories, peristyles for conversation and walking in wet weather, libraries and reading-rooms, a stage for the performance of comedy, gymnasia for athletes, an arena for running and wrestling: they had there, got together and administered by a numerous staff of virtuosi, artists, and slaves, all that could divert an indolent people and make it forget life. There were even picture galleries and museums of statues: it was pleasure raised to the rank of an institution and organised on the plan of an architect. For sovereigns who had to maintain a power, as absolute as it was fragile, over a corrupt population in whose breasts not even faith in their country had survived, the distribution of the public amusements on an enormous scale was a political interest of the first consequence.

Thus the more the nation abases itself and grovels, the more does the

CALDARIUM OF THE BATHS OF CARACALLA.

ministration of pleasure increase in importance : the despots could only

The Baths of Caracalla. 71

maintain themselves by becoming proxenetæ. Continued by Helio-

ALTAR OF ST. CLEMENT'S.

gabalus, the baths of Caracalla are the most magnificent of all:

several thousand citizens were able every day to exhaust there the varied cycle of the delights of mind and sense.

The exterior buildings form a perimeter of 4,200 feet. In the court thus cut off by these buildings there rose on Babylonian vaults another edifice in several stories, which was nearly 700 feet by 450 broad. The Caldarium, a rotunda lighted from above like a greenhouse, can only be compared to the Pantheon of Agrippa, which is purer in its ornamentation, but not so bold in construction.

Before 1857, when people wished to give the idea of a Constantinian church arranged as in primitive times, they chose St. Clement. It was known from St. Jerome that a church was built in Rome which, from an early date, perpetuated the recollection of the successor of St. Anaclete, and that in 417 it had acquired the rank of basilica when St. Zosimus pronounced judgment in it against Celestius, who had fallen into the Pelagian heresy. St. Leo speaks of this temple in a letter to St. Flavian; it is mentioned in 499, on the occasion of the council which Symmachus presided over; St. Gregory the Great, who had delivered two homilies in it, described the last moments, under the Clementine porch, of St. Servulus the paralytic. Adrian I., Leo III., in the eight century, Leo IV. and John VIII. in the ninth, did, as we know from Anastasius, the first of them restore the roofing the second and third enrich the church with sacred ornaments, with marbles, above all with paintings, whose loss was long deplored. The last of the four rebuilt the choir, as is shown by his monogram, which is repeatedly carved on the *plutei* or balustrades.

To justify these traditions the interior of the building displayed as so many witnesses the columns of its portico in grey granite, its pillars of cipollino and of red granite which separate the three naves, and which come from the ruins of pagan temples. Ancient friezes annexed to the entablatures, and inscriptions of the era of the martyrs set in the walls, added the proofs of a charter-house of stone, the antechapel, the first inclosure, in which the sub-deacons, minor clerks, and the chanters had place; at the two sides the pulpits, with porphyry plaques and contemporary with John VIII., in the loftier of which, on the left, the Deacons read the Gospel, proclaimed edicts, and denounced the excommunicated, while the other was only used for the Epistle; before the passage to the right, the desk; finally, the twisted pillar, destined for the Easter taper, a ribbon of mosaic under a Corinthian capital, bearing an ancient vase, decorated under Innocent IV. The sanctuarium appears equally decisive and curious, separated as it is from the naves, a usage still preserved in oriental churches. Cut off by the ancient railing from the transept,

PULPIT OF THE EPISTLE AT ST. CLEMENT'S.

the altar or confession is covered by a ciborium, supported on slender columns of violet marble; in the circle of the apse is the presbyterium, in the centre of which the chief seat is raised by three steps,—all multiplied proofs of a very lofty antiquity.

A few years ago in raising some pavement for the purpose of digging a well, the prior of the Dominicans of Ireland, to whom the convent was given by Urban VIII., discovered, buried under the present church of St. Clement, the real Constantinian basilica that had passed into a subterranean state. How could one suspect that, far from depreciating the monument which had been the object of so extraordinary a misconception, this discovery would soon give it a triple value! As they removed the earth with which the crypts were filled up, they perceived by the light of their torches the walls gradually peopling themselves with strange forms resuscitated from the darkness. The church above was a cabinet of curiosities, while the church underground is a gallery, and the only one which could by authentic pictures fill up the gap of between the fourth and eleventh centuries in the history of painting.

The edifice was buried in 1084, and, as the level of the soil had been greatly raised by the load of ruins, when four-and-twenty years after they wished to rebuild the church, instead of building other foundations, they completed the filling up of the hidden basilica, after taking the pains to withdraw from it the ciborium, the plaques of marble and porphyry which had separated the transept, most of the columns, and whatever else could, without destroying the edifice underground, contribute to the adornment of the new temple while perpetuating the memory of the old.

The church of St. Clement is situated between the Coliseum and the church of St. John Lateran. You enter to the left of an alley of monastic rudeness by a heavy porch, poor of aspect, though with fine columns that do not match, and of such primitive simplicity that we wonder if it may not have seen Pope Liberius pass. The atrium is joined to a much lower portico, of which the arches rest on ancient columns with Ionian capitals; this arrangement is the frame to a small cloister which usually stood in front of the first basilicas, and in which catechumens as well as penitents remained. A side-door gives access to the monastery, and here you must ring to have the church opened, as it is nearly always shut up. The homely roofs, arranged to cover the vaults, do so little to prepare one's mind for the dimensions of a rich church with three naves, that with the interest thus spontaneously awakened there mingles the magic of a supernatural vision. While the treasures of the place present the very ideal of a historical

Antiquity of the Church. 75

monument, various portions and their arrangement according to the primitive rites carry the mind back to the morrow of the catacombs. Even certain marks of barbarism contribute to the general effect. At what time, to level the unmatched columns of the atrium, could they have taken it into their heads, instead of shortening the shafts, to saw off the capitals in the middle? The ancient barriers of the transept,

STREET OF ST. JOHN LATERAN—SIDE ENTRY OF ST. CLEMENT'S.

with their Byzantine crosses, their plaited crowns, their untwined serpents, and their frames of glittering mosaic; the pulpits of so grave a form, the ciborium, the inscriptions, the funereal symbols of antiquity mixed with the bas-reliefs of the pagan era, that profusion of marbles of every age and every colour, would suffice to raise the value of the monument amply high enough. But it is to other riches that it owes the spontaneousness of effect. From the door of the church to the choir you tread upon the flowery garden of a tapestry of coloured marble arranged six centuries since, that is at the best moment of the *opus Alexandrinum*; and then, behind the tabernacle above the presbyterium, which was completed the beginning of the twelfth century by Cardinal Anastasius, the semicircle of the apse, a demi-cupola of dark gold traversed by arabesques in which mystic figures appear among the darkness of legend and of ages,—the whole of this portion of the church is one immense piece of mosaic, executed in the time of Jacopo da Turrita, that is, in the revival which crowned the thirteenth century. Displayed between these sumptuous pictures of Alexandrine pavement and of the tribuna, the smallest objects possess a strange value, for they are not overwhelmed. Time has gilded the fresh crudities of the marbles, and cooled the too glowing warmth of the gold of the mosaic; and these elements of what would have been an incongruous splendour have gained an intensity which wraps them in charm and mystery.

Below the ornaments of the cupola, where the cross rises from a scroll rose, a frieze rich in veined marble, marked by the uncials of an inscription, separates the neo-Greek emblems from the corresponding Latin realities. On the upper course are arranged in two processions on each side of the Lamb, who has a golden nimbus and is placed in the centre, the Twelve Sheep whom he bade follow him, and who eye him with an interrogating expression. Under the entablature Christ is seen with his mother, surrounded by the twelve disciples, separated from one another by as many palms. This decoration, due to Celano, belongs to the fourteenth century. On the pendants of the vault are certain apocalyptic figures with floating draperies spread forth like clouds. We recognise, over Bethlehem and Jerusalem, Isaiah, Jeremiah, St. Laurence, St. Paul, St. Clement, and St. Peter; Urban VIII. introduced St. Dominic. To the right of the altar, beneath the flourishes of a pilaster, is a ravishing tabernacle of mosaic and sculpture in the Gothic style of the Pisans, a gem that Cardinal Tomasio of the Minor Brothers had executed in 1299, at the same time as the great arabesques of the semicircle, " to please the city of Rome and his uncle, Boniface VIII."

In one of the chapels of St. Clement is the marble statue of St. John the Baptist, one of those living representations of asceticism and penance that no one dared approach but the supple and vigorous Donatello, with all his contempt for the traditions of antiquity. This figure is attributed to Simon, brother of that distant forerunner of Michael Angelo. In the same chapel have been erected, also in the fifteenth century, two Florentine tombs of admirable quality, especially that of Cardinal Roverella. Votive inscriptions exhumed from the catacombs revive upon the walls and recall to one's mind

EXTERNAL PORTICO OF ST. CLEMENT'S

ancient and romantic names that seem to have been gleaned from the poets.

It is not without an emotion above ordinary curiosity that you prepare in one of the low naves, while the guides are lighting their torches, to descend from the churches where so many antiquities have entranced you, down to a monument of a yet more venerable antiquity, in which time has displaced nothing on the evil pretence of restoring or beautifying. We are sure that the torches will light up halls in which St. Augustine, St. Sylvester, St Gregory the Great, made their voices heard; we know that for eight hundred years no eye beheld this sanctuary, in which Gregory VII. was the last to officiate.

When Pascal II. had the San Clemente rebuilt, they only left in the lower church some marble pilasters and a few columns, and these blocks still mark the separation of the naves. The rough casting of the walls, that is frequently peeled off, lets us see the irregular layers of a building formed for the most part of inferior materials, mixed with

FRAGMENT OF A FRESCO OF THE FOURTH CENTURY.

parts of much greater antiquity. As soon as the torches cease to wave in front of you, the compositions disclose themselves. We perceive that time and damp have wrought much destruction by making the pozzuolana fall away from the facings; but besides that whole pages have remained all but untouched; whatever is not destroyed has preserved the freshness of its colouring. The general appearance from this point of view is that of the mosaics of Ravenna, I would even say of the early frescoes of the Campo Santo at Pisa, if the usage of cruder colours, of ochres especially, which make deep reds and yellows, did not give to these pictures a more truly antique simplicity of aspect. As for the design, it has in general more suppleness of movement; in the less ancient portions the composition is more freely picturesque than it was under the hand of the contemporaries of Ducci and Giotti.

Let us proceed in the order of the dates, as far as possible, to a rapid analysis of these curiosities, that are too little known and that have not yet been explained. They lately found two heads of life-size, the one on a kind of island of plaster of considerable thickness, the other on a piece of very light rough cast, which permits the stones to be seen through it; these fragments are, so far, the oldest nobiliary

FRAGMENT OF A FRESCO OF THE FOURTH CENTURY.

titles of the monument. The one represents a woman, true type of the Roman matron, with black eyes, and eyebrows deeply arched under a low brow. This face, framed in a nimbus, seems to belong to the end of the fourth century, and it recalls with more art the processes used in the frescoes of the catacombs. The other reproduces them still more perceptibly; it is a man's head, with the bust draped in the Roman fashion; short hair marks off the brow, which is low, the nose is extremely aquiline, the chin salient and broad, the eyes finely cut, the mouth accentuated, and the mask joined to the shoulders by a well-set neck. This fresco is obtained by a succession of tones passed one over the other and forming flat tints, a process which characterises also the likenesses in the catacombs. The woman is, perhaps, Euodia or Eutyche, that St. Paul gives to St. Clement for helpers, or Domitilla, whom he converted. As for the man, it would be difficult to hazard any theory. Still, it may be said that in the opinion of the most competent this head, which is of a style and sweep purely Roman, can scarcely have been painted later than the year 310. The *vir togatus* permits us, therefore, to attribute to this portion of the church an origin anterior to Constantine.

LEGEND OF ST. LIBERTINUS: FRESCOES OF THE EIGHTH CENTURY.

The most ancient fragments, though sadly mutilated, that we next find in the northern wing date from the eighth century, and offer three subjects taken from the legend of St. Catherine of Alexandria. This is the most ancient iconographic mention of the virgin-martyr. These paintings, in which we find some hints of movement, are of a remarkable rudeness. They are more barbarous than those devoted to St. Gregory the Great, on account, no doubt, of the homilies which he pronounced in this church. The three others are taken from the numerous writings of St. Gregory, who, describing some traits of the holy monk Libertinus, recounts how the monk charged a serpent to watch the vegetables of the monastery of Fondi, which a robber used to come and carry off every night by scaling the walls. The serpent seized with his coils the foot of the offender, and hissed loudly by way of summoning Libertinus, who unbound the captive, and authorised him in order to avoid sin to come henceforth to the house for the fruit of which he had need. This Libertinus was of such humility that, after being beaten by his superior, he presented himself before him with as much sweetness as if nothing had happened, and the abbot was so moved that he prostrated himself before the simple brother, and besought his forgiveness. One day as Libertinus was entering Ravenna, a woman took his horse by the bridle, and forced the monk to come and bring to life again the child that she had just lost. These legendary stories, evoked by the writings of St. Gregory, were evidently painted subsequently to his death in 604; but they may have been painted less than a century after, under Gregory II., who was a Savelli, and who was, I believe, titularly of this church, for the popes gladly illustrated the canonised predecessor whose name they bore. These frescoes, in great part destroyed, are placed under the chapel of St. Catherine, and may have been executed between 715 and 730, for they recall pretty closely the Vatican manuscripts of the same epoch.

The neighbouring compartment, evidently executed to complete an exposition of doctrine, is more remarkable: it is the oldest known representation of the Assumption of the Virgin. Round the tomb the apostles express their stupefaction by their faces and by the attitudes of a movement that is as varied as it is energetic. Covered with an ample cloak, slightly lifted by her extended arms, with eyes raised to the sky, where she beholds her son seated in the midst of four angels and surrounded by an ellipsoid nimbus, the Madonna rises from the earth. The scene has a motion in it which is still far away from Byzantine immobility.

These compositions anathematize the heresies of the Pelagians and their errors touching grace, the holy sacrament, original sin, and the divinity of Christ. Close by they have introduced, armed with his Chronicle and his Poems against the deniers of grace, St. Prosper, who came from Marseilles at the invitation of St. Leo the Great to fight by the side of Augustine against the Pelagians. In order the better to show the invention, at one of the extremities of the picture of the Assumption they place St. Vitus, Archbishop of Vienna, who had destroyed as against the Arians certain analogous errors. He forms a counterpart to the illustrious Pope Leo IV., a Roman of old time, who resisted the Saracens, who fortified Rome, constructed the Leonine enceinte round the Vatican, and made great restorations in the church of St. Clement. The square green nimbus surrounding his head is a sign that, at the time he was painted, he was still living. Still we ought not in general to grant absolute authority to this presumption; it assists a probability without warranting certainty. Leo IV., who was canonised, wore the tiara from 847 to 885. It was he who had this fresco composed; the formal and curious inscription that

ASSUMPTION OF THE VIRGIN: FRESCO OF THE TIME OF LEO IV.

informs us on this point shows us Latin prosody in decay; it contributed also to prove the age of the paintings:

> QUOD HÆC PRÆ CUNCTIS SPLENDET PICTURA DECORE,
> COMPONERE HANC STUDUIT PRÆSBYTER ECCE LEO.

At the north of the crypt is a Madonna with a diadem loaded with stones or drachms; she is posed in full face, her eyes fixed in front of her, with her son below also in full face, and with that sphinx-like immobility to which these people systematically condemned their figures. To right and left two saints, of whom we only see that the heads are equally mummified; above, in a medallion, the Christ, beardless and draped as in the primitive times, belongs to another hand, if it is not earlier. Lower than the lateral figures, two subjects from the Sacrifice of Abraham form pendants to one another; we should suppose that they were copied from one of those sculptured *olifants* sent by Saracen art to the stout folk of the Carlovingian cycle. The purely Greek style of this little chapel in the form of a niche we shall soon see undergoing modification, because at that time those who imparted it were still open to the influence of the more free, more dramatic and living art of the Latin races; a tradition which was not entirely extinct at the end of the ninth or the beginning of the tenth century. Certain monuments, in fact, will disclose, at that distant date, the abortive attempt at renaissance; abortive because the Roman

BYZANTINE MADONNA: FRESCO OF THE NINTH CENTURY.

inspiration soon completed the process of its extinction, while the Greek school, remaining absolute master of the field, ended by imposing its iconography, in the symmetrical immobility of which the orientals satisfied their instinctive aversion for images. Of these last productions of a hybrid school, connected with the Roman tradition by its movement, its feeling, and its intelligence, with the school of

Byzantium by its mannerism and costume, no one would ever have suspected the existence if the crypts of St. Clement did not furnish proof of such a transition.

So far we have only seen Pope Clement in his church in an episodic state. The finding of the remains of this pontiff by St. Cyril the Philosopher, brother of St. Methodius, and the translation of the relics under Nicholas I., that is, between 858 and 869—this return of a patrician martyr to his home after seven centuries of exile gave a new impulse to the worship of the saint.

The event and its date are of extreme importance for settling the origin of our church and the age of the paintings that are left for me to describe.

It was, according to all appearance, between 900 and 940 that they set themselves to paint on the walls of the principal naves the series of illustrations of a legend suddenly become popular. These subjects, which are numerous and most interesting, are as a rule in good preservation. The first, which presents itself on a thick and very broad pilaster, quite close to the master-altar, is the most important page in the series; it is the Conversion of Sisinius, the friend of Domitian.

The principal subject is that of the centre, which represents a church lighted by seven lamps, answering to the seven gifts of the Spirit of Light; the lamp which surmounts the altar on which the missal and the chalice are placed itself consists of seven flames arranged in a circular lustre. They have chosen the moment when St. Clement, who is officiating, with the pallium on his shoulder and wearing a chasuble falling to a point, turns round with extended arms to chant the *Pax Domini sit semper vobiscum*, and when the pagan Sisinius, drawn to the temple by a malignant curiosity, becomes blind and deaf; his steps are uncertain, and a young attendant much marvelling leads him forth. The pious wife of the courtier, Theodora, beholds what has happened with a surprise that has nothing painful in it. The deacons and bishops, placed on the other side of the altar, present the givers of the fresco, who, in elegant apparel, bear crowns. They are in stature less by a half than the chief personages of the drama; an inscription that is over the arabesques on which the picture rests has transmitted to us the names of these persons Ego Beno de Rapiza cum **Maria Uxore** mea pro amore dei et beati Clementis. The space being too short to continue, the following character have been placed vertically over one another under the last letter of

Clementis: P. G. R. F. C. They offer by far the most singular method of abbreviation that I think I ever met, the initials of each syllable being included, *PinGeReFeCi.* Elsewhere the same formula in all letters, beginning by *ego Beno*, &c., ends by *fecit—Ego . . . fecit.* This is Latin in extreme decay.

But the subject treated *en prédelle* with more negligence will bring in philological curiosities of a different sort. Sisinius having commanded his attendants to strangle Clement, they bind and drag along the shaft of a column which, thanks to a miracle, they mistake for the saint.

The saint has escaped at the opposite end; he is only represented by his last words, pronounced as he crosses the portico on which the painter has written: "DURITIAM CORDIS VESTRIS (*sic*) . . SAXA TRAERE MERUISTI." The two attendants of Sisinius, who struggle to draw the column, are named Cosmaris and Albertel. The first has pulled the cord on to his shoulder, the other has it under his arm; "ALBERTEL TRAI," says the legend, written over his head, "Albertel draws." *Trai* is no longer Latin, but it belongs to vulgar idiom. On the side at which the saint has fled, a person, probably of his suite, and named Colopalo, is turning round. Rushing with a stick, as with

LEGEND OF ST. CLEMENT: EPISODE OF SISINIUS.
(TENTH CENTURY.)

a rope he shakes the base of the shaft, he looks at an attendant, who was drawing at the other end, and casts at him some words that are figured thus: "FALITEDERETO." To discover the sense of this queer group of syllables, I think we must decompose it to these four words, *Fali te de reto!* and translate it by this ironical phrase, "Cheat thyself by this delusion!" It is Italian, ill taken from Latin forms; *de reto*, instead of *di rete*, is explicable, by a propensity of the decline to assimilate the forms of the second declension to most substantives. That the inscription is in Italian one could show by that which is placed as a pendant, and as to which no uncertainty can be maintained, but the apostrophe of Sisinius is too rude to be reproduced. In the central composition the costumes are Greek; a certain unity presides over the arrangements; the frame is filled up with indisputable art, for the intentions, without being forced, are shown in a free and natural manner, and the heads are far from being inexpressive. Those artists succeeded better in young than in old forms, in the heads of women and the figures of men, in draped personages than in those which are not so—all of them characteristic traits of Christian art. The figure of Theodora is graceful, well draped, supple, and of a handsome cast.

MIRACLE AT THE TOMB OF ST. CLEMENT (TENTH CENTURY).

We shall see again, in the continuance of this legend, all the family of Beno de Rapiza, at the bottom of the representation of the miracle which took place before the submarine grave of St. Clement, when a widow finds there her child, who had been forgotten at the festivities of the previous year. Below the fresco, in a great medallion, is the pontiff, to whom Beno, his son Clement, his daughter Atila, his wife Maria, and the grandmother of the children, bring each a taper with crowns. These are priceless studies of costume.

The upper subject, destroyed as on the previous panel, represented the construction of the tomb by an angel, as the half-preserved inscription shows. As for the principal picture, the arrival of the clergy of Kherson, with the bishop at their head, to assist at the prodigy of the child found safe and sound, the work is one of the most remarkable, as much by the architecture of the little monument on which the altar appears, the curtains of the Tabernacle having been symmetrically looped up, as by the drawing of the figures, which are reproduced in a double action. The stooping mother raises the child extending its arms to her; then, standing upright, pressing it to her breast, she leans her head tenderly against that of her son. In the second subject, the group has a movement so faithful, and the draperies are of such a style, that this charming figure recalls the sculptures of Chartres and those of Erwin of Steinbach at Strasburg. It shows to an equal extent the thought and intelligence of the West applied to the art of Byzantium, but the artists who here reach this result are three centuries before Giotto. The miraculous shrine in which the scene passes is covered with large tiles, like the churches of Ravenna; four arches, in spite of symmetry, are only equipped with three lamps, because these lights symbolise the divine virtues. The anchor that they fastened about the neck of the pontiff when he was drowned by order of Trajan is fastened to a ring in the wall; peopled by fish swimming, the waves of the sea envelop the miraculous chapel. In the shape of epilogues are added the acts and deeds of St. Cyril, who died under Nicholas I. during his stay at Rome. A fresco, of which few traces remain, placed above an excavation by which we descend into the darkness of earlier times down to the Etruscan substructions, allows us to recognise Cyril, or Constantine the Philosopher, receiving from the Emperor Michael III., called the Drunkard, the mission to go and convert the Slavs and Bulgarians. Behind the apostle is, or rather was, for few fragments remain, his brother Methodius. Close by we perceive the King Bogoris, being baptized naked in a piscina in which he is plunged up to the waist. Let us further remark two extremely curious pilasters, which might very well date from Leo IV. On one are represented St. Giles and St. Blasius, one above the other; the Armenian bishop, at the prayers of a weeping mother, is drawing from the throat of her child a thorn which choked it. It is for this reason that, in order to be cured of quinsy, people go to touch at the church of Santa Maria in Via Lata the relic of the throat of St. Blasius. Below is drawn a kind of devouring wolf, which is carrying off a creature and scratching it with its whiskers; this subject is separated from the basement by an ornament taken from the acanthus, and inspired from the ancient arabesques. On the other pilaster, St. Antonine the Martyr, in the time of Diocletian, has beneath him Daniel, whose feet two lions of a heraldic make are licking, twisting themselves into the strangest posture. The prophet, who was minister to the kings of Babylon, wears the gay and half-warlike costume of the young Byzantine lords of the ninth century. A broad belt is over the surcoat; the breastplate is trimmed with ornaments; short open cuffs expose to sight long and tight sleeves, fastened at the wrist by an embroidered decoration; the buskins are elegant. In the lower compartment struggle five monsters that we might call man-lions, three of which erect on their hind feet try to devour Daniel, and open formidable jaws. The ornament of the base is of exquisite taste, consisting of curves which meet enclosing rosettes between denticulated cinctures. What would lead one to suppose that these pilasters are earlier than the

ST. BLASIUS PICKING A THORN FROM THE THROAT OF A CHILD: FRESCO ON A PILASTER (NINTH CENTURY).

second half of the ninth century is that there is no question of St. Clement, and that St. Giles of Nismes acquired renown in Rome at the end of the seventh. Let us not omit a composition entirely Greek and of later date, Cyril and Methodius presented to Christ; the one by St. Clement, whose relics he has brought back; the other by St. Andrew, the predecessor of Methodius in the apostolate to the Scythians. The Saviour, draped in the toga, is too short by more than a third considering the size of the head; he is blessing in the Greek manner, that is, the ring-finger bent under the thumb and the three others extended, a unique example of the oriental rite in the monuments of Rome, but not in the rest of the West, where we meet it from one remote time to another up to the twelfth century.

At the bottom of the church is a painting that can only be attributed to the authors of the miracles of St. Clement, already described. It is the representation of the funeral of St. Cyril, carried to the Vatican with face uncovered on a *cataletto*, covered by a rich quilt. The clerks in long dresses have torches in their hands; the incense bearers swing their spherical censors. In front of the altar of St. Peter is the Pope, who pronounce. the *Pax Domini*. This pontiff, who is Nicholas I., is also drawn at the head of the procession, with a mitre on his head, or pointed tiara with single circle, and wearing a white pallium sprinkled

DANIEL SPARED BY THE LIONS: PILASTER IN THE NINTH CENTURY.

with black crosses. At his right walks Methodius, the brother of the deceased, in deep sorrow. The two saints and the Eastern clergy wear the beard, while the Roman clergy are shaven. Behind the cross-bearer of the Pope rise banners of stuff sprinkled with gold, surmounted with a Greek cross. Under the frieze, which is framed by two inscriptions, we learn that " Maria the butcher's wife (Macellaria) for the reverence of God and the healing of her soul has had this drawn." Here, then, in religious buildings, long before the development of the monasteries and the impulse given by Franciscans and Dominicans, here are works of art due to the munificence of the Roman citizens. We may conclude from this that throughout the events of the middle ages the commune preserved a certain preponderance, and that the middle classes had gathered the spoils of the fallen patriciate. Nothing is truer; it was not before the end of the tenth century that civil discords brought Rome to ruin, sacked and destroyed property, and extinguished for two hundred years and more the intellectual lights which had begun again to shine forth.

Along the nave, perhaps to fill up an empty space, towards the same epoch, the end of the ninth or the beginning of the tenth century, they grouped into a single frontispiece the principal points in the legend of St. Alexius. They are painted in the midst of a ravishing ornamentation of rosettes and compartments decked with flowers, among which birds move, with a cornice, half destroyed, on which Christ figured, censed by the two archangels, Michael and Gabriel, who are accompanied by St. Clement and Nicholas I. The three acts of this edifying little drama pass in front of the house of the senator Eufimianus, father of the pilgrim who in his early youth quitted the paternal roof to exile himself in Palestine; the buildings of the palace occupy three-quarters of the background placed in the middle of a fresco. Under a window, from which, without recognising him, his betrothed, whom he abandoned on the day of their nuptials, is regarding him, Alexius, having returned to Rome, with the staff and wallet of the traveller, goes before the patrician, who arrives on horseback followed by an escort. The pilgrim without being recognised offers his services to his father, who receives him into the number of his attendants. This figure, walking and speaking, is posed with an ingeniousness which does not exclude observation of nature. We perceive that the young man solicits humbly and entreats warmly. He separates himself from a group on which he turns his back, and which represents another situation;—the Pope, followed by his clergy, and coming, warned by a voice from heaven, to release the body of a saint in the house of Eufimianus. They find at the door, resting on a mat, the poor servant who for seventeen years dwelt under a staircase in his father's palace. In the hands of

LEGEND OF ST. ALEXIUS: FRESCO OF THE TENTH CENTURY.

Alexius was folded a writing, which the pontiff unrolls and reads before the company and the sorrow-stricken kinsfolk : this third subject in the distribution of the figures is combined with the two others. The groups balance one another, and the scene is so skilfully occupied that we seem at first to have to examine only one homogeneous subject cleverly disposed. The blessed one is placed on a couch, covered by a counterpane with alternate medallions of Greek crosses and doves. The betrothed of Alexius, hastening up, presses him in her arms, while the father and mother have rent their garments and are tearing their hair.

This picture fixes the date of the adventure of St. Alexius; it must have taken place under Boniface I., who held the Roman bishopric from the year 418 to 422. The name of the Pontiff is shown thus: *Boniphatius*. This curious painting, in the inspection which serves for legend, offers the most singular example of the prosodical decomposition of Latin verse, and of the transition from scanned rhythm to syllabic and rhymed rhythm. The events traced by the painter are summed up in these two hexameters:—

NON PATER AGNOSCIT, MISERERIQUE SIBI POSCIT;
PAPA TENET CARTAM, VITAMQUE NUNTIAT ARTAM.

It can escape no one that each of these verses cut in two forms two versicles of modern structure with leonine rhymes.

Thus the church of St. Clement, a museum of archæology in its upper story, a gallery of paintings unique over the whole world in its crypt underground, furnishes, besides the revelation of certain unknown schools, precious documents on the decomposition of Latinity and specimens of the Italian tongue towards the end of the age of Charles the Great. The monument so recently discovered also throws a vivid light on the origin of the first basilicas, on the rites, usages, and costume of the obscurest epochs, as well as on the antiquity of legends. Only, to exhibit the whole interest which a Roman church may stir, it was necessary to leave nothing out, for here detail is the very web of history.

CHAPTER VI.

ON entering the city by the gate of St. Pancras you begin to hear sounds of a cascade, which announce the Pauline Fountain. The ornamentation of this waterwork has for its single purpose to accompany the inscriptive tablet, which is perhaps the most gigantic in the world. As the building is nearly on the top of the Janiculum, you will discover from a great

THE PAULINE FOUNTAIN.

distance this page of writing framed in marble vignettes, which are accompanied by six columns of red granite taken from the Forum of Nerva; the ostentatious style of the seventeenth century triumphs here by its size. Paul V., restoring life to the aqueducts of Trajan, and infusing Lake Bracciano into their arteries, did not mean it to enter Rome in poor guise; below the arms of the Borghese, illustrated

THE STATUE OF ST. CECILIA, BY STEFFEN MADERNO.

by the tiara crowning of the attica, there rush forth brawling from three open gateways three currents, and from two neighbouring niches pretty streams. Dragons also spout forth other streams. These masses of water, so unexpected on the bare summit of a hill, and pure as the crystal of the Alps, pour down into a vast marble basin. There was once here a Temple of Minerva. The Nympheum, a monument of the liberal foresight of the popes, nobly enough connects their power with the secular traditions of the emperors, by making the memory of Trajan flower again among the younger buds of the Borghese. The construction does honour to Fontana as well as to the sculptor-architect, Stephen Maderno.

You find this last artist again at the foot of the Janiculum in a very different and perhaps more original work, if after turning the base of the hill towards the south, leaving to the right the convent of Franciscans in which dwelt St. Francis of Assisi, and following the suburban street in which the great St. Benedict stayed in the sixth century, you finally enter the church of St. Cecilia.

What has made the legend of the virgin

PORTICO OF SANTA CECILIA IN TRASTEVERE.

martyr disputable is that her execution is imputed, under Alexander Severus who did not persecute the Christians, to one Almacus, a pretorian prefect unknown to history. Signor de Rossi has shown the error of the Bollandists on this point, and confirmed the statement of Fortunatus, who places the martyrdom of St. Cecilia under Marcus Aurelius. The place of her burial shows the family from which she sprang; but these are points to which we shall return as we proceed among the catacombs.

The church of St. Cecilia, which gives a title to a cardinal priest, passes as having been built by Urban I. towards the year 230, on the site of the saint's dwelling-place. They show you in one of the chapels to the right the remains of the baths of her house, and on a lower story some fragments of the primitive pavement. Pascal I. who rebuilt the temple respected, as they had done in the third century, the remains of the furnace, where we recognise the conduits for heat and water. Clement VII. presented St. Cecilia to the Benedictine Sisters; Clement VIII., in 1579, had opened the sarcophagus of their patron, the body of whom, intact and masked by the folds of a long robe, disclosed itself in an expressive and singular attitude, and this exhumation occasioned one of the finest statues that was executed in the beginning of the seventeenth century. The Pope being desirous that it should represent the saint in the vestments and the position in which they had surprised her, the task was confided to Stephen Maderno. This curious little temple rises in front of an apse of the ninth century, in which a mosaic has bequeathed to us, besides a portrait of Pascal I., the figures of St. Cecilia and her husband Valerianus, in the costume of the patricians and Roman ladies ten years after the death of Charles the Great. The saint wears a white mantle over a tunic of green, with a golden border; the robe and the peplum of Cecilia are of golden stuffs, and richly overwrought. Flowers are scattered on their way; by their side palm-trees laden with fruit symbolize the merits of martyrdom, while over one branch is the haloed phœnix, the emblem of resurrection.

At some distance from St. Cecilia, and at the end of the Lungaretta, rises the fine church on the right bank of the Tiber, Santa Maria in Trastevere. It is contended that on this spot there was erected under the first emperors a *Taberna meritoria*, a sort of hospital for the invalids of the army; and that this institution, having been abandoned at the time of Caracalla and Heliogabalus, no doubt because the number of cripples became too great, the building was conceded to the Christians by Alexander Severus, with permission to found an oratory there, a project that was realised by the pope St. Callistus. Anterior by nearly a century to the era of Constantine, Santa Maria in Trastevere ought to be the oldest church in Rome, and perhaps in the West. What is certain is that Pope Julius I. rebuilt this temple at an epoch when assuredly there was no other to reconstruct (349), and that before 1140 Innocent II. substituted for the monument of Pope Julius the present church, which is one of the prettiest in Rome, and one of the most interesting from the point of view of art and archæology.

It is one of the churches of character in which everybody can glean; the pavement of Alexandrine work contributes to its air of opulence. They have just finished decking it up afresh, but I rejoice at having seen it before it became superb. I remember that trying to go out, and having mistaken the entrance to the sacristy for a door, I observed in a passage some small tabernacles, on one of which some very charming but little-known bas-reliefs are signed OPUS MINI; for those who have studied Florence — necessary initiation for a journey to Rome—the name of Mino da Fiesole is placed under the banner Ghiberti, between those of Fra Angelico and the La Robbia.

YOUNG WOMAN OF THE TRASTEVERE.

You come out on the other side of the cross by a lateral door which joins the railing of a pretty little garden, that is made cheerful by an ossuary, furnishing an unexpected reminiscence of Lower Brittany.

One of the interesting pilgrimages from the Trastevere, and from that slope of the Janiculum on which gardens look towards the city, is the monastery of Sant' Onofrio, the witness of the agony of Tasso.

As soon as one has set foot in the little church of Sant' Onofrio, the comic element speedily puts romantic leanings to rout. The monument of Torquato Tasso, inaugurated in 1857 by Pius IX., does more honour to the sentiments of the Holy Father than to the talent of Giuseppe Fabrizi, to whom, for want of somebody better, no doubt, they had to confide its execution. His bas-reliefs and his figure of Tasso are of a smooth, scraped, and pomaded execution, and of a taste quite extraordinarily laughable. Close to the door is the ancient

SANT' ONOFRIO.

burying-place, where under a modest stone has slept for more than two centuries the author of the *Jerusalem Delivered*, at the foot of a portrait of the time, which is bad enough, but which may be a likeness.

In the passages of the monastery, where one loves to adventure in the footsteps of the poet, there is a little fresco representing the Virgin and Child, who blesses a donor at prayer. The picture is arched, and is surrounded with a frame in flowers and fruit on an enamelled ground, a rude imitation of Andrea della Robbia. The donor's portrait in profile, the infant Jesus from a soft model and of charming gesture, the fine movement, the delicate sweep, the lofty brow of the smiling Madonna—all reveal and proclaim Leonardo da Vinci, to whom this precious jewel is justly attributed.

The chamber in which Tasso ended his sad and glorious life is well placed. What he looked upon in his last dreams, we see to-day just as he left it. Leaning on the window where the lover of Leonore d'Este leaned, we beheld with rapture what he beheld with such gloom. The chamber is still just as he left it for the vault of Sant' Onofrio; a few pale marks on the walls show the place of things that have disappeared. Yet all has not been dispersed: certain objects have been preserved that belonged to the poet; his table, with an inkstand of wood, his great chair covered with Cordovan leather very worn, a small German cabinet, a mirror, an autograph letter, a large bowl, a crucifix. There is found also the original of a mask in wax, moulded from nature, and the copies of which known abroad have become much effaced.

PORTRAIT AFTER THE MASK OF TASSO.

The monks have placed this face on a clothed bust, an incoherence from which there springs a fantastic effect. The head is delicate, of a peculiarly spiritual beauty, and of a fascinating expression; the purity of the profile and the firmness of the mouth heighten the distinction of the poet's face.

Between the southern slope of the Tarpeian rock and the Fabrician bridge, near the Piazza Montenara, you come upon one of the pure monuments of the best epoch, the theatre dedicated by Augustus to the young Marcellus, his nephew.

Such is the perfection of this monument that the Doric and Ionic columns of the two superimposed orders which supported the arches have been adopted by architects since as models of proportion. There remains an enormous segment of this building, of which the Pierleoni and the Savelli made a fortress in the middle age.

When, doubling the round of the theatre of Marcellus, you proceed to lose yourself in the region of the Pescheria Vecchia, you discover a memento of Augustus in a colonnade once splendid. Octavius, who had dedicated to the son of his sister the neighbouring theatre begun by Julius Cæsar, placed under the patronage of Octavia the new portico, in which he placed together the altars of Jupiter and Juno. In an alley close at hand is the little church of St. Angelo in Pescheria, crowned by a covered belfry. It was from here that Cola de Rienzi, on the 19th of May, 1347, after hearing mass, came forth escorted by his adherents and the Vicar Apostolic, to ascend to the Capitol, where the populace whom he had convoked conferred upon him the lordship of the Roman Republic. Situated in a poor quarter with all sorts of incoherent masonry, the ruins of antiquity are connected on every side with buildings from the seventh to the thirteenth century. Under the pediment they have described an arch, by way of replacing two broken pillars; of the neighbouring colonnades there remain two capitals, one of them muffled in masonry, the other a fine piece crowned with acanthus, placed on a pedestal of brick; a pilaster disrobed of its surrounding of marble. The principal effect of these ruins comes of the contrast between the grandeur and the magnificence of the antique style, and the picturesque, sordid, and inveterate squalor of dens that are now given up to the fishery and Jewry installed there by the middle age.

Turning the corner of the portico and passing under a low arch, you suddenly come out at the head of a deep, narrow street, the houses of which, dark and of unequal height, are made yet more obscure by pent-house roofs and by clothes-lines set up, as at Smyrna, across the road, in the shape of ropes on which swing garments of varied hue. These abodes exhibit a complete harlequinade of all sorts of epochs and all sorts of purposes. The majority of them have been in turn palaces, convents, oratories, houses of business in many forms, and at last they are become garrets and dens for sheltering wretchedness. Everybody has patched up the walls for his own use, and such is the quality of the cement that a square of wall pierced, stopped, mined, torn away ten times in twelve centuries, remains solid as a

PEDIMENT OF THE PORTICO OF OCTAVIA.

rock, without there being any need to prop it. Hence, before each of these façades made up of pieces and bits, one recognises, as on an ill-scraped parchment on which various texts have followed one another, the plan and the appropriation of the previous dwellings. The small Roman bit, the remains of some *sacellum* of the lower empire, will form a kind of figured stuff with the narrow bricks of the thirteenth century and the large courses of travertine of the fifteenth. You will perceive from story to story spacious round windows stopped and replaced by tiny lattices, which are to-day in their turn condemned. Vast arches sketching their festoons in a wall pierced by a window will recall ancient porticoes. A console perched high in notched bas-reliefs, a shaft of syenite or of African granite coming out of the mosaics of masonry, will betray a whole mystery of vanished greatness. Marbles fouled with soot mingled here and there with the mud of the buildings; casting furtive glances to the bottom of the avenues, you will discover among the filth of a blind court captive colonnades and the crumbling scraps of some palace, such as those of the Governo Vecchio, whose porticoes are half concealed amid the hovels of the Pescheria. At Rome to build they never completely pulled down; erections having come from age to age to hive themselves one against the other like cells, it follows that the old quarters abandoned to the populace retrace the rank and tell the story of the life of the castes

GATE OF ST. ANGELO IN PESCHERIA.

which from century to century have been quartered there. Even the doors have been re-cut or re-hung; marvellous lock-fastenings,

COURTYARD IN THE PALAZZO DEL GOVERNO VECCHIO, VIA DELLA PESCHERIA.

antique and complicated gratings, will close sinks; a sarcophagus will serve for a trough, a gravestone for a basement, while dirty water will

have for gutters tombs that were contemporary with Gregory VII.
In this way the smallest bit of building may become a summary of
history, but you must inspect it close, for too often by dint of passing
from hand to hand the book has been effaced.

On each side of this curious street lie large flagstones of white
marble, gently inclined like tombstones, which forming a double row
at the foot of the houses take towards nightfall, when the street is
deserted, a most lugubrious look ; it seems that the graves of ancestors
are arranged before the doors. These blocks of Carrara or cipollino,
taken from the temples of the gods or the inferior palaces, serve as

BARBER IN THE OPEN AIR. BY HENRI REGNAULT.

stalls for the vendors of fish. When on these tables they cut up the
bronze-coloured sword-fish, sea-eels, doradoes with bluish gill, their
blood mingles in violet and rose-coloured webs with threads of
carmine over the delicate whiteness of the marble, composing bouquets
of colour which would have given delight to a rival of Van Ostade.
It was in digging at the end of this street that, in the seventeenth
century, they exhumed the Venus de' Medici at the entrance of the
rione of the Jews, who with an amazing thoughtlessness have never
thought of scratching the fruitful earth whose treasures they trample
under foot.

Rome allows the Israelites to keep open shop on the Sunday, and it does not forbid Christians to make their purchases in the Ghetto on that day, nor even to go and buy cigar-ends by the pound, or be shaved by the barbers in the open air, where people wait their turn with so much patience, while they gather from the lips of the inexhaustible Figaro the news of the quarter and of the two hemispheres. To have one's beard shaved is for the Romans the only toilet luxury over which their taste for dirt has not triumphed.

Above the Ghetto and Cenci Palace, between this piazza and the Via de' Pettinavi, are the lines along the Tiber with its deserted

A FISHERMAN ON THE WATCH BEFORE HIS GIRELLA. BY HENRI REGNAULT.

barges, of certain streets, still more curious than those of the tribe of the Hebrews. From the bank you see retreating in perspective a mass of habitations, one leaning over the other, as if they had been driven by a blast of wind. The sight continues as far as the Ponte Sisto, under which you may discover a fisherman on the watch before his *girella* stretched at the foot of an arch. Penetrating to the principal street, which is parallel to the stream, but sinuous and with a breach here and there in its line, this ragged quarter is alive with the noise of the people and with the incongruity of contrasts. There are deep lanes, showing at their mouths palaces without name, whose fifteen centuries of architecture tumble one upon another ; the lemon-tree and the laurel push out from clefts in the stone in the midst of filthiness and the creatures of the courtyard. These places are called the Rione della Regola, and are inhabited by tanners ; the sour and pungent odour of the tan and the hides mix with the accustomed perfume of the cabbage.

Not far from this, on the bank of the river, is the graceful Rotunda of the Sun, dedicated by some modern archæologists to Vesta, a gracious monument of the age of Trajan, very inferior to the more ancient marvel of Tivoli, but still attractive in spite of having lost its

FOUNTAIN OF BIZZACCHERI, AND TEMPLE OF THE SUN, OR VESTA.

architraves and its pediment. To save this pagan altar, of which the primitive institution ascends, they say, as far as Numa, it was placed by the popes under the protection of St. Mary of the Sun. This plaything in style has for pendant the basin, in the midst of which by order of Clement XI. Carlo Bizzaccheri placed high and dry upon a rock two sirens of no very dangerous beauty.

The bottom of this piazza is occupied by the porch of Santa Maria in Cosmedin. It is a common opinion that Pope Adrian I., in reconstructing this church, which was of Constantinian origin, enriched it with an ornamentation so splendid that it retained the surname, *in*

Cosmedin, from κόσμος, decoration ornament; but this designation is earlier than the year 780. Santa Maria, at the foot of the Aventine

SANTA MARIA IN COSMEDIN.

and the Palatine, at the end of the street Bocca della Verità and at the bottom of a piazza, surrounded by ancient monuments, has been installed between the Corinthian arms of a temple of Ceres and

Proserpine rebuilt by Tiberius. We can still distinguish a portion of the Cella in large blocks of travertine, as well as eight columns of the peristyle in white marble, fluted and of the composite order. Seven of them are set in the walls of the church, which itself contains two distinct kinds of construction. The small basilica, which is primitive and probably of the date of Constantine, is drawn across the ancient temple: it is narrow, deep, and divided from the lower aisle of more modern date by antique columns with various capitals. The pavement is Alexandrine work of hard stone of the richest and oldest sort; the pulpits, of the sixth century, were adorned in the thirteenth by some rows of mosaic; at the bottom of the basilica is placed the *cathedra* belonging to the first ages; it was here that Pope Gelasius II. and the anti-Pope Benedict XII. were proclaimed: the master-altar is surmounted by a ciborium, supported on four columns of granite. This church, on which the primitive times have left their mark, is a hundred steps from the school where St. Augustine professed rhetoric, and the adjoining street perpetuates the recollection, for it is still called the Via della Greca, though the Bishop of Hippo taught in Latin the lessons of Homer, whose own tongue he had not studied. It is under the vast porch of Santa Maria in Cosmedin, where we find a splendid tomb of the twelfth century, that there has been fixed against a wall the colossal mask in veined marble, from four to five feet in diameter, so well known under the name of the Bocca della Verità. It is a flat or slightly concave face, with a mouth opening in a circle in the middle, as if to serve for the funnel of some tube. At Rome they consider the Bocca della Verità as the ornament of a fountain-pipe in the funnel of a drain. As for the rather sibylline title that the mask has given to the open space in front of the church, it is less ambitious than you might suppose, the children of the neighbourhood amusing themselves by clambering on to the great lunar face and burying their fists in its round mouth. The grandmothers have fancied and repeated for centuries to these youngsters that if they put their hands into the *bocca* after telling a lie, they will never be able to draw them back again. The little folk believe, and to escape the terrible test they make up their minds to honourable confession.

Close by the side of the Temple of Fortune, some centuries of venerable antiquity have introduced the elements of an enigma that has a very different complication. Built with a collection of sculptured materials got from I know not whence, fragments covering a period between the fourth century and the thirteenth, the Loggia, surmounted with a curious erection which they call the Casa di Rienzo, would furnish the frame for a long lecture in archæology. An inveterate tradition assigns it to Colà di Rienzi, who governed the commune of Rome.

Before fixing himself at the Capitol and taking shelter in the castle of St Angelo, could the friend of Petrarch, Colà di Rienzi, when he was notary apostolic, have lived in this house? The thing does not seem improbable. Towards the year 1340 Rienzi, his imagination inflamed with the old Rome, with the orators of the queen of the universe, whose equal he claimed to be, with republican manners

HOUSE OF RIENZI, AND TEMPLE OF FORTUNA VIRILIS.

which he strove hard to restore with the view of rousing public spirit and suppressing feudal brigandage, Colà di Rienzi, who in preaching his crusade recalled to mind the Gracchi, the Fabricii, the Brutuses, the Scipios, this Roman of old time who appealed on behalf of freedom to inscriptions, monuments, ruins, may well have made his home in this house that had been built out of the ruins of Roman grandeur, at the bottom of the Velabrum in front of the camp of Porsenna, close to the Fabrician bridge, at the foot of the Tarpeian rock, before the rotunda of the Sun, at the side of the Republican temple of Fortuna Virilis.

CHAPTER VII.

CONSTRUCTED afresh by Borromini and Rainaldi on the great piazzi Navona, which is blocked with booths and stalls and animated with all the hum and noise of a market, the church of St. Agnes with its cupola, accompanied by two flashing belfries, its façade adorned with composite columns and joined to the palace which it overwhelms, St. Agnes, a mass of broken lines, of sombre openings and projections whence the sun flashes back his rays, bursts upon you between two fountains, whose bubblings play accompaniments to the chatter of the market-women. Around these market-women, encamped under enormous umbrellas of yellow chintz, stirs the tide of customers, housekeepers and servants, Franciscans foraging, women from the Trastevere or the Suburra, peasant-women with their traditional head-dress. As they march along with hand on hip and head laden with a basket of fruits, you would take them for canephoræ come out of Greek sculpture.

You can scarcely ever forget the day on which for the first time you tread the Roman campagna, especially if, directing your steps towards the Mons Sacer, who have gone out by the Porta Pia which replaces the old Nomentane gate by which the Emperor Nero, in full flight from his soldiers, who had at last revolted, made his escape from Rome followed by a slave. There still remain in the walls of Honorius some signs of their masked outlet, and in the projection of an embankment the remains of a camp occupied by the prætorians, under which the fugitive Cæsar passed so close to them that he could hear them shout, "Long life to Galba." It was there that in later times these troops sold the empire by auction: it was there, in the midst of this prætorian camp, that Caracalla slew his brother Geta in the arms of their mother, Julia, who was covered with blood and wounded in the hand in attempting to defend one son against the other. Built by Pius IV., the Porta Pia was designed by Michael Angelo, the great architect and painter.

To penetrate into the uncultivated regions of the great historic and

THE MARKET OF THE PIAZZA NAVONA. BY HENRI REGNAULT.

pastoral desert, you had not then to traverse that suburb of small houses and taverns which ends in the masquerades of the Villa

Torlonia, where its owner has constructed imitative ruins. To set up counterfeit in the midst of the richest necropolis of antiquity—what clumsy competition! A little beyond, on a low rising ground, let us observe an *osterie* where the peasants from the north of the Abruzzi make their last halt, when they come down from the counterforts of the Monte Corno to visit the great markets of Rome. The sluggish train of lean jades wait at the door with entire philosophy while the contadini drink. The country begins to afford glimpses of glorious landscape as soon as one reaches the church of St. Agnes. This

"WHILE THE CONTADINI DRINK." BY HENRI REGNAULT.

church is at the corner of a monastery, and its extremely sober walls would not lead one to guess half its antiquity.

When at the prayer of his daughter, Constantine, in order to discover the body of the saint, had the catacombs of the Via Nomentana explored, they took up from around the tomb the earth of the galleries, and the basilica imprisoned the mausoleum. One has, then, in order to reach this church, which comes after a series of caverns, to descend forty steps under a vault whose walls are adorned with fragments and ancient inscriptions. The basilica has three aisles with two stories of colonnades. Its pillars of granite, of violet marble, of porta santa, taken from ancient temples,—its seat of marble of the fourth century,—

—its mosaic of the year 626, representing between Pope Damasus and the first Honorius, Agnes crowned, wearing a golden and jewelled

PIAZZA NAVONA AND CHURCH OF ST. AGNES.

laticlave, with white borders and a violet tunic,—all contributes to the religious impression of a monument half underground.

Near St. Agnes and in the domain of the community is a monument of older origin preserved in greater entirety. To see it you must, by a path strewn with fragments of marble, make for a Christian cemetery that is open to the sky, and is perhaps the oldest that was ever established. It is bounded by a thick wall of brick belonging to the sixth century, supported on an embankment of more than a hundred feet. There rises a rotunda wholly Constantinian; it was for his daughter and his sister that the son of St. Helen erected the baptistery of Constantia, as Ammianus Marcellinus attests. The great porphyry sarcophagus of St. Constantia, placed in the Vatican by the order of Pius VI., has from the fourth to the end of the eighteenth century furnished on the spot a no less formal proof. When, in 1256, he erected this baptistery into a church, Alexander IV. had deposited under the altar in the middle the body of St. Constantia and that of St. Emerentianus. They are there still. A Christian church can hardly date from an earlier epoch than this, and among the basilicas of the same date there is none in a more satisfactory state of preservation. This baptistery, in which St. Sylvester christened the two Constantias, presents among all the edifices of the Roman decline the most ancient example of coupled columns. They are of ancient origin, and reach the number of four-and-twenty; their shafts of granite support over varied capitals very curious protuberant friezes, above which rises a cupola. The vaults of the Ambulatorium which forms the circumference are decorated with mosaics on a white ground, belonging to the first half of the fourth century—a specimen that

ST. AGNES, AFTER THE MOSAIC OF THE CHOIR
(SEVENTH CENTURY).

would be unique if those of St. Pudentiana had not been preserved equally, for the frieze of Santa Maria Maggiore can only belong to the end of the same century. The precious mosaics of the baptistery have for their subjects flowing designs formed by vine-shoots turned in various directions and laden with ripe bunches. Pagan genii at large, and angels latest born of the Mother of the Loves, gather the grapes from branch to branch; some interspaces are furnished with grotesque heads; some coffer-work frames rosettes connected by interlacings which form crosses.

Round the little convent of St. Agnes, over a space of two or three

ST. AGNES EXTRA MUROS ON THE VIA NOMENTANA.

acres on a road-side, you have the complete picture of the heroic ages of religion. The martyrs, the subterranean worship in three stories of catacombs, the symbolical inscriptions, the sacred paintings of the earliest centuries, all await you in the depths of the earth.

Below the ancient Rome, along the fifteen Consular roads which radiated from the Capitol as centre, there existed in the third century, besides a score of underground cemeteries consecrated to families, twenty-six great catacombs, which answer to the number of the parishes of that time. It has been calculated that these labyrinths must measure a hundred and fifty leagues of gallery, and must contain six millions of the dead. The average width of the corridors is nearly a yard; placed one over another, so as sometimes to form five stories, they are never dug deeper than about five-and-twenty yards, a thickness beneath which the volcanic crust ends to make way for humid clays.

Nothing can be more interesting than this cradle of religion, this elysium of the martyrs of imperial tyranny, ancestors whom all Christian communions venerate.

The cemetery where St. Agnes had her tomb, which, as it has been exposed, now serves as an altar for the church constructed about it, this dormitory, for such is the literal and spiritualistic meaning of the word, is situated a distance of two miles from Rome; you go down to it from the midst of a wild garden by some thirty steps. At the bottom of the cellar steps you penetrate a series of narrow corridors one after another, cut at right angels, intricate like a network of lanes, and whose complexities could certainly never have permitted any kind of working.

The Christians must then have chosen in the intermediate section of the volcanic stratum that porous marl which was of a sufficient consistency, while it was tolerably easy to chip away; a light substance, of which the fracture is soft, which does not split, and where one could work excavations without encumbering the passages with bulky heavy blocks which would be difficult to get out.

Such is the geological constitution of the catacombs. The useless matter of which they are formed was heaped up in the passages out of the way, or brought from the bottom of these sacred burrowings under some look-out hole, and from these the rubbish was raised by means of rope and basket, and mixed either with the sand of the quarries of the upper range or with the uncultivated ground of the surface. At any rate, it is certain that the catacombs could only have been established to serve as cemeteries, and to be expressly set apart for that purpose. Their use, for that matter, long preceded the Christian era; Pliny informs us that the practice of incineration was not very ancient, and that many great families had preserved the custom of burying their dead. Sallust had under his garden catacombs provided with *loculi;* the dictator Sulla was the first of the Cornelian family whose body was burned.

As we see with what economy they utilised space, leaving no more than the necessary room between the compartments, and taking **advantage of the** very smallest nooks for the burial-places of children, of which the number is prodigious, we are better instructed here than in any book as to the rapid propagation of the faith during the first

SUBTERRANEAN GALLERIES AND LOCULI OF THE CATACOMB OF ST. AGNES.

centuries. The complexity of the place explains how, under the territory of the ancient city alone, they could have made about three hundred and sixty miles of winding ways. Pagan Rome was simply mined by the catacombs.

If I add that before the year 316 these cities of the dead, where the holy mysteries were celebrated, and where catechumens were instructed, sometimes hid as many of the living as they concealed of the dead, we can understand how at the moment when Christianity was officially proclaimed, it had rallied all the lower and middle class, only leaving to pagan worship as the defender of ancient institutions the support of the old Roman aristocracy, which was the enemy of a dogma that, while it proclaimed equality and the fraternal possession of earthly goods in common, annihilated at once both large properties and the institution of slavery, the single means of working such extensive appanages. Thus Tacitus, the mouthpiece of the most oppressive tyranny that ever was, describes the Christians as "infamous and pestilent men, execrated for their crimes." In yielding to the necessity of attracting the Nazarenes to his party and placing the cross upon his standard, Constantine made sure of the empire; *in hoc signo vicit.* And we may imagine how imperious this necessity must have been, when we recall that more than a century before, under Septimius Severus, Tertullian affirmed that if the Christians were forced to emigrate, the Roman empire would become a desert.

Some visitors are so vividly impressed by the aspect of the catacombs, and so suffocated by the atmosphere of their narrow, low, and never-ending passages, where the air is made thick by the smoke of torches, that they beg to be allowed to make their way back. In truth, if the torches were to go out, one would be condemned to await death in this tomb of some millions of souls; if the old and bowed guide who went before us had by mischance been struck by apoplexy, probably not one of us would ever again have seen the light. The caverns of St. Agnes not being public, we had come alone to our appointment; and even supposing that a week after another guide should have brought a company, the party would most likely have directed its steps towards some different quarter. These are reflections to which people do not stoop until after the event. The tombs of martyrs and heroes often nameless draw ones attention specially; it is easy to make them out, for when the grave-makers closed them, they fastened in their cement by the side of the head an ampulla of glass in which the blood of the confessor had been collected. You still see on nearly every hand the mark and often the fragments of these vessels. When the martyrs had been drowned, burned, or put to death without spilling of blood, then in sealing up the burial-place the workman with the point of his trowel drew in the fresh mortar a

SUBTERRANEAN ALTAR, TOMBS, AND CHAPEL IN THE CEMETERY OF ST. AGNES.

rude sketch of a palm-tree, and a certain number of these are to be seen. Occasionally we recognise the calcined bones of a martyr burnt alive and it sometimes happens that the bones are crystallised to such a degree as to shine. Inscriptions give the name of the dead; those in Greek are usually the oldest, Greek having been the official tongue of the primitive Church. Many of the tombs are closed fast and untouched.

If you wish to penetrate further in the study of the catacombs and its symbols, it is necessary to return to Rome, cross the whole of the city, and reach the gate of St. Sebastian.

Forgotten for centuries, confounded even no more than twenty years back either with the cemetery of St. Sebastian or with that of Domitilla, the catacombs of Callistus were definitely discovered in 1852, by the most eminent of Roman archæologists, Signor Rossi. St. Callistus is one of the caves which help us best to understand what after the reign of Constantine was the fate of the catacombs. Pope Damasus and his successors decorate them and organise stations in them; light-holes are made above the monuments made illustrious by saints; they wall up corridors that had no interest, and which only added to the complications of the labyrinth; they allow new *loculi* to be hollowed out for the burial of pious families under the protection of the blessed patrons of the ages of trial. It was then that the faithful of the fourth century described this place as the Jerusalem of the martyrs of the Lord. Believers came thither from all parts of the world.

This catacomb was constructed long before the epoch at which Pope Callistus I.—sprung, they say, from the Domitian family, but who had directed a bank in the Forum—bequeathed his name to a cemetery lying under his vineyard; some *loculi* are closed with bricks, the stamping on which dates from Marcus Aurelius; everything shows that this cemetery of pagan origin was created by the Metelli on their vast territories, which extended as far as the mole of Cæcilia Metella.

As at St. Agnes, it is from the midst of an uncultivated garden that by the corner of a ruined country villa you descend into that legendary spot where the most modern restorations date from between 366 and 420. Half-way down the descent, along which the steps and the face of the wall are stocked with vegetation, as soon as you have lost sight of the city and its hills, the torches are kindled, and each visitor, flambeau in hand, penetrates into this labyrinth of sanctuaries very much as the subterranean processions used to go. Armed with torches, the guides who precede you plunge deeper and deeper into the sombre corridors, where the black smoke of the resin seems to throw them into strange and funereal perspective. For very nervous persons the sensation of fright is not less invincible here than it is at St. Agnes, and we frequently see women and old men so overwhelmed that they stop and pray to be taken back to the light of the sun. You are among not less than three rows of sepulchres one

VALERIANUS AND CÆCILIA. MOSAIC OF THE NINTH CENTURY, AT ST. CÆCILIA.

over another: skeletons are under your feet as over your head; they elbow you right and left. Men by hundreds of thousands have prayed and sung in these galleries, and now they sleep in them the sleep of death.

It is near the burial-places of St. Cyprian, Bishop of Carthage, and St Eusebius, who died in 311, that one of the inscriptions of

Damasus in six verses, engraved upon a tablet of marble, informs us that the bodies of St. Peter and St. Paul were long concealed in these catacombs.

In the second and third centuries the little underground basilica of St. Callistus and the chambers which surround it were the metropolis of the Holy See, and the centre of the pontifical administration. They still show there the little cell which served as working-room for these spiritual masters of the Christian world, reduced to this curious appanage unknown to the sun. They had as guardians, as soldiers, and as legates, mendicants posted from distance to distance who kept watch along the Appian Way.

The site of the tomb of St. Cæcilia is still marked at St. Callistus, as well as the spot where St. Lucina reposed. Around the loculus of St. Cæcilia, tombs and a multitude of inscriptions placed on the walls by enthusiastic pilgrims announce that famous personage, before, in a crypt adjoining the papal room, one has recognised the likeness of the saint and that of Urban who buried her.

The subterranean Vatican of the primitive church abounds in interesting epitaphs. "Here was laid to sleep Gorgonius, whom all loved and who hated none." This inscription, like many others, is in Greek; the following are in Latin, but without any date, which is a sign of great antiquity :—

"Too soon hast thou fallen, Constantia! Admirable for Beauty and for her Charms, she lived xviii Years, vi Months, xvi Days. Constantia, in peace."

There are some epitaphs which retrace the memories of the persecutions; such is that of one Marius, a young officer under Adrian, "*who lived long enough, for he spent his life and his blood for Christ.*" His friends laid him there with much wailing and many fears. This one, which comes from St. Agnes, and which is composed in Latin with Greek letters, has a very different significance :—

"Here Gordianus, Messenger from Gaul, Slain for the Faith, with all his Family. They rest in peace. Theophila, their servant, had this done."

The poor envoy from Gaul, put to death on foreign soil with all his family; the servant, left alone and far from her land, raising a monument to her master and adorning it with a palm—here is a touching episode in the inner life of our forefathers. The workmen of the catacombs, or grave-makers, formed not a corporation but a minor order of the clergy An inscription has been found at St.

Callistus with these words: "Diogenes the Gravedigger, in Peace, laid here the eighth before the Kal. of October."

This is placed above the delineation of the deceased. His tunic comes down to his knees, and he is shod with sandals. On his left shoulder is a piece of fur or stuff; on his right shoulder as well as above the knees are traced small crosses; in one hand he holds a mattock, and in the other a lamp hung by a small chain; around him are the tools of his business. The characteristic of most of the inscriptions is tender and consolatory thought; affection sighs its regrets, and faith breathes in hope. There is nothing pompous,

nothing to recall the dignities of this world; much cheerfulness, much simplicity, much sweetness. "To Adeodata, meritorious Virgin, who rests here in peace, her Christ having willed it so."

The virtues praised among the deceased are always amiable virtues; *friend of the poor, tender and blameless soul, lamb of the Lord.* A widower recalls fifteen years of union *sine lesione animi*; he was father of seven children, *but his wife has four of them with her with the Lord.* "May thy soul be refreshed in supreme bliss, O Kalemira!"

Certain names show how recent the conversions were. Two sons address this prayer over the tomb of their mother: "Lord, may the soul of our mother, VENUS, not be left in darkness."

It seemed to me that at St. Callistus the paintings were more numerous as well as more important than at St. Agnes. You come upon the Anchor, which symbolizes hope, and figures the cross; the Dove flying away with the olive-branch in his mouth, emblem of the Christian soul that quits this world in peace; the Ship at the foot of a beacon; the Fish, ΙΧΘΥΣ, whose Greek name recalls that of Christ and furnishes the initials of the formula, Ἰησοῦς Χριστὸς Θεοῦ Υἱὸς Σωτήρ; Bread, symbol of the Eucharist; the Rabbit gnawing, symbol of the destruction of the body. The Tortoise and the Dormouse signify that the sleep of death will be fo'lowed by an awakening; the Children in the Furnace remind the confessor that he must brave torment; Daniel given to the Lions is the patron of martyrs; Jonas is the emblem of regeneration by faith. In a vault distributed into compartments, a number of these subjects make a frame to Orpheus, who draws a crowd of animals and even turtles to himself. This curious vault, which Bosio first sketched, goes back, according to D'Agincourt, to the end of the first century.

JONAH AND THE WHALE.
PRAYER.
THE CHILDREN IN THE FURNACE.

The cemetery of Callistus makes us acquainted with the works of embellishment executed in the catacombs down to the pontificate of Pascal I. Starting from St. Damasus, described as the Virgin Doctor of the virgin church by St. Jerome, who was his secretary, and who remembered wandering in the catacombs in his childhood. This pope, who prevented the raising in the senate of a pagan altar of Victory, and who obtained from Valentinian in 370 a

PLAYING AT BOWLS. BY HENRI REGNAULT.

decree forbidding members of the clergy from receiving donations or testamentary bequests—Damasus, who regretted the purity of the old days of trial, wished to be buried, not in the cemeteries, even of Cæcilia and of St. Callistus, for which his humility disinclined him, but

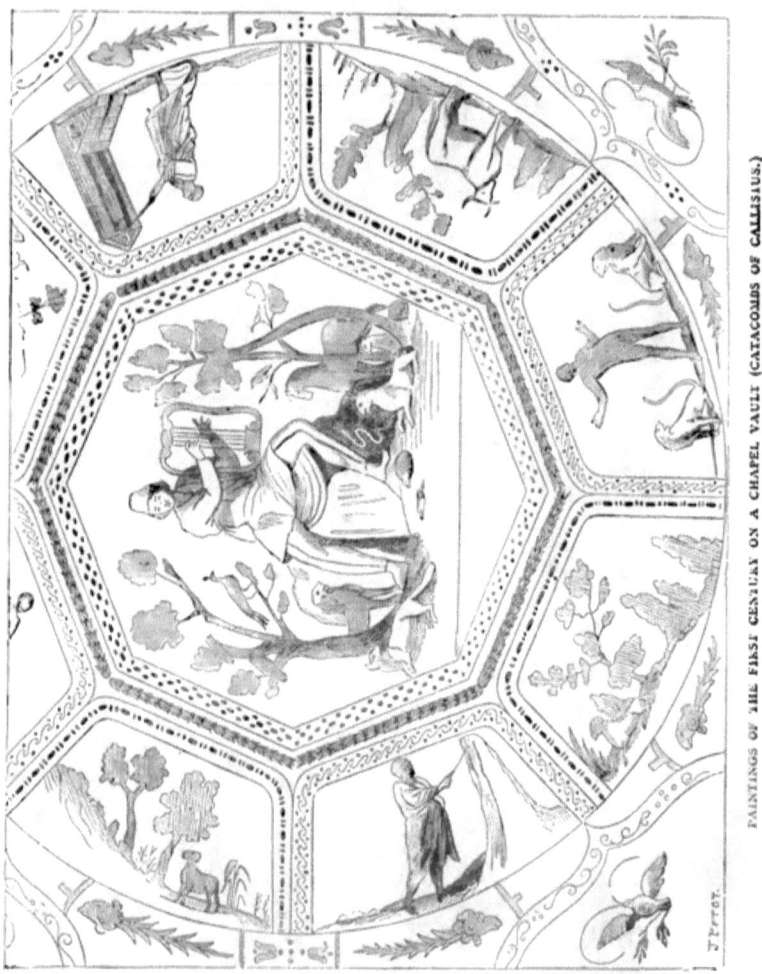

PAINTINGS OF THE FIRST CENTURY ON A CHAPEL VAULT (CATACOMBS OF CALLISIUS.)

in a small outside chapel near one of the light-holes. The four walls of this chapel still stand.

The Nomentane Bridge.

At a short distance beyond the basilica of St. Agnes is the Nomentane bridge which contributes with a massive tomb, in which the shepherds have hollowed out a hut for themselves, to give colour to a landscape of tranquil simplicity. Near at hand was the villa of Phaon, where the Emperor Nero found his last shelter and ended his life when pursued after his escape from the capitol by the Nomentane road and bridge.

In the neighbourhood of it, under the green arbours of a rural tavern, by the side of the Teverone, the Roman holiday-makers of modern days empty their flasks or quarrel over the points of a game at bowls.

Like the Great Desert the Roman Campagna is eternally unknown; no one crosses it without searching for something, and each year is witness of some discovery. It is a vast region of inexhaustible treasure.

PONTE NOMENTANO.

CHAPTER VIII.

THE Cælian being a melancholy desert, it is best to go there alone, so as to gain an impression in harmony with the look of the place. To ascend this slope, you leave on the right the monastery of rich and substantial aspect that marks the site of the house of the Anician family; and it was here that Gregory the Great was born. The street, which is shaded by trees, is commanded on the left by the lofty apse of the conventual church of St. John and St. Paul, which has belonged ever since Clement XIV. to the Passionist fathers. The tower-shaped chevet is crowned with a rounded diadem of arches cut in festoons and supported on little columns. Sometimes along the line of this road ancient pavement varies the chessboard pattern of the modern; the wall on the right, which separates various gardens from the street, is contemporary with Nero. This wall, mixed with *opus reticularium* of brick and peperino, shows against its thick and hollow sides the traces of a row of small habitations. To uphold the embankment and support the Redemptorist convent, which is on the edge of the street, they have thrown from one side to the other a series of flying arches under which you pass, forming a perspective at the back of which, set fast among buildings and in ruins, rises the arch of Dolabella.

A little above you arrive in the piazza where Leo X. had placed a small boat of marble, which has given a surname to the church, Santa Maria della Navicella, more commonly described as *in Domnica*, because it replaced the house of a noble lady, St. Cyriaca. This temple, supported on ancient columns of granite and porphyry, was restored by Leo X. from the plans of Raphael. The frieze above the architraves of the nave, although it is to be attributed to P. del Vaga and Giulio Romano, might well have been designed and even partially executed by Giovanni d'Udine. The mosaic of the choir, from the year 817 to 824, is all the more interesting, as the paintings of the ninth century are not very common in Rome.

STREET AND APSE OF ST. JOHN AND ST. PAUL.

It was the feast of St. Stephen, and to find the church I had only to follow the crowd along a battered street which footsteps had already made slippery; a true mountain pilgrimage *intra muros*. As this strange temple is only open once a year, the day of the

ARCH OF DOLABELLA AND GATE OF THE OLD CONVENT OF THE TRINITARIANS.

funzione, taverns and stalls where they sell small tapers are improvised at the approaches to the monument. Holiday-makers of the

Rione Toscano, coachmen, pilgrims from the country, all stop there to see the stream of people returning, and to gather a few baiocchi

ROMANS PLAYING AT MORA. BY HENRI REGNAULT.

from them upon occasion. You would sometimes imagine that these good folk are quarrelling and must be going to cut one another's throats; they are playing at *mora*, a word which, while expressing the idea of delay or check, describes a game that keeps the adversaries constantly on the alert and excites them to excess. It consists in presenting very suddenly to your partner your right hand, keeping one or two fingers shut, and in crying at the same moment the number of fingers extended. The adversary, who is obliged to seize your intention with magical rapidity, has at the same moment to imitate his comrade, and to pronounce the same number as rapidly as he. The left hand serves to mark the points gained. The precipitate haste, the tensity of mind required, the rapidity of the turns, make both players cry their words in jerks; the faces of the players become glowing and contracted, while their voices, breathless and hoarse, accent with a guttural dryness the numbers cried monosyllabically—*Du'!*—*Quattr'!*—*Un'!*—*Tre'!*—*Cinq'!* Animated by this trifling, which not seldom degenerates into a downright quarrel, so easy and so doubtful is a mistake, the Romans unconsciously assume postures and expressions of ferocious beauty At the street corners I was never weary of looking at them. It is said that their ancestors played at mora while besieging Syracuse, and they even talked of a Greek bas-relief where the petulant Ajax is beaten by the sage Ulysses in presence of the aged Nestor.

ENTRY OF THE CONVENT OF ST. JOHN AND ST. PAUL.

San Stefano Rotondo

The church of San Stefano Rotondo is extremely spacious, and a double colonnade surrounded it previously to Nicholas V.; its conical roof sloping on to an architrave which covers fifty-six columns, as well in marble as in granite, with Ionic and Corinthian capitals. The unequal dimensions of the shafts, certain disproportions between their diameters and those of the heads, the rude design of some of the ornaments, a number of incised crosses in the heart of the acanthuses, —all denote a Christian temple constructed of bits and pieces on a circular ground-plan at the end of the fifth century. It is said, in fact, that it was inaugurated towards 465 by Pope Simplicius, who as

SAN STEFANO ROTONDO.

a native of Tivoli might, before the Sibylline temple, have acquired a fancy for monuments of round form. This is surrounded by a perfect necklace of altars; one of them still preserves a mosaic of the seventh century. Let us also not forget to mention a very fine Bishop lying on a sarcophagus by Lorenzetto. But this is not the principal curiosity of San Stefano Rotondo, nor what makes it so popular. In old times, when spectacles were rare, the spiritual and temporal pastors of a people that were degenerate in their passion for theatres, in order to attract the populace, whose mind it was necessary to stir, had invested most of the churches with ceremonies and display of a peculiar character. At St. Peter, the regal pomps of the sovereign church; at the Ara Cœli, the pastoral of the Nativity; at St. Stephen the Round, they represent with all its terrors the melodrama of martyrdom, and this is quite naturally the spectacle which the populace prefer.

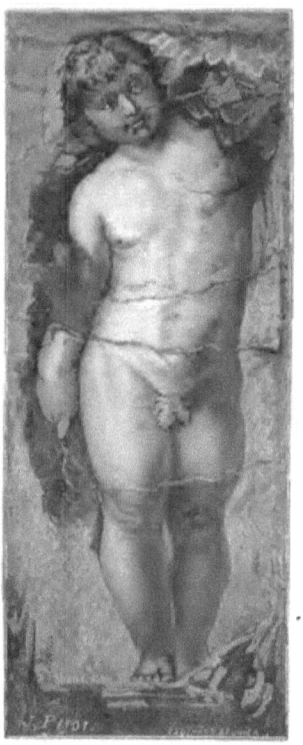

FRAGMENT OF RAPHAEL.

To enter the gallery of St. Luke, you have to ring at a modest door on the left of the Via Bonella, and once entered you find yourself before some cows that Berghem has brought to graze among the ruins. A fine shipwreck of Tempesta, a landscape of Salvator Rosa, a few country pieces of Blömen, instantly give you the key of the modern note and of simple nature.

I wish I could give some sketch of this museum, of the impression it makes, of the entertainment or use that one may find there, without believing myself obliged to mention this or that, under penalty of appearing incomplete. As for detail, there is a catalogue. The principal attraction of this collection comes of its diversity; it possesses something of every school, and the most thorough, rather than the largest, examples of each school—a rare circumstance in a gallery created with a view to teaching.

The sanctuary of the place is dedicated to Raphael on account of two important paintings; the one which represents a robust and beautiful child, naked, in the style of Farnesini, is a piece of fresco detached from one of the rooms of the Vatican, and which once belonged to Wicar, the benefactor of the museum at Lille; the other picture has been made common by engraving, and the painters have placed a copy of it in their church. It is the St. Luke painting the Madonna, who descends from heaven to pose for him; behind the evangelist a pupil, probably Raphael, looks and draws in inspiration; a charming head painted with much suppleness.

One of the gems of the Gallery is the portrait of the handsome Madame Vigée-Lebrun, whom I knew when she was nearly a hundred years old, at Louveciennes, where she died. A grey dress, a cloud of white muslin, serving at once for kerchief round the neck and coiffure for the head, constitute her négligé. This celebrated artist, who had exhausted all the triumphs that fame and beauty can confer, had cut on her gravestone the simple words, "*At last I rest.*"

Turn the street to begin the ascent of the Capitol; at the corner of the Via del Marforio, under the small church of San Giuseppe, a monument of an entirely different sort will arrest you on the way.

I mean the two dungeons, one over the other, which, by way of recalling their founders, bear the denominations of the Mamertine prison, in memory of the King Ancus Martius (issue of Mars, whom the Oscans called Mamercus), and the Tullian prison, because the king, Servius Tullius, they say, had the deeper of the two dug out under the first.

MADAME VIGEE-LEBRUN, BY HERSELF.

These caves of detention, the oldest in the world, are seen in the nakedness of primitive construction, and in the simplicity proper for the circumstances which their name is enough to make remarkable.

The Mamertine prison, properly so called, into which you descend at the present day by the church of St. Joseph, due to the corporation of the carpenters, is in the shape of a trapezium twenty feet long by about sixteen broad; the masonry consists of enormous blocks of volcanic stone or reddish peperino, cubed and arranged in the Etruscan way; the vault, which is semi-cylindrical (though irregular, the sides of the square being unequal), is formed of immense blocks. This chamber, where you recognise the traces of a window that has been long condemned, had no door; previously bound tight, the prisoners were plunged through a round hole into the Mamertine by means of a rope.

The Lucumos of Tarquiniæ were sprung of the Etruscan stock which permitted human sacrifices, and the crypt of the temple dedicated to their gods must have been a slaughter-house. Josephus demonstrates the duration of these customs. 'It is a pious usage,' writes the Jewish historian, 'to put to death in the Mamertine prisons the chiefs of the conquered nations, while the triumphant conqueror sacrifices on the Capitol to Jupiter.' For at the same time Pliny the Elder saw buried alive in the Forum Boarium, with the design of winning the favour of the gods, a man and a young woman born in Gaul, with which they were then at war; and this pious atrocity seems quite natural to Pliny.

ARCHES OF ST. JOHN AND ST. PAUL, AS SEEN WHEN DESCENDING FROM THE CŒLIAN.

This prison was exactly as we see it to-day four or five centuries before the Cæsars, in the time of the Decemvirs, when Appius Claudius slew himself in this prison. Who has not thought of the lot of Manlius Capitolinus, reduced to appeal in vain for his defence against the envious Camillus, to thirty enemies slain with his own hand, to his eight civic crowns, to his thirty-two military awards, and to the scars that adorned his breast? He was plunged into the frightful Tullianum. Then arrives in this hostelry of slaughter, before Syphax king of Numidia, Jugurtha, who carried on so long a campaign, and whom Marius and Sulla together would never have conquered, if the treason of the king of Mauritania had not delivered him to the Republic; as he came down from the Capitol, where he had figured in the triumphal car of Marius, Jugurtha, like an actor whose part is over, was stripped and cast into the Tullianum. 'By the gods!' he exclaimed, as they entered his name on the jailer's scroll, 'how cold your stoves are!' For death to come to him, six days of inanition were enough.

It was in the Tullianum that they strangled Cethegus, Gabinius, Statilius, and Ceparius, those hardy accomplices of Catilina, after Cicero had dragged Lentulus to the prison, whom he caused to be put to death first, proceeding in his own person to that swift transaction. Cicero scarcely foresaw that to punish him for thinking that he had saved his country, an exceptional

ONE OF THE TROPHIES, CALLED OF MARIUS, AT THE CAPITOL.

law would come, confiscating his property and driving him into exile. Aristobulus and Tigranes, after the triumph of Pompeius, were incarcerated according to custom in the Mamertine prisons.

After all, these Romans were a cruel people, and these great men had small souls. The valiant fair-haired warrior of the Gauls, Vercingétorix, who confronted Julius Cæsar with an enemy worthy of him, was transported to the Mamertine cage to await the ceremony of the triumph. It was put off for six years; Vercingetorix figured in it, and then Cæsar had him slain under the vault of the Tullianum. It has devoured people of every sort, this famous jail, and even criminals. Sejanus was put to death in it, as well as his daughters. Six years before the remnant of Israel had entered there, another Simon, Simon the Fisher, and Saul the converted philosopher of Damascus, had borne into these caves their last fetters. It is in memory of this captivity that the Tullianum has become a chapel under the designation of San Pietro in Carcere. It is said that St. Peter was bound to the pillar at the side of the altar. The tin bowl placed near the subterranean spring is for the use of the faithful who care to drink water which quenched the thirst of the Apostle and baptized his jailers, Processus and Martinianus.

As you reflect that at the dawn of the Republic these prisons already belonged to an earlier régime, that for five-and-twenty centuries so many illustrious victims have wept, raged, prayed, groaned in this cave with its soil kneaded with blood, you are profoundly moved at the contemplation of what has been looked upon by kings of Asia, by consuls, by enemies of Rome, by saints; by seeing them exactly as these men left them, by breathing in the atmosphere in which they lived, and by saying to yourself as you touched the walls that there perhaps where your hand lies, the first of the popes rested his head, which had been touched by the hand of Christ.

On the hill of the Capitol the Senatorial Palace, planted on that ancient base, has its chief frontage in the midst of the Intermontium. Cut down steep on one side on to the Forum, which it masks, this piece of architecture on the other side bounds a space, standing in the middle of which you have on your right the Protomotheca, founded by Pius VII., and the palace of the Conservators or civil magistrates. The left side is occupied by the museum of the Capitol. A little behind rises the church of the Ara Cœli, where the Temple of Jupiter used to be, a pendant to the Tarpeian rock, which was crowned of old by the Acropolis. The enceinte of the small central space has for boundary-marks balustrades guarded by lions, and some steps, above which rise the colossal figures of Castor and Pollux, adjoining those celebrated trophies which have retained the name of Marius, but which belong to the age of Trajan.

Between the steps and the principal palace rises the single equestrian bronze bequeathed to us by Roman antiquity. Yet this only owed its preservation during the middle ages to a mistake; the pseudonym of Constantine protected Marcus Aurelius. In the fifth

STEPS OF THE SENATORIAL PALACE: TARPEIAN STAIRCASE.

century, Totila is said to have carried off this statue, which was then gilded, and he was proceeding to put it on shipboard when Belisarius recovered it. In the time of Sylvester II. the pretended Constantine edified the faithful in the Forum Boarium; Pope Scolari (Clement III.) transported it to the front of the Lateran palace, the old abode of Constantine. The Marcus Aurelius stayed there until the time when, under Paul III., Michelangelo had it brought on to the Capitoline piazza, at the very spot where Arnold of Brescia had been burnt in 1155; near the steps at the foot of which, two centuries after, Rienzi, on his flight from the Capitol, came to his end under the knife of an artisan. When Andrea Verocchio, the best jeweller in Florence, came to Rome, the Marcus Aurelius made so vivid an impression upon him that he was emboldened by that revelation of equestrian sculpture to execute the Bartolommeo Colleone of the Piazetta Zanipolo at Venice, a truly incomparable masterpiece. The illustrious pupil of Ghirlandajo and Verocchio, Leonardo da Vinci, was likewise inspired by the Marcus Aurelius, and also, according to Paolo Jove, by the horses of the Dioscuri, when he offered to the admiration of the people of Milan his model of the equestrian figure of Francis Sforza, which, when exposed to view in 1493, seemed superior to the Donatello of Padua (*Gattamelata*) and even to the Verocchio of Venice. The revolution of 1499 hindered the execution of this masterpiece: nothing is left of the sculptures of the great Leonardo, and it is only from the testimony of Ludovico Dolce that we know to what a point this artist, the only one of the three greatest contemporary painters whose school maintained itself without degeneracy, was '*stupendissimo in far cavalli.*'

JUNIUS BRUTUS.

At the very first we are attracted by the singularity of another bronze, the bust of Michelangelo in his old age, from a marble sculpture from life by one of his pupils. It is surely the most extraordinarily constructed head, the most gnarled skull, the most violent,

PIAZZA OF THE CAPITOL GALLERY OF ANTIQUES.

the most diabolic outline. As a pendant to it there rises another still

THE DYING GLADIATOR.

more striking figure, Junius Brutus, founder of the Republic. His short, flat hair, his brow with its acute angles, his frowning eyebrows, under which there shine out in the tawny glow of the bronze black eyeballs on an enamelled crystal; the severe shape of a very aquiline nose, the broad chin, the iron lips, the firm-set lines of a jaw that stands out under a short bristling beard—all impresses upon this physiognomy, which has a beauty incompatible with grace, a really terrible character.

Descending from the museum you enter a court decorated as they all are by antique fragments. I remarked among them a group energetically cast, representing a horse devoured by a lion; the important restoration of this piece, corroded by damp, is attributed to Michelangelo. Not far off is the statue of the Ocean, which they call Marforio, and which has given its name to one of the neighbouring streets. It was found in the Forum of Augustus, or of Mars, Marte-Foro, and hence according to some the name of Marforio; but this etymology is barely satisfactory. We decipher in this court a number of inscriptions of prætorian soldiers; we find in it sarcophagi, statues, bas-reliefs; but what I observed there particularly were the ornamented fragments of the Temple of Concord, cut with marvellous art. An amateur

FAUN, AFTER PRAXITELES.

will scarcely omit to look at the fine tomb from which the Portland vase was taken. The staircase has for its decoration those plaques of marble which were taken from the Temple of Romulus, and which preserve for us a plan of Rome engraved under Septimus Severus. In a saloon that was arranged ten years ago for works in metal, you will find with interest, marked with an undeniable Greek inscription, the strange and noble bronze that Mithridates gave to the gymnasium of the Eupatorists. There are also graduated weights and measures of ancient Rome; an admirable Hercules in gilded bronze; the Greek Child holding a comic mask, by which Raphael

THE AMAZON.

MESSALINA.

was more than once inspired; and the Ariadne, the ideal of fascinating beauty. A mistake has given a name to the chamber of the Gladiator. The warrior mortally wounded, that for so many years has been admired in the Capitol under the designation of the Dying Gladiator, does not in truth represent a gladiator at all, but a Gaulish chieftain. The collar or torques leaves no doubt on this subject. One may compare this type with the combatants of the battle of Telamone, fought with the Gauls 355 years before our era by Attilius Regulus, who was killed there. The figures of this curious sarcophagus recalled, by their type and their curling hair, this dying warrior, in whom we see one of the ancient heroes of the French race. Here also is an old reproduction of the Faun of Praxiteles; some Etruscan fragments and a quantity of works from Greece, including even archaic pasticci, initiate the visitor into a multitude of forms, schools, and practices. It is in a chamber of this museum that the Antinoüs is to be found, the ideal of sensual beauty; there the bust of the murderer of Cæsar, Marcus Brutus, a fine, intelligent, marked, and sombre head, strangely recalling the features of Armand Carrel; also that statue of a Roman lady, so naturally posed and so well draped, in which without valid reason some people have pretended to recognise

MARIUS.

AGRIPPINA, DAUGHTER OF DRUSUS.

Agrippina, others Domitia. We will only cite, by way of enumeration, the figures of Flora, the Amazon, and the infant Hercules.

The inhabitants of Olympus are no more than the lares of this palace; in proportion as the great personages of antiquity are resuscitated by the excavations, our popes send them to recruit the lofty society of the Capitol. How, in the midst of so noble a population, can we help believing with the contemporaries of Apuleius, with St Augustin himself, that the spectres of marble are tenanted by souls? Etiquette has formed two distinct salons: in one of them the writers and philosophers of Rome give hospitality to those of Greece; and this areopagus forms an assembly in which more than eighty celebrities shine. There you visit Socrates, Seneca, Agrippa, Diogenes, Theophrastus, Apuleius, the architect Posidonius, Demosthenes, Sophocles, Cato, Thucydides, Antisthenes, Terence, Apollonius of Tyana, Aspasia and Pericles, Archytas, Sappho, Periander .... we cannot cite all of them. In the middle sits Marcellus, the victor of Syracuse; while on the walls are bas-reliefs: among them a Sacrifice to Hygieia, marked by Callimachus.

It does not take very long to come down from a mountain whose summit is not more than fifty yards above the level of the sea. Near the foot of the Capitol is the hospital of La Consolazione, belonging to the sick of the weaker sex, where a dormitory opens on to a piazza in direct continuation of a long street.

Rome was the first to organize and develop genuinely special hospitals.

ROMAN LADY, TAKEN FOR THE FIRST AGRIPPINA.

As you enter Rome by the Porta Portese, situated at the southern extremity of the Janiculum, you leave to the right the Tiber and the vast hospital of St. Michael, which occupies at Ripa Grande, a port constructed by Innocent XII., part of the site of the Prata Mutia. It is here that legend places the camp of Porsenna and the royal tent where Mutius Scævola thrust his hand into the flame. St. Michael is a reformatory for young prisoners, combined with a conservatory of industrial craft and the fine arts, while they also receive into it the poor, the aged, and the infirm of both sexes. Four hundred indigent children are collected there, educated by the most skilful masters, and kept until the age of twenty-one, when the lads, provided with a position, go away with full purses, and the girls receive a dower of a hundred crowns.

THE HOSPITAL OF ST. MICHAEL.

I have reserved what concerns the ordinary object of charitable establishments, the treatment of the patients and the administration of the numerous hospitals. The most considerable is that of the San Spirito, which contains also a refuge for foundlings.

NEST OF HOUSES ON THE BANKS OF THE TIBER. BY HENRI REGNAULT.

It was in 1198 that, as he was walking on the banks of the Tiber, Innocent III. came upon a fisherman who had just brought up in his net three dead infants. Deeply moved, the Holy Father immediately had established on a barge contiguous to the hospital of San Spirito, which he had just instituted, a movable turning box lined with a mattress, in which they might at any hour place abandoned children; at the same time he forbade, under severe penalties, all inquiry as to who placed them there. The children are kept at San Spirito till they are old enough to be sent to the asylum at Viterbo, where they are taught a trade. At seventeen they receive enough to live upon for a year. The girls are the object of a still more paternal solicitude. We cannot either too much admire, or too warmly praise, or be too much struck, as we recognise that Rome has constantly directed the Christian world in the path of charity; if religion has truth for its basis, that was bound to be so; and the thing being so, to state it becomes a duty.

On the banks of the Tiber, adjoining the Vatican, in the place where the Gauls and Germans who were brought by Vitellius perished of fever, and sought, according to Tacitus, in the waters of the stream, a disastrous relief from the summer heats, there is the hospital of San Spirito. It would be out of place here to describe this vast establishment. It is situated on the abrupt corner which separates the Vatican Hill from the northern extremity of the Janiculum, where it occupies a triangle as large as a small town. Marchione of Arezzo, Bacio Pintelli, San Gallo, perhaps even Palladio, worked successfully at this charitable institution. To establish it, Innocent III. chose a site already consecrated by a Saxon king, who in the year 717 set up there a hospitium for his countrymen, and hence the name of San Spirito in Sassia which the house still bears. The bull of foundation bears the date A.D. 1198. At San Spirito, whoever is suffering is received and tended, whatever the position, nationality, age, or even the religious creed of the patient.

CHAPTER IX.

ALTHOUGH the Capitoline promontory, looking on the Tiber and the Palatine, is nearly to its top scaled by houses of tolerable height, the Tarpeian rock has not disappeared; to see it quite close you have to go by the lane of Torre de' Specchi, in front of a religious house, which depends upon St. Francesca Romana. There, under the escarped terraces of the hill, opens an irregular court, encumbered with old buildings, sheds, and penthouses, which seem to carry on their roofs the little gardens of this point of lugubrious memory. The rock, of which the citadel followed the outlines, is porous and of a dark shade, being a tufa like that of the Tullianum. It bounds abruptly on the plateau the garden of the old Caffarelli Palace, whence the eye can measure, above plenty of other ruins, the ruins of a precipice so deep that by jumping down one would be perfectly sure to break one's bones. It was there that in old times ingratitude and envy used to launch into eternity the great men who had done too much for their country, and genius that was too embarrassing for the ruling mediocrity. The anfractuosities of this aerial cemetery of glory are scented with yellow violets and rose-coloured gillyflowers.

Seen from a slight distance the rock by no means discloses its size, because it is masked; but in entering at the back of the hospital della Consolazione, in a lane which comes out upon the Via Bocca della Verita, you measure better the real height of the Tarpeian rock, with one or two cavities in it, and veined with sewers of an indefinite age. Although the grounds of the **Velabrum** and the neighbouring quarters have since the time of **Sulla been** raised forty-two feet, the Tarpeian rock is less changed in appearance than might be **supposed**. In his description of the siege of the citadel by the **partisans of Vitellius**, who wished to recover it from the soldiers of Sabinus, and who set fire to it, Tacitus represents the besiegers as climbing 'the hundred steps which separate the sacred wood of refuge from the Tarpeian

VIEW ON THE TIBER IN FRONT OF THE CLOACA MAXIMA.

ock,' and he adds that the soldiers mounted to the fortress 'by the roofs of houses, which, owing to a long peace, had been built close to the walls, so high that they reached the level of the Capitol.' If this description dated from yesterday we should think it exaggerated.

FRONTAGE OF SANTA MARIA IN ARA CŒLI.

The best-fêted saint in the Capitoline Church is the Bambino, for whom the pifferari form a procession when he makes his visits in a gala coach, which was acquired by the Franciscans in a singular enough manner. In 1848, the people having set to work to burn the pope's carriages, one of the triumvirs bethought him, in order to save the finest, of making a present of it to the Bambino. On his return Pius IX. had some scruples about taking back what had been offered to God. The Bambino, cut from a block of cedar by a monk of the sixteenth century, is transported in his royal equipage to the bed of the sick, who send for him when medicine has no power. Only he is not moved while the exhibition of the crèche lasts; and when the first day of the year comes, it is the sick who set off to convey him their homage.

THE BAMBINO.

To build up the bric-à-brac of antiquity called the Ara Cœli at a distant and undeterminate period, for the first known dedication dates from the year 595, they dug among a quantity of ruins, which makes this church strangely furnished, hybrid, and curious. Different in module, the columns do not present three capitals that are alike: one of them, above the third column to the left as you enter by the great nave, bears on the abacus this equivocal inscription, though the cha-

INTERIOR OF THE CHURCH OF SANTA MARIA IN ARA CŒLI.

racters seem ancient enough: E CVBICVLO AVG. Gilded with gold taken from the Turks at the battle of Lepanto, the church is richly paved, but the borderings, in *opus Alexandrinum*, are reduced to patches by the profusion of sculptured tombstones; those of the fourteenth century, which abound in relief, are so numerous, that in going through the church one is caught at every step. These reclining figures, which replace under your eyes in the churches the society that once frequented them, render them more animated. The Temple of the Ara Cœli is a veritable museum. It would take too long to enumerate all; but we cannot pass over, towards the top of the lower aisle on the right, the tombs of the Savelli from 1260 to 1306. That of Pope Honorius IV. and the monument raised to his father present a small model of the frontage of a Pisan church, in the style of San Miniato; adorned with rosettes and bands of mosaic, the little temple is of marble, and

HOLIDAY CARRIAGE OF THE HOLY FATHER—THE EQUIPAGE OF THE BAMBINO

is an authentic work of Arnolfo. This pope Honorius, who reposes among his kinsfolk, is a fine figure that the trumpet of the last day will not awake without trouble, in such deep slumber is it plunged. The tiara of 1290, by its rudimentary shape, adds still further to the verisimilitude of this repose, for it is like a cotton nightcap. There reposes, too, the first pope of the house of Savelli, Honorius III., who, in 1216, succeeded Innocent III.; this chapel belonged to the family.

Let us not forget near the pulpits, which are of the twelfth century, and which are remarkable, a tombstone set against the wall, which must oblige the Queen Catherine of Bosnia to sleep standing, widow

of that King Stephen whom Mahomet II. had flayed alive ; nor, in a
chapel to the left, the mausoleum of Philip of Valla, a Florentine
monument of rare delicacy. The two weeping genii who bear the
scutcheons, the reclining statue, the arabesques of the lower part, are
treated with a master-hand. At the bottom of the nave close to the
door, the chapel of the Bufalini, at the invitation of St. Bernardin of
Sienna, was decorated
by Pinturicchio with
frescoes which ought to
be fixed upon as among
the finest inspirations of
this genius : the death of
the saint, who has had
himself laid out in a bier,
where he expires in
the midst of his religi-
ous comrades, is a most
skilful composition.
You enter by a charm-
ing doorway, which
admits you to the
church as well. I re-
call wide corridors with
ogival vaults tinted by
pale gleams of light,
along which one would
summon the shade of a
St. Bruno ; as well as a
cloister in two tiers,
austere, of fine style,
which has an air of a
Thebaid, three paces
away from the Capitol
and its museums. The

PRINCIPAL DOOR OF THE ARA CŒLI.

convent, at the time of the jubilee of 1450, when St. Bernardin of
Sienna was canonised, received in general chapter three thousand
brethren from the houses founded by this blessed patron.

The Tiber, which is rapid, large, and deep, divides into two arms
in the midst of Rome, and thus leaves an isle which is tolerably
populous ; you reach it by a bridge of stone, built by Fabricius, under

the Republic; you leave it by the Ponte Cestio, that Valentinian, Valens, and Gratian constructed, to come out upon the right bank where is that Trasteverine quarter which Ancus Martius fortified against the Etruscans. In the present day the bridge of Fabricius is called Quattro Capi, because they have kept at the extremity of its parapet a couple of Hermes with four faces, which in old days held

OGIVAL VAULTS IN ARA CŒLI.

the balusters of bronze. As for the foot-bridge of Gratian, it is now the bridge of St. Bartholomew, a titled borrowed from the adjoining church, of which we shall say a few words, after observing that Rome possesses four ancient bridges, the oldest of which, the Ponte Rotto, was finished under the censorship of Scipio Africanus, and that this city furnished the model of all the stone bridges constructed in the ancient world. St. Bartholomew replaces, at what may be called the stern of the island, a temple to Æsculapius, erected in the year 401 of Rome, an age already respectable; but the isle itself is an historical monument of a more remote century.

It has been asked whether the granite columns which separate the aisles of St. Bartholomew of the Island were not a portion preserved from the temple of Æsculapius. They are small, which diminishes the improbability; but their too cylindrical proportions seem more

The Island of the Tiber. 157

ISLAND OF THE TIBER, ST. BARTHOLOMEW, AND THE QUATTRO CAPI BRIDGE.

recent. Two of these pillars are of the marble called onion-peel;

cippolino, and even granite, under the republic before the dictatorship of Sulla, were not in frequent use. It is a church of the early lustra after the year 1000. It has for its gem, and probably for its very reason of being, a large and fine urn of porphyry, on which rests, the master-altar, and in which are collected the relics of the four martyrs, Bartholomew, Paulinus, Exuperantius, and Marcel, which the Emperor Otto III. is supposed to have brought to Rome. This church during the last week in December receives also preachers fresh from the nurse, and offers amid a childish setting the spectacle of the Nativity. But its cradle and even that of the Ara Cœli are nothing compared with the one which chance discovered to me on the top of a dungeon. This is the most original, the most popular, and the least known by strangers, for it has never been described by any one.

UPPER GALLERY OF THE CLOISTER OF THE ARA CŒLI.

It is before the not very interesting church of St. Eustace, and in the street of the Caprettari, that the end of the Christmas festival takes place, concluding with the rejoicings of the Epiphany, or the day of the kings. These small spaces, irregular, long, choked, contrived in the midst of a labyrinth of alleys between the Pantheon and the Piazza Navona are the theatre of a popular diversion which opens on the 5th of January, and is prolonged throughout the entire octave. The *mise-en-scène* is of a Gothic simplicity. Round the piazza booths are set up in the open air, where they sell an immense number of dancing jacks, punchinellos from Naples, and grotesques of every sort; eathernware bells with a sweet ring, little drums, steel trumpets, Bambini of coloured plaster, and so on; they present too fried pinocchi

LA PORTA SETTIMIANA, IN THE TRASTEVERE.

and confetti, and things fried in oil, the equivocal incense-offering of the solemnity.

At the third hour after the vintiquattro, the crowd collects at the approaches of St. Eustace; everybody is provided with noisy instruments, and until after midnight this assembly, which includes every class as well as every age, moves and tosses about with immense tumult in the narrow space; all try, along the illuminated street where they

VIEW OF THE VILLA PAMPHILI-DORIA.

are trampling and elbowing one another, who shall produce the most formidable uproar. They whistle, they howl, they imitate by means of calls the cries of savage beasts, they stamp and bellow, they push and are pushed ; the tumult is diabolical, the image of violence is on every side, but there is no temper ; brawls are uncommon, and it would be to fail in the etiquette of this feast of unreason to get up a quarrel.

I had been present at so many church ceremonies, at so many civic festivals, that I was impatient to discover at the villa of the Farnese the divinities of Olympus, those finished models of the perfect form, so prodigal of attractions for initiating mortals into the science of the beautiful. It was then with a certain satisfaction that, remaining in the tranquil region of the Trastevere, in order to gain the perspective of the Lungara, I passed under the choked archway and dovetail battlements which in the middle age travestied the Porta Settimiana, which got its name from the father of Geta, which was restored by Alexander VI., and then condemned under Urban VI., to be no more than an ornament of the quarter.

In the Farnesina Palace that Peruzzi built for a friend of Raphael, for the banker Agostino Chigi who survived him only a few days, we come upon that pagan Renaissance which so dazzled the Valois. Described as a villa, although it is in the city nearly in the front of the Corsini Palace, but because it is in a garden, the Farnesina has a very gloomy aspect from the outside. The purity of the lines and pinnacles impresses an eternal youth on the edifice, which for all that has a dilapidated kind of physiognomy ; the neglected aspect of the uncultivated grounds contributes to the same impression. As soon as you pass the staircase, twelve great subjects designed and begun by Raphael, and then executed by the eagles of his school, fill the roof of the vast hall which serves for vestibule. Two great compositions divide the ceiling—the Marriage of Psyche, the piece which has suffered most from retouching, and the Assembly of the Gods, where the figure of Mercury, that of Cupid, and the head of Venus, are of exquisite line. This vigorous and free piece reminds one of certain freaks of the audacious naturalism which delights Michelangelo.

To see again for a few moments green fields and fresh waters after one has been so busy exploring a city, to end under the shade of trees a day where one has summoned up all the visions of mythology in company with Raphael, and laboriously scanned the frames of a gallery, is a temptation that a man hardly resists, especially if you remember that the Farnese and the palace of the Corsini are not far from one of those fairy works where the mind is so ready to call up the divinities of woods and fountains.

You know, reader, that in the Roman Campagna the small properties described elsewhere as orchards, meadows, lodges, are called vineyards; hence so many bas-reliefs and statues found *among the vines*.

A garden is a very different thing. This term often means enormous spaces, comprising groves, meadows, hills, ponds, and rivers, with ruins and scattered monuments; such are the Pamphili gardens on the site of those of Galba. Under the rampart of Rome, a few yards from the gate of St. Pancras, of warlike memory, they present

GARDENS OF THE PAMPHILI VILLA.

the close dales, the woody shades, the plantations of genuinely rural solitude. As the approach to the domain is at the back of the plateau which bounds Rome on this side, you no sooner enter the park than the city disappears from the horizon, except towards the north, where at the extremity of a valley shut in between hills rises solitary the enormous mass of St. Peter, flanked by the Vatican, and framed on every side by meadows, fields, and gentle slopes, like a colossal Chartreuse lost in the midst of a Thebaid. Between the rose-hued Soracte and the Monte Mario, the dome rises into the clouds supported by masses of trees and bounded by the Leonine city, which winds across the slope, its lands of brick running from distance to distance by keeps of the ninth century.

The ruins of a villa restored in the manner of a triumphal arch furnish an approach at present to those groves of oak, of planes, of great spreading pines. At the back of these wooded plains, long avenues spread out unseen by the day, aisles in which the birds sing, and dividing a slope at the end of which the plain extends far out of sight, a kind of solid ocean which the other ocean made level in old times. This shady labyrinth, which goes up and down by turns, will show you the snows of the Apennines through the breaks in the trees; to perspectives of verdure will succeed perspectives of water. Under the cool freshness of the waters and the tall trees the grass gets a fineness and brightness which recall the Alps; in the dawn of spring, the anemones, violets, periwinkles, primroses, and cyclamen display their mosaic on the turf. Further off the walls of the embankment are crowned with camellias; the arabesques of the parterres of the flower-beds, the enamel of their compartments, which frame bas-reliefs and statues, cause the surprises of art to come upon the poem of nature.

You recognise, from having seen it in pictures, a certain semicircle of architecture reflected with its garlands of trees in a sheet of water; the rest is unforeseen, and causes new sensations; you believe you walk in a dream. The gardens of Rome were assuredly thus in the time of Virgil and the poets of the Empire.

GARDENS OF THE PAMPHILI VILLA.

CHAPTER X.

THERE are in Italy a dozen churches which, like Santa Croce and Santa Maria Novella of Florence, like the dome of Sienna, like St. Clement and Santa Maria Maggiore at Rome, are for architecture, painting, and sculpture, true museums by the aid of which one might unfold all the annals of modern art. Such is the church of the Dominicans, Santa Maria sopra Minerva, so called because it replaces a temple erected by Pompeius to the Virgin of paganism. Nothing is so unexpected as the first aspect of its three ogival aisles supported on pillars without either capitals or bases, like huge trunks reflected in the polished marble pavement. The vault and walls lighted dimly from above are of a bluish green, and shining like the moist walls of a marine grotto covered with lotus, seaweed, and scolopendra. The monks in 1855 had the temple covered with a kind of stucco, imitating with an excessive brightness the tint and veining of green porphyry. The date of the building is about the end of the fourteenth century; the nave is wide and fairly high; the choir, more modern and recently harmonized with the ogival style, is of fine proportion; a series of chapels very highly decorated cluster in the rather narrow side-aisles. But as you enter, you are so struck with the green and lustrous colour of a nave that doubles under your feet in a mirror of polished marble, that the church under its skylight seems dark and empty; to commence to make it out, one must acclimatize one's eyes. As often happens to people who pry, one of the first monuments that I proceeded to discover was one of those most hidden. On a tombstone set up in a deep chapel in the left transept is represented in relief a monk, an ascetic with hollow cheeks, with delicate and angular features, with a large arched brow which gives accent to a pensive expression, while the slender and knotty fingers indicate at once manual activity and the sentiment of the ideal. It is the only known portrait of the angel of Florentine painting, of the blessed John of Fiesole, the painter of souls and the heaven of which he had had glimpses. Who does not now admire this holy artist? The President de Brosses, Dupaty, Beyle, have never even pronounced his name. I insisted on keeping the epitaph

ST. JOHN OF THE FLORENTINES.—TRASTEVERINE BANK.—SLOPE OF THE JANICULUM.

of the patron of religious artists composed by his venerable friend Nicholas V., who died the same year.

HIC JACET VENER. PICTO. FR. JO. DE FLO. ORDIS PDICATO?

> Non mihi sit laudi quod eram velut alter Apelles,
> Sed quod lucra tuis omnia Christe, dabam :
> Altera nam terris opera extant, altera cœlo.
> Urbs me Johannem Flos tulit Etruriæ. MCCCCLV.

The cenotaph of Cardinal Orsini goes back to the end of the fourteenth century. The monuments of that age are superior to those of the following century by their collected gravity ; the last slumber is profound then ; later on death becomes a triumph, first for its victim, and next for the artist charged with commemorating him ; the hero continues to act, to live, to command. We may associate with this school the mausoleums of the two Medici who are not at Florence—Leo X. and Clement VII. Of the two statues in sitting posture and confronting one another, attended in the air by figures of saints singularly twisted and tormented, the best is that of Pope Leo, which seems to have inspired François Bonivard, the prisoner of Chillon, with that other Portrait recently published at Geneva: '. . . . savant en lettres grecques et latines et davantage bon musicien . . . . à la reste, bel personnage de corps, mais de visaige fort laid et difforme ; car il l'avoit gros plutôt en enflure que par chair ni graisse ; et d'un œil ne voyoit goutte, de l'autre bien peu, sinon par le bénéfice d'une lunette de béryl appelée en italien un *ochial;* mais, avec iceluy, il y voyoit plus loin que homme de sa cour.' The author of the *Advis et Devis* might, when he was prior of St. Victor, have seen Pope Leo X. close.

St. Andrew of the Valley, its façade full of sweeping architectural floridnesses, is a large and very rich church where Zampieri painted the Evangelists on the pendentives of the cupola. These figures might make one think that the imitator of the Caracci ventured this time to raise his eyes to Michelangelo ; for the rest, we find here the serenely bright colouring which goes so well with the architecture. The effect of these qualities is still more perceptible in the vault of the choir and on the apse, where the same artist has distributed in compartments, elegantly marked out by garlands of arabesques, his figures of the Virtues and various points in the legends of St. Peter and St. Andrew. Whatever the merits of the personages and the compositions, qualities that are hardly to be disputed, it happened to me to forget the actors of the scene, and Domenichino will often occasion these distractions to people with a passion for a certain interpretation of nature. In the subject which represents St. John pointing out the Saviour to Simon and Andrew, the landscape has a charm and invention that are admirable ; the Crucifixion of St. Andrew rises from architecture that forms a splendid decoration. The Florentines of the famous epoch had not so much style ; nor the Veronese so much purity.

The Convent of the Philippines possesses a very fine library, in which also they preserve some unpublished works of Baronius. I only entered this establishment once, accompanying one of our artists who was anxious to buy an old tapestry, which the society was willing to part with for a very moderate price, so it was said. But as soon as we came into the presence of the father manager, whose ascetic leanness I have still before my eyes, he gradually raised his pretensions so high, that in spite of the efforts of a young frater who pleaded for us, it became necessary to give up an acquisition that was too visibly desired. As we parted in mutual dissatisfaction, I lost an opportunity of seeing the famous Bible of Alcuin which is there; the young artist recompensed me by the expressive sketch below of our little scene.

A large framework of wall, under which are two wide arches, having at their sides three small gates, crowned with pediments resting on columns; there in all its simplicity is the Porta Nevia, better known as Porta Maggiore. Its austere and solid character, and the roughness of the outlines, give full effect to the façade which three emperors left unfinished without ordering it to be roughcast: the Romans concerned themselves before all else with utility, with just and practical appropriateness. This façade is reduced to what may be called a speaking ornamentation; three inscriptions placed one over another, cut in handsome capitals on that white page, describe from two thousand years ago the consolidation of the monument as well as of the aqueducts by Claudius,

THE FATHER MANAGER OF THE PHILIPPINES.
BY HENRI REGNAULT.

the son of Drusus, by Vespasian, and by Titus. The middle age reduced the dimensions of the porticoes by inscribing in them smaller arches, surmounted by embattled copings of extremely unhappy effect.

Out of the Porta Maggiore, set with antique pavement, and parallel with the aqueducts, of which Aurelian and Honorius made a rampart, the old Præneștine road begins. Five or six aqueducts cross one another in this plateau, and their great arches rise against the sky, and are continued in the background by other ruins.

I have reserved to close this chapter, and serve for introduction to

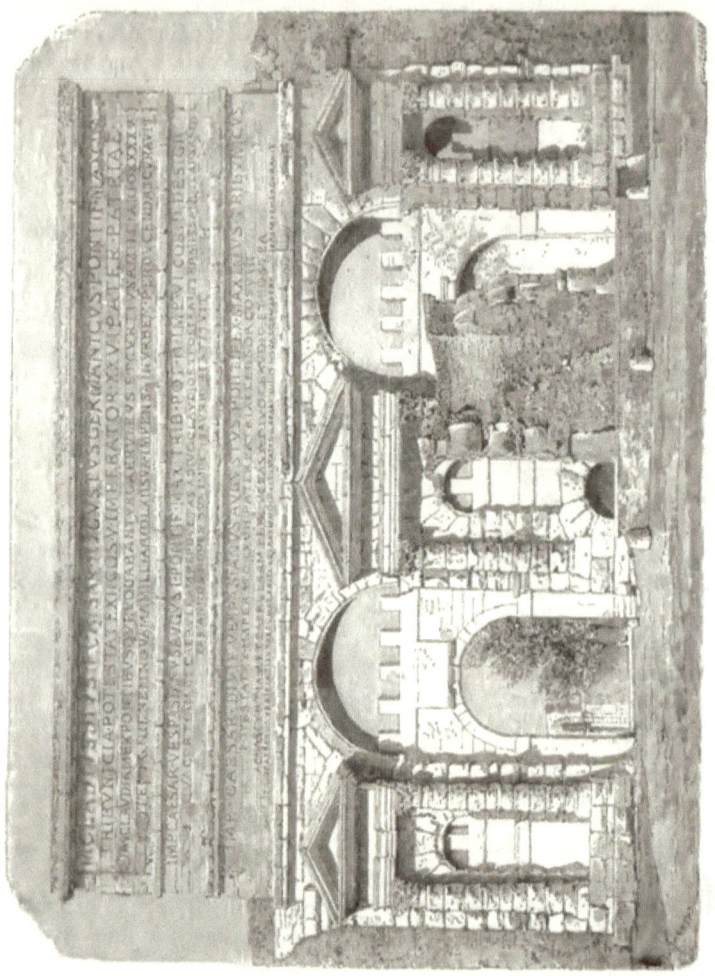

PORTA MAGGIORE.

the next, a small church of which, after passing under the arch of Gallienus, I proceeded in search in a recess of the Vicolo delle Sette Sale. You make your way through a square court into the impoverished Temple of San Martino ai Monti, and you can come out of it, by the side of the apse through a small door, at the end of a claustral-

FAMILY OF BEGGARS.

looking alley. On one side as on the other this place is solitary to a degree rarely equalled. Yet I found there, grouped as for a picture, a beggar-woman with her three children.

St. Martin tries the sagacity of archæologists, because there are in this place two or three churches one over another. In reconstructing

ARCH OF GALLIENUS.

the oratory at the beginning of the sixth century, St. Symmachus prepared at the Baths of Trajan a burial-place for Martin I., who was actually buried there one hundred and fifty years later. Below the church which Symmachus dealt with, there is another that Peter of

Cortona totally disfigured; from this you descend into a crypt where St. Sylvester has his tomb, and where he is said to have presided over

the council of Rome in 424. It is paved in black and white mosaic. Remaining poor, though twice decked out in the finery of the deca-

INTERIOR OF THE MINERVA MEDICA.

dence, St. Martin has neither vaults nor ceiling; the wood-work of the roof is by an original contrast supported on twenty-four ancient

St. Martin ai Monti.

Corinthian columns of precious marble. They preserve here the seat

VIEW OF ST. PETER'S AND THE VATICAN.

of Pope Martin whom Constant II. sent to end his days in exile in the depth of the Chersonese, because he had condemned the heresy of the

THE PIAZZA OF ST. PETER'S AT THE GREAT BENEDICTION.

Monothelites. Let us also note a small mosaic of the seventh century

which is very curious though damaged. As at St. Agnes for Honorius
I., as at Santa Maria in the Trastevere for St. Cornelia, I remarked
that the Pope always wore a slipper with a cross embroidered on it, and
that, as in all the other figures of the sovereign pontiff, the metro-
politan of Rome has no crosier. A cross is drawn upon the slipper,
so that when people kiss the foot of the father of the faithful, the
homage is addressed to the symbol and not to the man. There have
been refinements in humility resorted to, ever since St. Gregory the
Great adopted and transmitted the formula, *Servus servorum Dei;*
they are more laudable in intention than in appearance, for the cross
might be more suitably placed than on a slipper. The absence of the
crosier among the insignia of the papacy is explained by a legend that
Innocent III. will tell us in a very few words. 'The Roman pontiff
has no pastoral staff, because the blessed apostle Peter gave his to
Eucherius, first bishop of Trier, to awake from the dead Maturnus,
whom he had sent with Valerius to preach the gospel to the Teutonic
nation, and Maturnus succeeded Eucherius. This staff is still preserved at Trier with the greatest veneration.' (*De Sacrif. Miss.*, c. vi.)
St. Thomas Aquinas completes the story in the following terms:—
'The Roman pontiff does not use a staff, because St. Peter sent his to
resuscitate one of his disciples, who was made Bishop of Trier. This
is why the popes only carry the pastoral staff in the diocese of Trier,
and not in other dioceses.'

FACCIATA INTERIORE DELLA CHIESA ANTICHA DI S PIETRO IN VATICANO E SVO ATRIO

CHAPTER XI.

LET us examine first what concerns the general appearance of the work; then let us point out the most remarkable of the numerous objects of art which the Basilica of St. Peter's contains, with the hope of calling especial attention to works that are either not appreciated at all, or not appreciated as they should be; finally, let us do our best to rise to the idea which presides over this conception, which gives it a unique significance, and which constitutes its grandeur.

At the exit of the Piazza Rusticucci, at the moment when, facing the dome, you proceed to make your way into the round of Doric columns which mark the ellipsoid outline of an immense space, you are struck with the apparent unity of so vast a construction, commenced in 1450 and continued over two centuries and a half. The more we look at these erections, the more astonished we are, as we recall the names of Bramante, of the two San Gallo, of Raphael, of Peruzzi, of Michaelangelo, and of Vignola, the principal masters of the first century of the construction. The circular colonnade of Bernini, nearly three hundred columns set in four rows, and leaving between them a central passage for carriages—this enormous phantasy is the manifesto of a style which subordinates utility to symmetry, and rules to decorative effect: these two hundred and eighty-four columns, which are strong enough to support the palaces of Semiramis, support nothing at all; they are placed there for show; they are the feet of two banqueting tables set for a congress of giants, on which are drawn up in a row ninety-six statues of between three and four yards, which from a distance cannot be distinguished, and which you do not see any better when you are near. For that matter, no one looks at them; and such is the fate of works of art that are lavished out of place.

The façade is not a success, as everybody has remarked; it masks the dome, its pediment is abortive, its attica ill accented by a row of

UNDER THE PORTICO OF ST. PETER'S (SIDE OF THE SACRISTY).

small, low, and misshapen windows; its top is ridiculously equipped by the thirteen colossal figures of Christ and the apostles gesticulating on the balustrade. I like also the interior gallery running the length of the façade and ending at the extremities by vestibules, at the foot of which appear two weak and characterless equestrian statues. One of them, the work of Bernini, represents Constantine; and the other, Charles the Great. Above the great door they have replaced the Barque of St. Peter, a mosaic executed in 1298 by Giotto for the old basilica; the work has been so re-handled as to have lost its character. The last door on the right is walled up, with a bronze cross in the centre; it is that of the Jubilees; it is only opened in the holy year, four times in a century.

In Italy they do not shut the churches by a system of small doors soon made greasy by the hands of the populace. Giving a literal interpretation to Christ's saying, 'My Father's house is always open,' they are content with a curtain; but in order to prevent it from flying about in the wind this curtain, especially for doorways of great size like that of St. Peter's, is a sort of canvas with lead at the foot of it and doubled by a piece of leather. The process is dirtier than ours, for, as it falls back on you, the leather, which is plastered with all the filth from people's hands for centuries, often gives you a brush in the face. However, there is no noise; you enter as if you miraculously made a hole in a wall that instantly closed up again. The sensation is particularly striking at St. Peter's, where you are dazzled with a mass of splendour, and it would be still more so if the longest of naves, and one of the highest, since the vault is over fifty yards from the pavement, disclosed to you instantaneously its astonishing dimensions.

Is it true that you have no suspicion of the immensity of the church, before you have measured yourself with Liberoni's angels in yellow marble, seven feet high, which support against the first pillar a vessel for holy water in the shape of a shell? This is not quite accurate; the thickness of the air which makes the bottom of the nave cloudy, the microscopic smallness of distant passers-by, have already given you warning. The Angels in question occasion a peculiar illusion; the mere prettiness of these naked children, recalling a number of analogous subjects smaller than nature, hinders you at the first glance from conceiving that a pier should have been exaggerated to such a point. To understand what must have passed here, and to explain their disproportions, which are real in spite of the theories which are strained for their justification, it is indispensable to describe the various phases which the structure has passed through.

Rossellini and Alberti, the first interpreters of the intentions of Nicholas V., confined themselves to raising from the ground the walls of an enlarged apse, when, to answer to the vast designs of Julius II. and to efface the renown of Brunelleschi, who had constructed the cupola of Florence, Donato Lazzari, called Bramante, proposed to raise in the middle of a Greek cross formed by four long naves in the style of Constantine, a cupola on the model of that of Agrippa, but enlarged to untold proportions. Such was his ardour, stimulated by the large and ambitious character of Julius II., that in 1513, after seven years of work, the cupola without supports launched its arches into the sky, but erected too quickly, and on unsure foundations, the Babel threatened ruin, and had to be demolished. Raphael, the successor of Bramante, who in taking his flight, "dreaded," he wrote, "the doom of Icarus,"—Raphael, assisted by Giuliano da San Gallo and by Fra Giocondo, strengthened the pillars; curtailing the chevet and the transepts, he adopted the design of a Latin cross; his design has not been preserved. Balthazar Peruzzi erected the apse, and returned to the idea of a Greek cross less developed; consequently Antonio da San Gallo, when he replaced him, preferred the Latin cross. They still show his plan in relief, rich in belfries and pyramidal outline, a scheme that Michelangelo depreciated by accusing it of savouring of Gothic. San Gallo showed himself more penetrating than his predecessors; divining the rock on which they had split, he supported the building on formidable stays, and excavating the mysterious soil of the Neronian Circus, which was furrowed by the graves of martyrs, he solidified the whole of the circumference down to an extreme depth. After that they could build on substantial foundations.

This was preparing the glory of Michelangelo, who did not fail to return to the Greek cross, and who ended the drum of the cupola, to which the rest was subordinate. It has been maintained that he meant to raise a portico with columns, in the style of that of the Pantheon; but the elevation of his plan, executed in colour under Sixtus V. against one of the cartouches of the Vatican Library, contradicts this assertion. It shows us four small bays in a cross terminated by semicircular apses, and the great cupola surrounded by a circle of statues at the base and accompanied by four small domes. All these rounded masses were to be isolated in a quadrangular space of a calm and severe architecture. Vignola and Pirro Ligorio who came next, in accordance with the wishes of Pius V., conformed to the plans of Michelangelo; but as soon as Giacomo della Porta had finished the dome, Carlo Maderno, left too free by Paul V., made haste, in order to

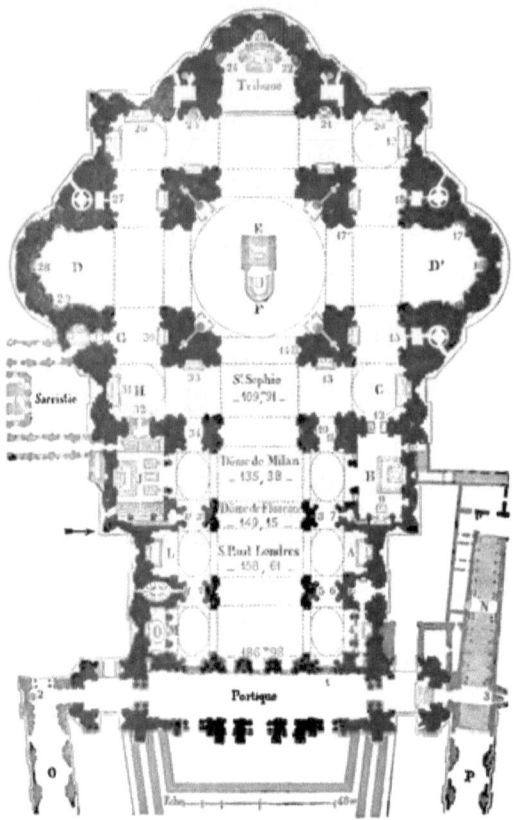

PLAN OF THE BASILICA OF ST. PETER'S.

A. Chapel of St. Sebastian.
B.   "   the Holy Sacrament.
C. Gregorian chapel.
D D'. Transepts.
E. Pontifical altar.
F. Confessional of St. Peter.
G. Entrance to Sacristy.
H. Clementine chapel.
I. Choral chapel.
L. Presentation chapel.
M. Baptistry.
N. Scala Regia.
O, P. Galleries of Bernini.

v. Urn with remains of last pope.
x. Tomb of Innocent VIII.
y. Entrance of stairs to dome.
z. Tomb of the Stuarts.

1. The Jubilee gate.
2. Statue of Charles the Great.
3.   "   Constantine.
4. Chapel of the Pieta.
5. Tomb of Christian of Sweden.
6.   "   Leo XII.
7.   "   Innocent XII.
8.   "   Countess Matilda.
9.   "   Sixtus IV.
10.   "   Gregory XII.
11.   "   Gregory XIII.
12.   "   Gregory XIV.
13. St. Jerome.
14. Bronze statue of St. Peter.
15. Tomb of Benedict XIV.
16. Martyrdom of St. Processus.
17. St. Erasmus.
17'. Statue of St. Bruno.
18. Tomb of Clement XIII.
19. St. Michael (Guido Reni).

20. St. Petronilla.
21. Tomb of Clement X.
22.   "   Urban VIII.
23. Pulpit of St. Peter.
24. Tomb of Paul III.
25.   "   Alexander VIII.
26. Bas-relief.
27. Tomb of Alexander VII.
28. Crucifixion of St. Peter (Guido Reni).
29. Stigmata of St. Francis (Domenichino).
30. St. Peter and St. Andrew (Pomeranico).
31. St. Gregory the Great (Sacchi).
32. Tomb of Pius VII.
33. Transfiguration (Raphael).
34. Tomb of Leo XI.
35.   "   Innocent XI.

show his genius by a novelty—a novelty four times tried—to return to the Latin cross by elongating the great nave. He ended it by that frightful façade which Bernini connected with a bracelet of columns.

It was not without good reason that the most expert, Peruzzi, Michelangelo, Vignola, Della Porta, were bent on avoiding a conflict between so enormous a dome and the longest nave that had been seen. As it was necessary, after the death of Bramante, in order to support a cupola nearly as high as the Great Pyramid, to more than double the thickness of the pillars of the choir and make them terribly massive, these great men understood that it was necessary to bring the supports of the nave into proportion, and that it would be crushed by them. Such the peril that Maderno braved, being obliged, in order to bring himself into harmony with the end portion, to give to the pillars of his nave a volume so monstrous, that only three could be arranged on each side, and it is these enormous supports which do more than anything else to make the gigantic church look small. In fact, who will dream of suspecting that a nave whose length only divides into three arches, is the longest in the world! I was bent on measuring these blocks of masonry which give the nave so short a perspective; each pilaster measures thirty of my steps, and the pillars of the cupola are two hundred and six feet in circumference.

As for the traditionally professed opinion with reference to St. Peter's, that these dwarfing deceptions are the valuable result of an ideal harmony of the proportions, that is a piece of nonsense begotten of the servility of inferior schools, and we should not trouble ourselves about it, if it were less widely spread. Surely there would be a ruinous inconsistency in laying out money to erect the largest religious edifice in the world, and yet to do so in such a way that it should appear small. We should rather incline to the contrary idea: to build the edifice as vast as possible, and try by a skilful combination of lines to make it seem even larger that it is. How can we help perceiving, in the course of this long undertaking, the continual influence of personal vanities? Bramante and Maderno claim to surpass, the one all the cupolas, the other all the naves, and their ambition comes to nothing; the cupola of St. Peter's is higher, but it is neither so deep nor by any means so wide in diameter as that of Florence, by the great and simple Brunelleschi; the nave of the basilica exceeds all others in length, but we only set forth this advantage to mark an effect that has completely miscarried.

In the accomplishment of this work, in which pride ever went before, the error of the popes lay in putting into a position of rivalry with one another a series of men of genius, who were too illustrious to consent to execute with docility a rival's conception. Each of them on coming forward claimed that he was the bearer of new prodigies; the people were full of joy, the pontiffs were radiant, and it cost them dear; for towards the end of the seventeenth century, Carlo Fontana calculated that the expenses up to that time mounted to nearly £6,080,000 sterling. To meet this demand it was necessary, from the reign of Leo X., to coin money in every fashion, and hence the traffic in indulgences, which furnished such dangerous weapons to Luther. Rome thought she was raising on the tomb of the apostle the monument of triumphant unity; she was working for the Reformation: the breach between modern art and religious sentiment, of which the last champion perished on the scaffold of Savonarola, was to be consummated for ever by the pompous style of the edifice that was consecrated to the temporal glory of the popes.

When you pay a visit to St. Peter's, you might imagine that you were come to pay court to some one. So many prelates and pontiffs in their dresses of ceremony seem still to exist there, the statues of an illustrious congregation of saints unite respect for ceremony with attitudes so deliberate that, the great man driving from the mind the ascetic or the martyr, and the astragals making the idea of the palace master that of a temple, the place invites less to prayer than to conversation; the basilica is the vastest reception-room on the globe, and people will understand the necessity of self-restraint on the subject of a church where we count forty-four altars, seven hundred and forty-eight columns, and a council of three hundred and eighty-nine statues.

The old basilica, situated in the same place, lasted for eleven hundred years, when Pope Nicholas V., though with pious designs, committed the archæological impiety of presuming to substitute for it a temple superior to that of Solomon. By good fortune the Constantinian basilica was only pulled down proportionally with the works, and fifty years after the death of Thomas of Sarzano one-half of the church still served for worship; and these delays still permitted the replacing in the new church of various monuments which it was good to preserve. The statue which people generally visit first, by way of paying dutiful respect to the patron of the place, is the seated statue of St. Peter, a bronze of the fifth century, which, towards the year 445, Pope Leo placed in the basilica.

At the bottom of the nave the eye is attracted to the front of the master-altar, at the foot of which are the eighty-seven lamps, perpetually burning on the circular balustrade of the crypt or Confession; you would take them for a mass of yellow roses. Their stems are gilded cornucopias. At the foot of the steps is Pius VI. kneeling in prayer, his eyes fixed on the tomb of the apostles: his last desires, as he lay dying in exile, were a dream of this burial-place. Canova has impressed on the martyr's features a sublime aspect of devout meditation and fervour.

The Confession gives access to a fragment of the primitive oratory raised by Anacletus on the monument of his predecessor, and the tomb of Peter and Paul serves for an altar to that chapel of the Grottoes, above which they have replaced the master-altar of the new patriarchal church, in the very spot where the successors of St. Sylvester officiated.

I have mentioned the dimensions of the canopy; that estimate adopted for a standard, you take in almost with terror the height of the

CURULE CHAIR ATTRIBUTED TO THE APOSTLE PETER.

vault, beneath which this toy of thirty-one yards is lost. The apse is one hundred and sixty-four feet long. At the back is the presbyterium, where in the days of pontifical solemnity the sacred college is ranged around the pope. There is in it a sumptuous altar, and, in the middle of a glory, the Chair of St. Peter, sustained by four colossal figures of bronze and gold, which represent two fathers of the Latin and two of the Greek Church. The Chair, by Bernini, is only an outside case, containing the curule seat of Egyptian wood faced with ivory, which is supposed to have been given by the senator Pudens to his guest, the apostle Peter. They show in the sacristy a model of this precious piece, which is rarely exhibited, as well as some of the small ivory facings that have been detached from it; they represent the Labours of Hercules, and are of an indisputable antiquity.

Let us come down the church again, and turn to the right to the back of the transept, at the entrance of which on Holy Thursday is erected the seat of the Grand Penitentiary, who on that day after public confession gives absolution to some great sinner muffled up as a pilgrim. We will pass before the chapel of St. Leo without allowing ourselves to be dazzled by the queer cleverness of Algardi; his bas-relief of Attila is a virtuoso's trick and nothing more. At the foot of this altar is, not the tombstone, but the commemorative monument, of Leo XII., with the following votive inscription which he wrote a few days before his death:—"Leoni magno patrono celesti, me supplex commendans, hic apud sacros ejus cineres, locum sepulturæ elegi, Leo XII. humilis cliens, heredum tanti nominis minimus."

Before the Choral Chapel, where each day, with a view to hearing the practice of singing, strangers go and seat themselves in white ties and dress coats, we at last, against the pillars of an arch, come upon a work of a pure time, origin, and style, the tomb of Innocent VIII. Antonio Pollajuolo at the end of the fifteenth century made it in bronze for the old basilica. What grandeur, after so many vulgarities, has this Florentine jewellery! Compare these four Virtues in bas-relief with the great Bellonas of the Barberini, and mark the nobleness, the personality, of these two statues of the pontiff, the one representing him full of life, the other extinguished in death. In its elegant refinement, the ornamentation waits without solicitation or stir for the eye to come and rest upon it. Opposite is a door, and above it a coffer of stucco, which contains the corpse of the last Pope deceased, until the demise of his successor.

Before coming to the baptismal fonts, remarkable for their porphyry basin, which is the upturned lid of the sarcophagus of the Emperor Otto II. (a gem twelve feet long cut in the tenth century, and set by Fontana in a fine mounting), you will pass before the pillar against which lean the tombs of the last of the exiled Stuarts. People were in the full fervour of monarchical restorations, when Canova, having to portray these three princes, bravely gave to the children of James II. the titles of Charles III. and Henry IX. Rome professes the eternal perpetuity of right, and only confers the absolution of the *fait accompli* by favour of repentance. Above these two Augustuli, an Angel and Religion exhibit in a Louis XV.

frame a fine medallion in mosaic of Maria Casimir, the inconstant and adventurous grand-daughter of John Sobieski.

We pass in front of the chapel of the Pietà, a word that we ought

TOMB OF INNOCENT VIII.

to translate by Pity, if you prefer the real sense to a nonsense of custom. It is so called because on the altar is a marble group representing the Mater Dolorosa with the dead Christ. When he thus ventured to cast this corpse across the knees of a divine mother, Michelangelo was not four-and-twenty; hardy, already original, but

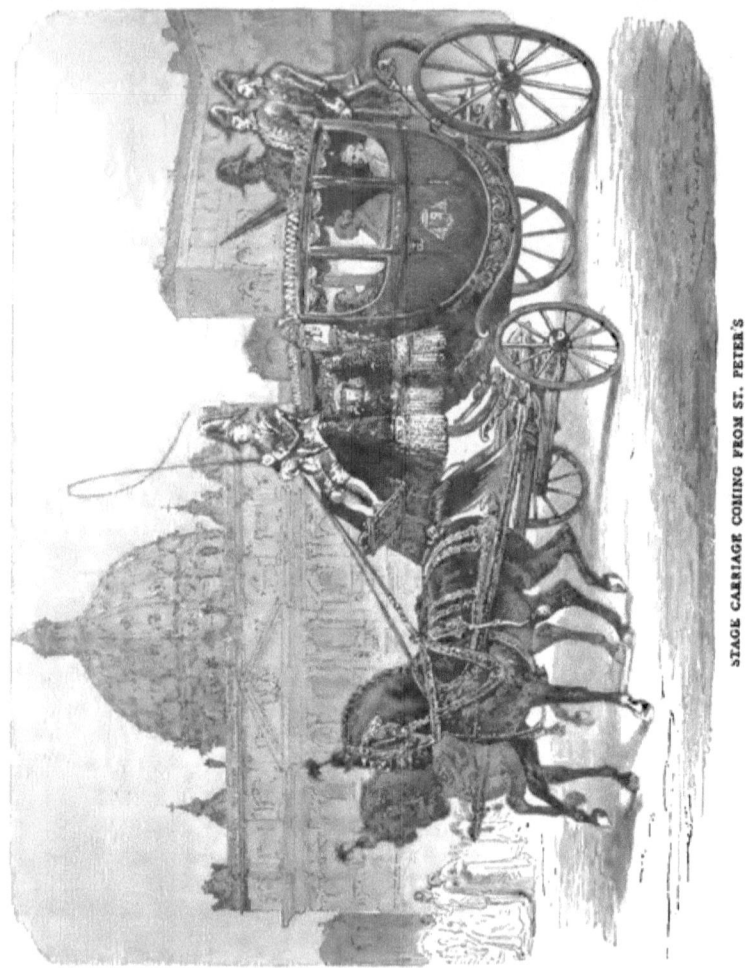

STAGE CARRIAGE COMING FROM ST. PETER'S

ingenuous; stirred by ancient beauty, but imbued with Christian sentiment, he enlarged the expression without as yet altering it. If I note in passing the triumph of the Cross that Lanfranc painted on

The Chapels.

the vault, it is to rectify the widely spread error that all the paintings at St. Peter's are mosaics.

The finest and one of the most spacious of the chapels is that of the Holy Sacrament, where in front of a copy in mosaic of Caravaggio's Descent from the Cross, and at the foot of the altar which it decorates, is a monument in bronze, very lowly since it lies upon the ground, and very simple as you take it in at a glance, but which is in my eyes the marvel of the basilica: the true amateur has already named the tomb of Sixtus IV. which Antonio Pollajuolo executed.

ANGELS OF THE CUPOLA, AFTER MELOZZO DA FORLI.

The construction, which has a very wide and open pedestal, rests on large feet attached to the corners by foliage; in the middle the pontiff slumbers on a simple truckle bed. But to the right and left, on the border of the pedestal, seven Virtues surround him, and as these are not enough to illustrate the life of a sovereign, the arts and sciences are added, forming the subjects of admirable grace: the little figure representing Music is one of the gems of the Renaissance. This composition is rich without confusion, noble with simplicity, delicate without dryness.

In the chapel of the Virgin, on the inscription of Benedict XIV., we notice the appearance of a practice that was introduced by the impoverishment of the pontifical families, who were no longer rich enough to erect royal mausoleums to their celebrities. Those who acquitted this debt to Benedict XIV. were his natural clients, *Cardinales ab eo creati*. Such is the custom at the present day, whence it follows that long reigns create many donors to the profit of their memories.

In a niche near the altar people greatly admire the large figure of St. Bruno by Michael Slodtz of Paris, latest born of those Slodtz of Antwerp who worked so hard at the sculpture in the gardens of Versailles under Louis XIV. and Louis XV. This figure is well worth looking at; it is the apogee of anecdotic and amusing statuary: that is its merit, and perhaps its slight defect also. St. Bruno refused to be pope, for which reason Slodtz represents him as tempted by an angel who offered him the tiara and the keys. The saint, whose posture is somewhat mannered, turns aside and refuses with undecided gesture, all the more expressive as it is not free from a certain clumsiness. To be ashamed of the triple crown in the beard of so many pontiffs who have worn it, and in their own basilica, would, without the introduction of certain forms, be to teach a lesson to the spiritual sovereigns; so Bruno refuses with hesitation, feebly, while his master lets fall a tender smiling glance on the pontifical ensigns from which he has difficulty in taking regretful eyes. But then where would be the merit if Bruno was not tempted?

Let us finish with an incomplete work, in which what is defective is more widely renowned than what is sublime. Canova was in his early maturity when he designed the monument of Clement XIII.; the great sculptor then worked under the influence of the Mæcenas of the north and academic theorists; I fear that he was bent on surpassing himself. Whatever it was, this construction, which is too big, too empty, too rectilinear, with its virago who is too short, and whose skirts are too short, and who personifies Religion; with its two figures fixed in bas-relief to the sarcophagus, and its too smooth and intelligent lions, of which one watches while the other slumbers with one eye open; with its Genius of Death, who weeps as he turns down the torch of life,—this affair has a coldness, an insipid attempt at poetry, and a past taste which will never return. But above the sarcophagus the kneeling statue of Pope Clement is avowedly the finest representation ever executed of a priest at prayer; this figure, which prays with so much fervour of soul, would be less expressive if the attitude did not exactly harmonize with the radiant spirit of the countenance.

Such are, so far as I remember, not all the important works contained in St. Peter's, but at least those which it is essential to study, to preserve the recollection of it. My involuntary omissions will give pilgrims a better chance of making discoveries; my notes, by the elimination of a mass of secondary works, will help people to find with less trouble what are of a truly superior kind by each master of each school.

Pope Pius VI. put an end to the buildings by making Marchionni erect sacristies, which are of a purer taste than the earlier portions. Towards the end of the eighteenth century, architecture, making a supreme effort, seized more closely and with a less mixed taste the ancient traditions.

The clerks and canons are lodged in these vast buildings, which contain a small world; besides the common sacristy, which is octagonal in form, there are three others for special purposes. You reach

PASSAGE UNDER THE PORTICO OF ST. PETER'S.

them by galleries adorned with antique inscriptions in the space between the columns. The capitals of the pilasters bear the complicated arms of Pius VI.: palms rolled in volutes, a star for the *eye*, and the branch of lily in the centre. In the sacristy of the canons there is in front of the altar, which is decorated by a picture by Fattore, a painting by Giulio Romano, the Virgin with the infant Jesus and St. John, which deserves a special place in the work of a master whose too ostentatious science is not always tempered by sentiment and charm. In the chapter-hall is the reproduction of the ancient Seat of the Apostle, with a host of precious objects which it would take too long to enumerate. These Italian sacristies are at once cabinets of curiosities and private apartments; the priests dress and undress; they write, they hum, they despatch their breviary; and if your discretion detains you on the threshold, they bid you enter.

Fully to appreciate the extravagant immensity of the basilica it is not enough to saunter there for long hours; you must wander all round it, and contemplate from the gardens the dome and one of the apses, falling formidably and as at a single cast down to the branches of the great green oaks, which are made to look like mere shrubs; you must pass under the portico which from the outside leads to the sacristy, and from the basement of the church watch at the end of the piazza the distant houses, which look like German toys; you must in descending laterally from the portico count the twenty steps of a staircase, which does not reach up to the stylobate of the neighbouring pilaster; you must estimate the little space which is taken on its pedestal by the equestrian figure of Constantine, entirely absorbed as it is in the thickness of a pillar. But above all do not shrink from the ascent of the cupola of St. Peter's. Let us conclude by examining this monument.

A gentle interior slope, cut by some very low steps, and that sheep might ascend, raises you to the platform between the summit of the façade and the drum of the dome; it is the first plateau of this artificial mountain. Advancing immediately towards the piazza, to throw a glance from this height upon the pavement, I leaned against an upright rock, posted there like a Druidical altar; and as other similar masses disclosed their outlines at my side, I recognised the twelve statues of the apostles which crown Maderno's façade. Turning right round, I had in front of me a sort of plain, ending in the monstrous tower of which the cupola is the roof. To the right and left, like hills, the small octagonal domes, now become considerable, bound the valley, which is the flattened roof of the three aisles. The country is inhabited; there has been formed in it a small hamlet, with workshops, huts, sheds for domestic beasts, a forge, a carpenter's stores, wash-houses, ovens; some little carts are stabled; a fountain sparkles in a rivulet which conducts it to a large basin or small lake in which the dome mirrors itself; you feel that there is up here an organized existence. For several families, in fact, it is a native land;

the workmen of St. Peter's, called San Pietrini, succeed one another from father to son, and form a tribe. The natives of the terrace

TRIBUNA AND CHAIR OF ST. PETER.

have laws and customs of their own. From this spot, whence you discern the height of the building in full development, there are still two hundred and eighty-five feet to climb.

Another point of view over the interior of the church is contrived in the entablature which describes the circumference of the cupola. This border is more than six feet high, although from the pavement you would take it for a simple moulding; it seems narrow up here, when you undertake on such a slip a circular walk of three hundred paces. From this height the church seems to you like the bottom of an abyss; the canopy of the altar sinks into earth, the pillars, attenuated at their base by a retreating perspective, form a reversed pyramid, and the faithful are dots; a bluish haze increases the enormousness of the space. And as your eyes ascend the walls of the dome, the frieze discloses in capital letters seven feet high the famous inscription, Tu es Petrus, which from below does not seem more than six inches high. On the pendentives I had remarked a St. Mark of a reasonable stature; seen from here it stretches under the cupola like a cloud; the pen with which he writes is a yard and a half in length.

At length the real ascent begins between the two shells of the cupola, and this strange journey, in which as you climb you lean over curved and inclined planes, at last by a curious sensation robs you of all feeling of a horizontal line, and consequently of a perpendicular. You are then in a state of considerable amazement, when you come out upon two sights of a most singular effect: in the inside, seen from a circular balustrade devised in the lantern, the pavement of the church as if seen at the end of a telescope with the object at the small end; outside, from a narrow gallery round the lantern, a perspective that is almost unbounded; it embraces all the old Latin world from the Sabine hills to the sea, and from the heights of Alba to Etruria. Only when you come out from the inner arches into the full and dazzling sun of this eagle's nest, you are not only dazzled, but almost lifted up in the air by hurricanes of wind which come from the Mediterranean to dash themselves against this height. You have now only to seek the ball of bronze, which from below has the effect of a melon, and which is capable of holding sixteen persons. You reach it by an iron ladder absolutely perpendicular.

The concussion of the wind makes this iron globe constantly musical; it is pierced with loopholes invisible from below, and through which, seated on an iron ledge, you prolong your gaze far over the mountains. Seen thus from the blue tract of the skies, the Roman Campagna loses its russet glow in a green mirage; the flattened slopes no longer justify the many windings of the Tiber, and the seven hills of Rome—which are in truth ten—are no longer distinguishable. These perspectives are still more magical from the

OBELISK OF CALIGULA AND FOUNTAINS OF THE PIAZZA OF ST. PETER'S.

Giro dei Candelabri, where, commanding the cupola with its arches descending like the slopes of an escarped island from a lower height, you measure the extent of the Borgo and the Vatican palaces, which with their square buildings and labyrinthine gardens produce the effect of a heavenly Jerusalem in the illuminations of some old missal.

The most ancient monument of the Vatican that is still standing, is an obelisk to which the authors of the first century first called the attention of posterity; Pliny tells us how, to bring it from Egypt, Caligula sent to sea the greatest ship that ever existed. The obelisk disembarked, they set it up at the Spina of the circus which Caligula had established in his gardens in the Vatican, and this circus took the name of Nero when the successor of Claudius received through his mother Agrippina the inheritance of Caligula. But before, as after Nero, the hill was always desert and of evil name. Under the republic people heard voices there; *vaticinia* were given there, and hence,

FAN-BEARERS.

according to some, the origin of the word Vatican.

All then began in these gardens in Nero's circus, at the foot of the obelisk that still remains standing; for in the middle of the ruins of the Vatican, which was abandoned at the end of that reign, the witness that had been sent from Egypt never fell. Sixtus V. found it in its place, close to the present sacristy, in a court where it con-

tinued to mark the Spina of the circus which had been the theatre of
the first martyrdoms. It was here that the Christians dug graves for
their brethren, under the very ground on which they had confessed to
their belief. The spot was henceforth consecrated; when its abandonment by the emperors had left it desert, the faithful brought
hither the head of St. Paul,
which had been buried near the
Salvian springs on the Ostian
Road; it was the same with St.
Peter, whom his disciples hid
for some time, before burying
him on the Vatican with the
other victims of the first persecution. Evidence shows, so far
as testimony of that sort is
evidence, the authenticity of
this burial-place: four-and-twenty years after the execution
of Peter, Anacletus marked it
by a small oratory, of which a
portion remains; for this monument was preserved by Pope St.
Sylvester when he had the
Vatican catacombs excavated,
in order to lay the foundation
of the basilica erected by command of Constantine on the
ruins of the oratory of Anacletus.
Eleven centuries later they
overturned the ground still
further for the commencement of a larger basilica, but

OLD NOBLE GUARD.—BY A DE NEUVILLE.

on the same spot, still continuing to respect the tomb of the apostle,
round which there still remains in the grottoes the pavement of the
Constantinian church: finally, three centuries ago the grave was
opened, and the presence of the bones established.

This is the basilica of St. Peter, and this is what that obelisk of
Caligula watches, which saw all done at its base, and all grow over a
tomb once dug in a garden, it will soon be two thousand years ago, by
timid and disquieted shadows.

When a long residence at Rome has familiarised you with the basilica of St. Peter, the monument acquires an extreme importance in your mind; under the naves where one loves to wander and think, all concurs, the moment you are free from the minutiæ of analysis, to raise you to the feeling of a truly universal conception, uniting all peoples in a common fraternity. Certain practices contribute to this impression: round the arms of the cross, here as at St. John Lateran, the priests of ten nations, almost in permanence, hear penitents submissive to the same dogma, and coming to profess it in all tongues; the dialects are marked by a sign on the front of each chapel.

THE POPE'S OLD SWISS GUARD.—BY A. DE NEUVILLE.

The custom of exalting on a *sella gestatoria* the fathers of the Roman country, the sovereign pontiffs, the patricians; and the emperors, has its origin under the Republic, in the time when Sulla was dictator: was not the first seat of the Popes, lent to St. Peter by Pudens, a curule chair? On a *Pontifex maximus*, a title perpetuated to our own day, in the year 511 of Rome, was conferred for the first time the privilege of being carried in a chair to the senate; at the time of a conflagration in the temple of Vesta, Cæcilius had at the peril of his life saved the sacred things. Since then the dignitaries of state have claimed a privilege first enjoyed by a supreme pontiff and which only the sovereign pontiff has retained. On either side of the "sella" huge fans of feathers are carried, and the rich and picturesque uniforms of the Guardia Nobile and the Pope's Swiss Guard have, added much to the effect of the shows, when the Pope was carried in procession.

Assisting at the offices of the great festivals in the Roman basilicas, one wonders whether the columns of their naves, refugees from pagan temples, have not seen something analogous to the display of the Catholic ceremonial. Do you wish to assist in our own day at the Lupercalia, the feast of the shepherd and tillers of the soil, older than Rome, celebrated since its foundation on the Palatine by the Quinctian clan in honour of Ceres or Faunus, and of Pan, the destroyer of wolves? Then go to high mass at St. Peter's on Candlemas Day.

On that day the cardinals wear a violet chasuble richly embroidered with gold, and mitres like the bishops, who wear copes to match. When the holy father is installed on the pontifical throne, the ceremony commences by the benediction of a multitude of torches; at the Introit, the priests and the deacons of the choir come and fall on their knees in turn before the Pope, who supports in his two hands

THE POPE'S BEARERS.—BY A. DE NEUVILLE.

a taper placed horizontally, to which they have fastened crosses and Madonnas at each of the ends. It is offered to the prelates to kiss,

A BENEDICTION FROM THE LOGGIA BY POPE PIUS IX.

after which, as the postulant kneels before him, the Pope, raising his arms, places the taper above his head; then one of the officials takes it and hands it to the recipient. The cardinals and bishops, the chamberlain, the heads of orders, the senators, the prince assistant all come for a taper; after them defile in the train of the mace-bearers, the conservators, ambassadors, and generals; each in turn accomplishes the same ceremonial. During the formalities of this homage to the pontifical throne, tapers are distributed to personages of lower dignity; the cross-bearers resume their advance, and a new procession of torches, starting from the right of the baldacchino, completes the circle of the church, returning by the left. Cardinals, mitred bishops, to the number of some fifty, in their chasubles and copes all glittering with gold, surrounding the curule chair of the sovereign, this time wearing a mitre of gold; foreign princes, ambassadors, officers, men-at-arms in their uniform,—all compose a most striking spectacle.

On the return of the procession, all the ecclesiastical ornaments, the chair of the holy father, and the back of the papal dais, suddenly change colour; white has replaced scarlet. Returning to the choir, the holy father is robed afresh in a long silver cope, while the cardinals, quitting the chasubles, resume their long purple cloak with ermine hood; the mitre is replaced by a biretta which they hold folded up, and which looks like a fan. This public change of toilettes produces

TIARA-BEARER.—BY A. DE NEUVILLE.

a half-comic kind of animation. The high mass of Candlemas is

INTERIOR OF ST. PETER'S.

celebrated by a cardinal wearing a mitre of gold on which in relief stand out ears of corn and flowers; he is assisted by four deacons and as many sub-deacons. The Pope gives the benediction, after intoning

NAVE OF ST. PETER'S.

the accustomed *Te Deum* in commemoration of the earthquake of

1703. The ceremony offers nothing else that is very peculiar, unless it is that at the *Confiteor*, the *Credo*, and the *Domine non sum dignus*,

DISPLAY OF THE GRAND RELICS.

the cardinals, leaving their seats, descend rapidly in a circle to the middle of the choir, where, half turning to one another, as if to call one another mutually to witness, they recite with loud voice the sacramental prayers; the Pope does the same with his assistants; and the sound of the words crossing one another in this way is very singular.

Raised on several steps, the high altar at St. Peter's has an inevitable bareness, because in the patriarchal basilicas they celebrate so as to face the faithful assembled in the nave. Tiaras and precious mitres taken from the treasury are placed in dishes at the angles of the altar—a usage that rather surprised me.

On these occasions a great variety of sacerdotal as well as military costume is to be seen. On occasions when the "Grand Relics" are to be displayed, the whole show is grouped below and in front of the statue of St. Veronica, below the cupola.

A MACE-BEARER.—BY A. DE NEUVILLE.

THE MOSES OF MICHELANGELO.

CHAPTER XII.

ONE would be more eager to enter the little church of San Pietro in Vincoli but for the temptation to seat one's self on the steps outside, before a vista contrived at the bottom of a rather steep space, half shut in by old buildings at the foot of which grass springs up in the pavement. This piazzetta is a sort of embankment over an uneven street, and above it there come

PIAZZA OF SAN PIETRO IN VINCOLI.

into outline the Capitol, some houses perched on the Tarpeian Rock, and the distant monastic grounds of the Janiculum. In the foreground are grouped the irregular roofs and square clock-tower of a monastery, from which a fine palm-tree stands out, enriching the background with an elegant setting off; here and there certain enclosures are marked with orange-trees, cypresses, and laurels; the picture is bounded to the right by the patched and ancient walls of the palace of Lucrezia Borgia, under which you go down to the Via Scelerata.

Cross the threshold of the church and go up the nave: you are before the Moses of Michelangelo.

The monument, which occupies the right side of a well-lighted choir, is placed well in front of a marble recess; seated before you on the same plane of the horizon, the figure is colossal and animated by a superhuman power of execution: thus, as one is not accustomed to see one's self face to face and so close to giants, the first impression is one of stupor. To the amazing grandeur of the style, which characterizes a conception as singular as it is naturally worked out, is added the finish of this most delicately wrought piece of rock; no lapidary ever caressed with such affection the model of a cameo. The Moses is eleven feet high; the polish of the marble makes it shining as an onyx.

VAULTED PASSAGE UNDER THE PALACE OF LUCREZIA BORGIA.

The church celebrated for the possession of this masterpiece is not without interest. An execrable woman founded the church of San Pietro in Vincoli, to be the reliquary of the chains by which the first apostle had been fastened.

It was, I suppose, Athenais-Eudoxia, wife of Theodosius II., who, having withdrawn into the Holy Land, whither she came to seek a refuge and a tomb, sent her daughter Eudoxia the chains which St. Peter had borne at Jerusalem.

Here is buried the jeweller, the sculptor, the bronze-worker, the painter, Antonio Pollajuolo (*Pullarius*), by the side of his brother Peter, who initiated him in oil colours, recently revealed to his master Andrea del Castagno by Domenico, whom Andrea assassinated, that he might remain the solitary possessor of the secret. The inscription of Antonio, which recalls the tombs of Sixtus IV. and Innocent VIII., tells how he wished to repose by the side of his brother. The two died within a few months of one another in 1498; but this text shows against all the notices that Peter preceded Antonio.

WELL IN THE CLOISTER OF SAN PIETRO IN VINCOLI.

Finally you return to Moses. The structure of which it occupies the centre was meant to form one of the sides of the four-fronted tomb which Julius II. promised himself in the middle of the nave of St. Peter's: the scattered materials of this vast design contribute to the adornment of the Palazzo Vecchio at Florence, of San Lorenzo, and even of the Louvre.

ARCH OF DRUSUS.

As you leave this church and its little-visited cloister, in the middle of which is a well with a remarkable brim, you are pleased to see the little piazza again, before plunging under the black vault which ends in the Via Scelerata, bounded by Etruscan substructions, which brings you down into the still-plebeian quarter of the Suburra, whither flocked in old days the companions of the seven guilds already constituted under the Tarquins, namely, the flute-players, the jewellers, the carpenters, the cordwainers, the copper-workers, the potters, and the dyers.

From San Pietro in Vincoli, by the arch of Drusus, I wandered to the Porta Appia, rebuilt by Narses, and the triumphal arch decreed by the senate to the father of Claudius, to Drusus Germanicus after his victories over the Germans and the Alpine tribes. The son of

THE APPIAN WAY.

Livia, adopted by Augustus, is the first Roman leader who sailed on the North Sea. His monument, under the arch of which the Appian Way retreats in perspective, is topped by an appendage that bristles with brambles—an addition of unhappy effect due to Caracalla, who made the triumphal arch of Germanicus serve as a support for the aqueduct of his baths.

As far as St. Sebastian the aspect of this never-ending suburb is that of a poor and half-abandoned faubourg. You follow, without diversion, the road which the censor Appius Claudius, after digging the first aqueduct to direct the waters of Præneste on Rome, opened and paved three hundred and ten years before our era. It has kept the name of its founder, though Cæsar prolonged it far beyond the country of the Volsci, while Augustus, that is to say Agrippa, who had the honour of finishing it, carried it as far as Cumæ. The road is broad and very straight, with remains of paths and open spaces in Visigothic pavement; the grass is green on the way, but the track remains definitely marked with a melancholy grandeur by two avenues of mausoleums in ruins of every shape and size, which, from the gate of St. Sebastian down to the foot of Albano, are counted by thousands. In the middle age, some feudal bandits having transformed several of these tombs into fortresses for detaining travellers for ransoms, the latter deserted a sinister avenue bristling with strong castles; they gradually wore to the left the present road to Albano, and even the very track of

MAUSOLEUM OF CÆCILIA METELLA.

the Appian Way at last was effaced by grass and brushwood. We owe its exhumation to Pius IX., who has had it cleared, who has had the tombs repaired over a space of five or six miles, and who has given back to the civilised world the most splendid of historical promenades. Excavations have been carried on along this avenue, where thirty thousand mausoleums are to be counted.

At the end of the rise in the ground the outline of the mole of Cæcilia Metella is seen. This turriform mausoleum is not less than one hundred feet in diameter, and it must be a third more in height; the walls, which are thirty-five feet in thickness, contained until the reign of Paul V. the fine sarcophagus that is to-day to be seen in the court of the Farnese Palace. This tower is the oldest Roman building of an assured date, where the use of marble is shown.

The temple of Romulus Maxentius is close to the circus bearing the same name. They made some noise in 1825 about the discovery of these curious ruins, but what was really found were the inscriptions which decide archæologists as to the date of foundation. As for the circus itself, it could never have been lost; the whole arena and its circumference came out in the grass, to a length of 1,680 Roman feet, and a breadth of 250. This circus of Romulus the son of Maxentius, where vast populations used to throng, is now only the haunts of birds and adders.

CIRCUS OF ROMULUS MAXENTIUS.

CHAPTER XIII.

IMMEDIATELY after exploring the funereal rooms of the Latin way, one ought to carry the memory of one's impressions in all their freshness before the decorative paintings of the school of the Sanzio, either in the Vatican galleries or at the Villa Madama, decorated for Julius de' Medici by the pleiad of Raphael. This excursion, which is one of the most interesting to be made in the environs, will take us out of Rome in an entirely opposite direction; by the Porta del Popolo, or else the Porta Angelica.

At the time when Cardinal Julius, who became Pope under the name of Clement VII., leagued himself with Charles V. against Florence, to seal that honourable pact, he married Alexander de' Medici to a natural daughter of the Emperor, and endowed her with the villa, which was still Margaret's when, having become a widow, she married Ottavio Farnese. Having quitted the government of the Low Countries, she came to end at Rome, in 1586, a life of many and chequered days. The title of Madame was preserved to this daughter of the Emperor; hence the designation still preserved by a residence that recalls unhappy times and sinister figures.

To gain the Monte Mario, at the back of which the Villa Madama is situated, we took the way of scholars, for the course was towards the Ponte Molle, that Milvian bridge of which Livy speaks in his account of the second Punic war, and at the end of which you come upon the Flaminian Way. Our first pause after leaving the Porta del Popolo was in front of the Villa of Julius III., a casino built by Vignola, who from an architectural medallion has sent a fountain bubbling forth, where the peasants refresh their beasts before entering the city.

On the side of the hill which has kept the name of *Mario* Millini, some thickets end in a rustic gate contrived in the broken walls of the

Villa Madama. When the gate was opened we entered a high-vaulted apartment, a splendid state-chamber.

In the darkness, there opened a door the bottom of which was broken into a fringe, like a beggar's skirts; all at once we came out with dazzled eyes into full light of day, by the back of an enormous

BETWEEN THE PONTE MOLLE AND THE MONTE MARIO.

Loggia divided into three lobes, painted and carved like the porch of a palace of fairies, and whose arches, grouped in broad shadows on the pavement, threw a pure outline against the ethereal depth of the blue sky. This masterpiece of ornamentation was designed by Giovanni da Udine and Giulio Romano; we should be tempted to assign it to the artists of the first century who executed the chambers since discovered on the Latin Way, with such success did Raphael and his

FOUNTAIN AT THE VILLA OF POPE JULIUS III.—BY HENRI REGNAULT.

group, impregnated as they were with the ancient arts, proceed perspicaciously from the known to the unknown.

By way of the Borgo the way back is short, and we went so quickly that the day was not far advanced when, having passed the Porta Angelica, and turned the colonnade of Bernini, we passed at the feet of St. Peter and St. Paul, coming from off the bridge of St. Angelo. But at the end of the Via de' Coronari, we chose for our halting-place Sant' Agostino.

Now what all the world will go to see at Sant' Agostino is that abjuration of his own principles and sentiment which Raphael expressed in his famous fresco of the Prophet Isaiah; an inexplicable piece, if he did mean to prove that the style, which consists in twisting the body and loading it with sculptural draperies, only to produce the travesty of a prophet, is no difficult task. Let us hope that such was the intention of the painter-poet Giovanni Santi, whom Pietro Bembo insisted for love of euphony in calling Sanzio, so delicate

CASINO OF JULIUS III.

was the ear of the author of Gli Asolani, the Ciceronian prelate who was so hostile to bad Latinity that he never read his breviary, and described the Epistles of St. Paul as Epistolacee.

If Raphael meant to strive with Buonarotti on the same ground, he was venturing into perilous games, for the figure has neither the nobleness nor the biblical majesty of his rival, and his glory will always remain under the slur of a semi-abdication before Michelangelo.

To estimate the pretensions of Raphael, in presence of his terrible
rival, it is enough on leaving Sant' Agostino to go as far as the church
of Santa Maria della Pace, the foundation of Sixtus IV. You will
see there one of the most important frescoes of the painter of Urbino's
Four Sibyls, which he painted because Michelangelo had painted
Sibyls. Only he seems to me this time to have been inspired by
designs more worthy of his genius. At Santa Maria the impressionable
young man shows himself a proselyte to the idea that it is necessary,
even in religious paintings, to rival the statuary of the ancients in
beauty of form; and the pagan subject of the Sibyls, in which the

ST. PETER AND ST. PAUL, BY THE BRIDGE OF ST. ANGELO.

æsthetic of the two religions is united, seemed to him a happy occasion
for affirming these doctrines. But he does not renounce his own
manner of sentiment, his theological prepossessions, or even the
habits of composition which he inherited from the painters who were
impregnated with the teachings of Savonarola.

A little distance from the church of San Luigi dei Francesi, and in
the neighbourhood of Pompey's theatre, a swarming quarter of which
the Campo di Fiori is the centre, we come across some French
memories in the Riario Palace, which in our own days witnessed the
end of a tragical adventure.

Here are to be seen a fine Florentine tomb, the exquisite bust of a princess Massimi, the tombs of Sadolet, the diplomatic cardinal and poet, and of Annibal Caro, who translated Virgil; finally, the mausoleum of a scholar, a jurisconsult, an economist, an Italian statesman, who made himself celebrated in three countries—in Geneva, in France, and at Rome, where he died from the blow of an assassin. Tenerani has carved a bust in a lofty style on the tomb which Pius IX. erected to his minister, Count Pellegrino Rossi.

The memory of this tragedy still gives a certain sombreness to the church and palace where the crime was perpetrated. Like the

first of the Cæsars, Rossi was warned five times in the same day of the lot that awaited him; the public was in the confidence of a plot against which no obstacle was interposed. Devoted to the task of obtaining for Italy by means of negotiation the liberal conquests, for which he doubted the chances of war, and of organizing at Rome a parliamentary system by moderating the excesses of revolution; hostile like every lover of freedom to the tyranny of the plebs, and the victim of the demagogic party, spurred on, they say, by the aristocratic faction, Rossi was immolated exactly as he would have been in the time of the Gracchi or of Marius.

He went straight to the Riario Palace, where there was a great crowd, for the anticipation of a sight which was vaguely hoped for had brought together bravoes and the curious in a throng under the portico, on the steps, and as far as the gallery of the first story, in presence of the civic guard, which was drawn up in the court, and which, without clearing the peristyle or protecting the minister, saw the preparations for the murder and looked on without an attempt to hinder it.

Count Rossi entered by the great door; immediately he was greeted by loud shouts and some thirty Bersaglieri cut off his retreat, while the other conspirators threw themselves in his path. He passed

RIARIO PALACE (CANCELLERIA).

the portico with deliberate step, and with his head upright; and as he was proceeding to mount the second flight, and passed by a small round door let into the wall, the Bersaglieri rushed upon him and thrust him against this wall. Then one of the bravoes, slipping between Rossi and the door, struck him rudely on the left shoulder. By a natural movement Rossi turned his head, thus exposing his neck, when one Jergo took advantage of this expected motion to plunge a poniard of great length into his throat, and thus the Italian from Modena, who had gained high posts in the administration of the Gauls, was stabbed at a distance of a hundred paces from the curia where, under the steel of the accomplices of Brutus, Julius Cæsar had fallen of old at the feet of the statue of Pompeius.

THE FARNESE PALACE.

Let us proceed to seek the statue which thus beheld the murder of Cæsar.

To find it, you must go to the Spada Palace; but if the little spectacle of popular manners displayed in the piazza Campo di Fiori do not make you forget your object in amusement on your way, the

LOGGIA OF THE FARNESE FROM THE BANK OF THE TIBER.—BY HENRI REGNAULT.

Farnese Palace, before which you will come out before turning the Via del Mascherone, solicits a visit that you will hardly refuse.

The Farnese Palace.

I will beg all travellers given to art to study this monument: the vast edifice of which Alexander Farnese, before becoming pope, that is before 1534, confided the plan to Antonio San Gallo, is one of those classics which it is well worth while to read over again. When Quatremère de Quincy wrote, the Farnese was considered the finest palace of modern architecture.

It has a colour which animates and increases its charm: brick mixed with stone forms the ground of the façades; the entablature, the bands, bossages, windows columns, are of travertine taken from the theatre of Marcellus, and even from the Coliseum, which still seems all but untouched, and from which centuries have drawn supplies as if from a quarry. There is now nothing to be seen in the cloister but two sarcophagi: the one with perpendicular flutings is a Christian monument of the third century; the other, in the form of a gondola, loaded with sculpture and ornaments, has acquired a great celebrity; it is that assigned to Cæcilia Metella, if we may believe scholars, who by multitudinous dissertations have confirmed this account of its origin.

THE EXCAVATED HERCULES.

It cannot really be thrown further back than the time of Adrian.

The Righetti Palace contains deep cellars of two stories, which wind under the court. I saw these caves, remains of the portico and the theatre, rising at the back of an opening pierced to enlarge the Hotel Pio. As they were clearing away to come upon foundations that should resist them, the workmen struck upon what seemed a block of gold; under the gilding they recognised bronze. At length they made out a Hercules, fourteen feet high, whose face, hands, and arms are intact, and which only wants one of its feet. The skull with a circular hole behind denotes that the statue delivered oracles; the son of Alcmena has on one arm the skin of the Nemean lion.

In crossing the piazza Capo di Ferro I had already noticed the Spada Palace. Buried a certain depth down, the Colossus of the defeated of Pharsalia was exhumed in 1552 in the street of the Leutari, near the Palazzo Riario, and nearer still to the theatre of Pompeius, among the substructions of its portico and of the chamber, where was perpetrated the classic model of the assassinations called political. The attitude of the statue is majestic without being forced; the features have a striking mark of individuality, an expressive and severe physiognomy. The triumvir carries the object of his cheated ambition—the globe, an attribute that he may have appropriated to himself by having his head placed on the decapitated trunk of some god; for the head is fitted on, and Pompeius was not too modest. Such substitutions became frequent under the emperors.

THE SPADA POMPEIUS.

So far as concerns the identity of this figure with that which saw Cæsar expire under the blows of Cassius and Brutus, the presumption may be reasonably upheld. It was exhumed near the spot where the murder was committed; Suetonius informing us that he saw it "in a palace adjoining the theatre of Pompeius, whither Augustus had had it transported." As it is not very probable that the hero, at a time when they did not multiply statues, would be represented twice under the same portico, we have good grounds for admitting, in spite of a school that is ready to deny everything, that the colossal Pompeius of the Palazzo Spada may have seen the fall of Cæsar. The monument is not very familiar, the Spada princes never having allowed it to be either modelled or copied.

The attraction which led me out of my way across the inexhaustible bric-à-brac of the old quarters brought me out, near the Piazza Montanara, by a stall, where, under awnings erected at a street corner, amateurs and clerics disputed a few smoked and trashy

BROKERS AND BOOKWORMS IN THE OPEN AIR.—BY HENRI REGNAULT.

pictures, antiquities of modern date, and old books ill used by time. Much theology, which was not my affair, but which interested seminarists, a Dominican, and some Philippines, who, for cheapness, read the books on the spot instead of buying them; one of them, however, pressing three small books to his heart, was driving his bargain with much fury and gesticulation. The group formed so good a subject that a painter posted ten paces off maliciously took out his pencil, producing a very clever and characteristic sketch.

As I followed the labyrinths of streets that end at the back of the

FOUNTAIN OF THE TORTOISES.

Capitol, a wrong turning brought me to the Fountain of the Tortoises, that a little while before I had been vainly seeking. Imagine two basins, the upper of which is supported by four young Tritons, their feet on the heads of four dolphins; these aquatic divinities are thrusting tortoises into the upper vase, from which the water flows over. The complexity of the arrangement does not obscure the clearness and graceful movement of the figures; all is animated, unusual, and charming.

Giacomo della Porta designed the Fontana delle Tartarughe, but the bronze figures are the work of Taddeo Landini, of Florence.

Close at hand rises the lofty and sombre gate of one of those palaces which have fallen from their high estate—proud homes of families that have vanished, on which time and misery imprint their marks: it is the ancient Palace of the Mattei. The court, which is

COURT OF THE MATTEI PALACE.

surrounded by a peristyle contemporary with Pius V., still preserves some statues, and a few busts on consoles.

To go in to the church of St. George in Velabro you must seek at a neighbouring house a Portinaio, who seems surprised at your visit. Then, under a charming porch of the thirteenth century erected by Stefano, prior of St. George, you enter a temple with three aisles marked by twelve columns of granite and four of violet marble, fluted, the shafts of which, without stylobates, bury themselves in the mosaics of the pavement, like trunks of trees in a flowery sward. Heavy arches trust themselves to these rather slight pillars; the old and decayed ceiling matches the dilapidation of a pavement patched with inscriptions, and made green by mould that is impregnated with the myste

PORCH OF ST. GEORGE IN VELABRO.

rious perfume of old marbles, the chilly incense of the buildings of a thousand years ago.

Next let us cross, past the street of the Greeks where St. Augustin professed, the Marrana stream which Cæsar banked in, and, turning from the shores of the Tiber, having caught a glimpse of the Aventine, let us on that bring to a close a journey marked by so many miscellaneous recollections. If chance had turned us to right or left, the harvest would have been just as fertile; when you have worked through the streets of Rome, and explored them house by house, you know too well that the task of describing everything can only end in skimming a subject whose real extent is boundless.

The Aventine, where three convents stand out on a deserted

IN THE PALACE OF CALIGULA.

plateau, was once one of the plebeian sections of Rome. It was there that, 630 years before our era, King Ancus is said to have quartered the inhabitants of four conquered or destroyed Latin cities. Rome thus became for the conquered first a place of exile, then a colony, and finally a country. Historians contend that in order to put this suburb out of danger of foreign incursions, this king surrounded the Aventine with a strong wall, and Dionysius of Halicarnassus even traces its outline. But the traditions of nearly a fabulous epoch are almost always suspicious, especially when they are supported by no palpable proof.

The priory of St. Mary replaces the Bona Dea, a temple celebrated by Cicero's epistles: St. Sabina rises between the Temple of Juno and the remains of the fortress of Honorius III., as the convent which replaces the house where St. Peter baptized St. Prisca rises between Minerva and Diana.

PORCH OF SANTA SABINO.

CHAPTER XIV.

HALF-LOCKED within the modern city, the Palatine, round which the seven hills group themselves, is, as we know, the primitive site of Rome. It was there, according to the legend, that the twin sons of Mars and Sylvia were suckled by a she-wolf, then reared by the shepherd Faustulus; and it was there that, after their recognition by Numitor, they founded the new city under the guidance of favourable auguries. The site determined on, Romulus proceeding to trace the *pomœrium* or sacred enclosure of the future capital, harnessed to the plough a heifer and a bull without blemish, and then he raised his wall on the furrow which the share had traced between the rising and the going down of the sun. Although, according to all appearance, this line describes an elongated trapezium with a break towards the east, the city of Romulus owes to this enclosure its designation of *Roma quadrata*.

Among the legendary stories invented to occupy our minds, the most seductive are those which project historic proofs into the domain of fable. To allow that Romulus ever existed is a condescension that has gone out of fashion. Livy, Dionysius, Plutarch, Tacitus even, raise a smile by their credulity.

As you sit facing the Aventine, residence of Remus and the Fabii, on the remains of the *pomœrium* of Romulus, you may fairly imagine that on this very spot, for having contemptuously climbed over the growing wall, the brother of the first king of Rome was struck down by his twin brother, crying, 'Thus perish whosoever shall cross this wall!' We shall not be sorry, thanks to this discovery, to gain an honourable pretext for seeking some other traces of the primitive reigns, that for thirty years have been reduced to myths. It was above the cavern of Cacus, celebrated by Hercules, and not far from the *ficus ruminalis*, that tradition placed the hut of the shepherd Faustulus, covered with reeds, according to Dionysius of Halicarnassus, in whose lifetime they showed both the fig-tree and the hut piously preserved. To the north-west of the Porta Mugionis, at the very spot indicated by Livy, they have exhumed the peribolus of the temple dedicated to Jupiter Stator by the founder of Rome, when the god made the fleeing Romans resume the offensive. In the time of Pliny the equestrian statue of Clœlia rose opposite to their temple, reconstructed by Regulus after the war of the Samnites. More to the west and near the Via Sacra, to the right of the Temple of Vesta, the ruins of Castor and Pollux mark the spot where the Dioscuri appeared for the first time.

EXHUMATION OF THE HOUSE OF LIVIA.

Before letting our feet stray at will in so renowned a spot, which has just acquired a double interest, thanks to the excavations of which we have just described the results, let us sketch some of the present aspects of this Palatine, which is less spacious than the garden of the Tuileries, and which has held all the grandeurs of Rome.

An embankment-wall, in the centre of which Vignola has set one of the correct doors such as are given to pupils in art schools to draw,

RUINS ON THE PALATINE.

separates the Palatine from the Via Sacra. At the very entrance you ascend a slope divided into green compartments; then you

mount by broad steps, on the top of which is planted a casino, well
situated as a point of view for antique Rome, and which the Farnese
constructed when they transformed the Palatine desert into an historical
garden. Verdure had long enveloped the enclosure of Romulus, too
great for modern generations; they moved away from the terrible
shadows which its ruins summoned to the mind. It seems even that
our religion, the faith of slaves and the poor, fell back before the
sanctuary of monarchical unity and Roman pride; this *pomœrium* is
the only consecrated ground of which Christianity did not take possession. No pope touched the Palatine before Paul III., who in an age

REMAINS OF THE PUBLIC PALACE, AND LOGGIA OF THE FARNESE.

that had become reconciled to the gods of Olympus, built a villa there.
But it was the destiny of the hill to remain a royal appanage;
the last heiress of the pontiff and the Farnese, Elizabeth, brought
the Palatine to the King of Spain, Philip V., and through Don
Carlos it entered into the possession of the kings of Naples.
Then, by a singular play of fortune, the cradle of the Cæsars passed
from the house of Bourbon into the hands of Napoleon III., who chose
the ingenious Pietro Rosa, epigraphist, geographer, consummate
Latinist, expert geologist, and descendant of Salvator Rosa, to direct
the excavations which he proposed to undertake in the Palatine, and

installed him in the midst of the Farnese gardens, which in the space of eight years Rosa turned up, to disclose in their place another Pompeii.

Let us saunter among these thickets of ruins and flowers, as we verify without trouble all that has been cleared, for each fragment finds

REMAINS OF THE PUBLIC PALACE OF DOMITIAN.

its identity guaranteed by a citation from some annalist or poet of antiquity. Romulus inhabited the summit of the plateau between the peribolus of Jupiter Propugnator and the spot where Tiberius afterwards built his palace; Numa, the corner of the Via Sacra and the Velabrum, towards the Temple of Vesta: *Hic fuit antiqui regia parva Numæ*, said Ovid. The Temple of the Penates, says Solinus, under Heliogabalus, replaced on the Velia (eastern slope) the dwelling of Tullus Hostilius. It is lower down than the Porta Mugionis, above the Summa Via Sacra, near the altar of the Lares, that Varro fixes the dwelling of Ancus. Tarquinius Priscus installed himself more at the back, at the Summa Via Nova. It was there that the children of Ancus had him slain by shepherds; you may mark the spot from a high window looking on to the Via Nova, for the king was quartered close to Jupiter Stator. Tanaquil addressed the Quirites and caused Servius to be proclaimed king. The site of the temple has been restored by Rosa, as well as that of the Porta Mugionis indicated by Solinus.

When the Republic had fastened the nation under the yoke of a rapacious aristocracy, persons of mark who were rich enough to pay for the usurpation of authority sought a dwelling on the Palatine. There dwelt, besides the chief dictators, the Gracchi, as well as Catullus, Flaccus, Hortensius, Sulla, and even Catiline, in the neighbourhood of Marcus Tullius. This last built facing the Via Sacra, below the house of Scaurus, bought, as Asconius tells us, by the tribune Clodius, against whom Cicero pleaded. 'I will raise my roof higher,' wrote the great orator, 'not from contempt for thee, but to veil from thee the view of the city which thou wouldst fain have destroyed.' Violets grow there under rose-trees, and the substructions mark the compartment of a parterre.

Below the roof of Cicero, more to the right, 'to the east of the sacred wood of Vesta,' Julius Cæsar came and established himself as soon as he was in possession of the pontificate. Before, adds Suetonius, 'he had lived in a modest habitation among the plebeians of the Suburra.' Marcus Antonius resided on the Palatine; Claudius Nero, the father of Tiberius, and Octavius, father of Augustus, built on the eastern and southern slopes of Roma quadrata. The Cæsars having come to resume on the Palatine the thread of royal tradition, Augustus extended his constructions as far as the slope facing the Circus Maximus; and to prolong his palaces to the east to the intermontium, he displaced a street, the Via Nova, without suspecting the cruel mistakes to which he would expose the archæologists of the future.

Domitian was the first to build a public palace in the dependencies of the imperial quarters. His constructions occupy a vast space to the north-west of the house of Augustus, on which they possibly encroached: for below the Flavian ruins you find galleries which they consolidated by filling them up from top to bottom with masses of mortar between planks, of which the imprint still remains. The walls were so thick, the pillars so robust, the pozzuolana so tenacious, that before building they did not take the trouble to pull down. Each generation settled over the quarters of predecessors. In the early times of the Empire the hill of Romulus shakes off the patrician residences. Tiberius, who built between the Auguratorium and the old houses of Clodius, and who surrounded his edifices to east and south with a half-subterranean portico, still left at the corner of his Cryptoporticus a private habitation that has been exhumed, and which is the most curious and considerable discovery of the Palatine.

In liberating it from the earth with which it was filled up, the excavators at once observed that it was contiguous to the buildings of Tiberius, that it was approached by the very portico, and that, as it was placed on a lower level, they must have set up some steps in order to go down into it. These circumstances showed that it must have belonged to the successor of Augustus, and was older than the palace; for they would not have erected it lower down, except to make the best of an inconvenient arrangement. Other circumstances persuaded them that it had had for its owner Claudius Nero, the first husband of Livia; the pursuit of the excavations brought to light a subterranean passage, round which, in the direction of the ancient palace of Augustus, were the leaden pipes that used to bring water to the pretended Domus Tiberiana. On these pipes we read from distance to distance IVLIAE AVG. As the name of the owner is constantly inscribed on pipes of this kind, this inscription is a genuine proof of ownership, and 'informs us that the house in question belonged to the Empress Livia, Julia Augusta; means, in fact, Livia, widow of Augustus.' When he instituted her heiress to a third of his property, Augustus prescribed that she should take his name.

Livia wished to be the first priestess of her husband after he was raised to the rank of the gods. This explains the subterranean passage which went from her house to that of Augustus; she probably had it constructed so as to be free to go, without passing through the public street, to fulfil the ministrations of her function. This passage is now interrupted at the junction with the *ædes publicæ*, erected in the reign of Domitian. But shortly before arriving at these *ædes*, we observe the passage branch to the right, which was most likely made in order to turn them.

The exhumation of a Roman dwelling-house of the time of

Augustus, the date of which is known, is an interesting fact. If we add to this that the residence of Livia contains the finest and most ancient pictures bequeathed to us from such distant ages, the reader will hardly reproach us for having edified him with proofs as to the origin of the building. You approach by the south side of the Cryptoporticus of Tiberius, going down four steps, to reach a vestibule opening on to the Atrium in which figure the altars of the Lares covered over with minium, as well as their foundation. You then front the Tablinum (chambers of honour), in which the master of the house kept his family archives and received his guests; to your right is situated the Triclinium. These porticoes, near which space for an antechamber has been procured, form four apartments, the only ones decorated. At the back of the three compartments of the Tablinum, which adjoin chambers belonging to the private living-place (Cubicula), is situated the Peristylum, in the middle of which a staircase with two flights led up to the stories where guests never entered. Of these quarters there remain thirteen chambers without any ornament, faced with a brown pigment. They had outlets both on the peristyle and on a long corridor (*Fauces*) which, constructed between the Tablinum and the Triclinium, and traversing the extent of the buildings, furnishes an approach both right and left to the apartments on the ground-floor. These comprise two bath-chambers, narrow and dark as they are described by Seneca, until Mæcenas had, according to Dionysius of Halicarnassus, set up the first Caldarium that the Romans ever saw. Let us proceed to the most interesting part of this exhumation, to the painted chambers opening on to the Atrium. They are not very large; they have greater depth than breadth, and the height of the walls does not exceed four yards. Their decoration is distributed in panels separated by figured columns of which the entablatures bear cornices and rest on stylobates, also painted. Among the decorative subjects, we observe large transparent Pateræ, filled with fruit piled up pyramidically—the simple indication of the vessels in which they presented fruits at their banquets. One of the panels contains a fanciful landscape in which trees, terraces adorned with statues, bridges thrown out into space, rockeries, and flowing waters make up a site that would delight a Chinese: in the foreground three ducks are coming out of an aquatic grotto, leaving long furrows in the water. Animals run along the cornice. At the bottom and on the sides of the left wing, at the entrance to which survive the fragments of a mosaic pavement that Livia once trod, the panels are surmounted by a series of cartouches with a clear ground, on which Genii stand out in pairs with wings of blue, green, and rose-colour, recalling some of the small figures of Raphael; they sport too among the arabesques. These cartouches have a purple framing, and are separated by mouldings with a gold ground with griffins running, from brown panels, marked by a line of lotus of a bluish tint, and divided by garlands of leaves of pale green : the lower portions, red upon red, are detached from the panels by a broad plinth of a chamois tone. The whole decoration is rich, bold, and harmonious.

In the right wing the chamois panels are enriched, by way of a simple ornament, with thick garlands of flowers and fruits succeeding one another in festoons and bound with ribands. On a band above these compartments, and under a frieze of dark yellow, defiles a curious procession of tiny figures, such as are to be seen in the Egytian hypogea; they represent scenes borrowed from the daily movement of the popular life of the streets. A consul, escorted by lictors without arms and preceded by an accensus, is attending to his private business; matrons go to the neighbouring temple; others along the Appian Way visit the tombs and

LIVIA'S HOUSE (LEFT WING).

carry offerings to the altars; women of the people go with their

PAINTINGS OF THE TABLINUM OF LIVIA.

STREET VIEW. SACRIFICE OF A LAMB. IO AND ARGUS.

baskets to market; lawyers make their way to the Forum, of which you see the outline in front of them; merchants come with their camels laden with wares; the freedmen go about their affairs, hunters are on their way back to town, a fisherman spreads his snares. Nothing can be more lively than these revelations of popular habits at the end of the Republic.

It is for the central compartment of the Tablinum that art has reserved the principal subjects. Starting from basements of brown framed with scarlet, the false columns, whose flutings are broken by rings of foliage, support cornices equally illusory, and of strange opulence: between the panels of a brighter red, set off by friezes of a delicate blue and varied by yellow coffer-work, between these architectural caprices so elegant in their strangeness, is a succession of well-preserved paintings. The finest in point of style represents, seated at the foot of a column, and watched by a draped Juno, Io, the daughter of Inachus, watched by Argus and just about to be taken from him by Mercury. The Hermes and Argus are naked and of superb design; the first has his name inscribed at his feet.

Between this painting and that which represents Io, and on the same wall, is a subject that gives us all the representation we have of the external aspect of the bourgeois dwellings of the seventh century of Rome. Two houses issue on the street by small square doors of a single leaf; the upper stories, pierced with small windows, fall back and leave projecting terraces, one of which forms a covered gallery supported on two pillars; a cordon divides the first floor from the second. At a window and on balconies five persons follow with their eyes down into the street a becomingly draped lady, who, fanning herself with a *flabellum*, has just gone out, followed by a little girl.

These paintings are of a rare delicacy; their colouring, even in the tones of minium, which often grows black, has preserved all its freshness, the ochres possess a good deal of liveliness; and the ensemble of tints presents a sprightly variety. Such, then, is a nearly unique monument of an early school imported from Greece, described by authors of the first century, and of whom nothing else has been left. These works, existing in the only ancient house of which we know both the exact date and the owner, are superior to all that Pompeii has bequeathed to us.

Let us return to the ruins of the palace of Tiberius, continued on a vaster scale by his successor as far as the extremity of the Palatine, breaking down on to the Via Sacra. It is on this side that you pass through guard-houses, where to pass the time the soldiers used to

RESTORATION OF THE CLIVUS VICTORIÆ.

draw on the walls confidences and emblems, sometimes with their signature, and sentences that are easily deciphered. There has lately been found here a caricature of Nero; a small narrow brow with a garland, and a chin tufted with a growing beard; the profile is very lifelike. The excavations around the modest house of Livia have brought to light a marble bust of the same emperor, the only one which goes back with certainty to the time when he lived.

VAULTED PASSAGE BETWEEN THE PALACE OF TIBERIUS AND THE PUBLIC PALACE.

Caligula brought under his gigantic palaces the Clivus Victoriæ and the Porta Romana, which Romulus opened at the western corner of his wall to go down into the Forum. In keeping his palace on the level of the summit, by means of galleries as high as the mountain itself, the successor of Tiberius, to unite the Palatine to the Capitol, undertook above the Velabrum that immense bridge whose abutment has been brought to light, and which was demolished by Claudius. It was in clearing out the accumulation of this precipice erected by the hand of man, that Rosa, sustaining galleries and vaultings with as

RUINS OF THE PALACES OF TIBERIUS.

much art as economy, succeeded in extricating from a mass of débris the most ancient portions of the imperial residence. Bas-reliefs, a few cartoons of stucco representing wanton scenes, corridors terminating in small chambers, enable us to recognise the haunts out of which, according to Suetonius, the emperor raised a tax, and where the senators made it a duty to degrade themselves in order to please Cæsar. The coffers of the vaults formed a decoration of a purer kind than the ornaments of Pompeii. As to the Argiletum, Caligula prolonged his palaces, according to Suetonius, towards the Forum as far as the Temple of Castor, to which he made a vestibule, where he exhibited himself as an object of public adoration, under the title of Jupiter Latinus

REMAINS OF THE LIBRARY OF THE PUBLIC PALACE.

After the great fire of the year 64, described by Tacitus, Nero rebuilt on plans of such immensity, that they invaded the valley and assailed even the Esquiline slope as far as the ancient palace of Mæcenas. Otho installed himself in a section of the palaces of Tiberius, that Messalina and Claudius had once inhabited. Vespasian, Titus, Domitian, and their successors, must have enlarged their dwellings on the side of the Auguratorium, and continued the porticoes, which had then become subterranean, from which another gallery branches out. Covered with a low vault and lighted from above, it allowed the emperors to proceed, without being seen, from their private dwelling to the throne-room, by penetrating, at the back of the Tribuna of the basilica, into the palace appropriated by Domitian for audiences and receptions.

RUINS OF THE PALATINE, TOWARDS THE CIRCUS MAXIMUS.

In the public palace the lower courses of most of the rooms have been brought into daylight: the stumps of the columns still mark the galleries; the levelled soil is the rough-cast in which the mosaics were

VIEW FROM THE PALATINE, TOWARDS THE COELIAN.

laid, of which a few scattered bits are still left. At the Tribune of the Triclinium, which was surrounded by columns projecting from broad pilasters, a pavement of mosaic marks the spot where these masters of the world used to feast. Beyond, a second portico covering foundations of the date of the Republic, and further on the Library, reconstructed at the very place where Augustus established two— one for Greek books, the other for Latin. It is contiguous to the Academia, a room for reading and dissertation upon poets and philosophy; it was separated from the Libreria, so that the noise might not disturb the readers; and it was brought next to it so as to have the documents close at hand.

OLD TOWER OF THE PALATINE, FACING THE CIRCUS MAXIMUS.

Beyond this hall for conversation, the ground falls away, and at the bottom of a ravine of buildings in fragments, your eyes wander over the narrow valley of the Circus Maximus. Close by at your right is the peribolus, with three steps, of the Temple of Jupiter Victor, erected by Q. Fabius Maximus; the Cæsars respected it.

In ordinary language we have come to confound circuses with amphitheatres. Among the Romans the circus was not a round monument, but a very elongated enclosure (about a mile), making a course for chariots, men, and horses between the terraces covered with seats, and nearly parallel to one another. The circus is wider at the entrance than at the other end, which allows the cars to be arranged at starting in the shape of a fan, so as to equalise the conditions of distance between them. To mark what we should now call the course, a road divides the circus in two throughout its length, only leaving at the extremity room for the course or arena, which turns the spur of it. This kind of causeway, called the Spina, was

STAIRCASE IN THE PALACE OF CALIGULA.

drawn rather obliquely, in such a way as to leave more breadth at the starting-post, where the cars were not yet in a file, than at the goal, where they would only go out one by one. The principal ornament of the circus was this Spina, which was less than two yards high, and in breadth only from eight to nine, and on which from all sides the eyes of the onlookers were directed, because it divided the arena. So on this long causeway art had collected all the charms at its disposal; there were ranged, round the narrow channel filled for irrigation, the masterpieces of Greek statuary and the curiosities of the East. It was there that they found the obelisks that decorate the Piazza del Popolo and that of St. John Lateran. Thirteen arches on a segment of a circle formed the Carceres, from which the cars, to the number of twelve, shot forth; the arch in the middle only introduced the festal procession, *pompa circensis*. At each end of the Carceres rose towers, on which they stationed fifes, drums, and trumpets, to animate the horses by their fanfares. Under a small portico the charioteers prepared themselves, divided by their colours into four *factions*, Albata, Russata, Prasina, Veneta (white, red, green, and azure). Above the Carceres, and between the towers, on the terrace of the Oppidum, gathered the privileged amateurs, betting-men, and owners.

The circuses were not used merely for races of chariots and horses: wrestling, boxing, foot races, the chase after ferocious animals, varied the spectacles.

ANCIENT PROCESSION TO THE LATERAN.

CHAPTER XV.

AFTER some months of residence at Rome, after incessant occupation amid ruins, basilicas, galleries, libraries, one is struck with a desire to be among fields and woods; so one morning we started for Albano and the forests and lakes of the Alban Hills. Our first walk was by the charming road called *La Galleria* to Castel Gandolfo.

As at Rome and its environs, this district and its hamlets are full of historic memories, of monuments, of mysteries unfathomable in these solitudes, where the sovereign aristocracy of the world concealed its inmost life. These country scenes, that nature has clothed in supreme beauty, have not been disfigured by the modern time; as we go through them, we smile at their striking resemblance to the pictures that the Latin poets have drawn of them.

In the early morning we again saw from another point, and in the lights of a different hour, the profound hollow of the Lake of Albano. On the terrace of the Capucins, the point of view is higher and the solitude more complete, and you can observe geologically the bizarre configuration of a region that volcanoes have overflowed twice or thrice.

The way back is shortened by three viaducts, and that of Ariccia is so deep, that it has required one of those bridges of three superposed ranges of arches, which figure among the wonders worthy of comparison with ancient achievements. The splendour of the site enhances the style of the erection.

On the morrow we wished to employ the day in going round the lake through the woods, in identifying the ancient *via triumphalis* of the Alban Mount, in ascending the deserted counterforts of the Monte Cavo, as far as Rocca di Papa, an escarped hamlet to which the landscape-painter enticed us.

250   Rome.

At the Madonna del Tuffo (a votive chapel commemorating a fall

ROAD TO CASTEL-GANDOLFO: LA GALLERIA.

of rocks, which the virtue of a prayer stopped before two cavaliers) there is a new point of view. You then find yourself under the Monte Cavo; a small convent of Passionists replaces the Temple of Jupiter

ARICCIA AND ITS VIADUCT.

Latialis, where in old times the Feriæ Latinæ were celebrated. The sun having cleared a portion of the plain, we perceived the enormous dome of St. Peter's rising out of the mist with its Vatican pedestals:

of the whole eternal city, at that distance this is the only building you

LAKE OF ALBANO AND PONTIFICAL VILLA (EVENING).

can distinguish; the rest was dissolved in the soft undulations of the Etruscan Hills.

Rocca di Papa presents the sight of a pyramid faced with brown houses, and terminated on the summit by a ruined fort; you climb up here through a labyrinth of alleys by forty steps. While the goats pressed round the hovels the men played at mora; the sound of songs came out of the houses; girls, in holiday attire, kept going to the fountain and running from house to house in sportive bands, many of them so handsome as to provoke a cry of surprise; the more calm among them returned from the water, bearing on their heads the handsome copper amphora, which we knew from the Etruscan bas-reliefs and the paintings of Pompeii.

We offered the guide refreshments, but he declined: he even dissuaded us from stopping because it was late and it were better not to be overtaken by night too far from Albano. This prudence struck me as opportune enough; we had met in the forest some woodcutters, of whom their guns had made me a little suspicious, because after all it is not by gunshot that

AT ROCCA DI PAPA—BY HENRI REGNAULT.

one fells trees. We made therefore a hasty survey of Rocca di Papa, an Alpine village from which, with feet in the snow, you could see eighty yards of olive-trees. But this poor place, with its striking style, its concentric alleys, its old and low gateways, and its roofs pointed as in the north, left on me a very vivid impression.

YOUTHFUL SHEPHERDESS.

From Albano to Frascati over the mountain, the journey even in winter is varied and interesting. It introduces you to hamlets more or less populous, but more curious than this renowned patron of so many places of pleasure. It was on the slope of Palazzuolo that they showed us the exact position of Alba Longa, built by the son of Æneas, and which long after its destruction by Tullus Hostilius, bequeathed its name to the hamlet formed round an entrenched camp, established to protect the Appian Way at the time of the second Carthaginian invasion. These recollections brought us to the entrance of Marino, by the valley in which still runs the spring of the goddess Ferentina, the Venus Genitrix of the old Latins; it was there, before the foundation of Rome, that assembled, under the presidency of Alba, the representatives of the thirty cities of which the Latin confederation was composed. Tarquin reddened with the blood of Herdonius that water to which we saw two she-goats going down, pensively tended by a girl of fourteen. She did not at our approach raise her pretty head, bent over the spindle which her fingers turned; you might have taken her for a little princess playing at being shepherdess.

No place has been more extolled for the mildness of its temperature, sheltered as it is from the cold winds of east and north, than Tusculum, which was incorporated in the Roman State 381 B.C., and which at that epoch retained its walls and its municipal independence. The flowers and trees of this little town were the delight of Cicero; Hortensius had a house there, to which he added a chamber for Cydias's picture of the Argonauts; thither withdrew both pleasure-seekers and sages—and the two were often only one in the times of Augustus. So to symbolize this happy vocation of a town of pleasure, people assigned its foundation to a son of Circe the sorceress, by Ulysses the eloquent—to that Telegonus who, when pressed by hunger,

OXEN OF THE ROMAN CAMPAGNA.—BY HENRI REGNAULT.

slew his father by mistake in his search for a meal. The palace ruins, discovered almost at the summit of the mountain, where the wind moves noiselessly over the bare ground, may go back to Cicero as well as to Tiberius, that sombre and skilful administrator who made choice of three great workshops for landscape-painters—Rhodes, Tusculum, Capreæ. The *opus reticularium* is everywhere; the Schola has left circular traces: some mutilated statues have been found, with which they have decked and supported the four corners of a house of a custodian, whom the winter had put to flight—a building crammed full of pieces of old marbles. Against the wind, laden with snowflakes, we had no shelter but the wall-side. To the left of the theatre, along a pathway hidden by brushwood, still exists a fountain in peperino, in a broad style.

The theatre of Tusculum remains nearly untouched; the outline of the tiers of seats came out very softly and almost effaced from under the snow, whence rose on the proscenium the shafts of some Doric columns, fluted, massive, and without stylobates; the art of Magna Græcia, brought into fashion by the villeggiature of Pompeii, of Baiæ, and Pæstum, must have smiled at a Hellenized aristocracy. Here and there rows of pillars, sunk partially underground and surmounted by their capitals, rose from a dark pavement like huge mushrooms. We next descended to Frascati. We came to the villa Rufinella; then the villa Mondragone, so vain of its three hundred and seventy-four windows; and the villa Taverna, and I know not what others; for as you enter Frascati, the villa of the Belvedere, designed by Giacomo della Porta for the Cardinal Aldobrandini, drives all the rest from your mind.

THE SALITA OF MARINO.

THE PIAZZA OF ST. JOHN LATERAN.

CHAPTER XVI.

IN the midst of the stirring quarters lying at the base of the Quirinal, you come out upon a great piazza which you name at once without ever having seen it before: Trajan's Column serves as ensign for a forum, of which Apollodorus of Damascus erected the porticoes. The lines described by the remains of a plantation of pillars will help you to identify the perimeter of the temple which Adrian consecrated, and the site of the Ulpian Library which was divided into two chambers—one for Greek books, and the other for Latin; and finally the situation of the basilica, of which the entrance was to the forum and its apse in the north-north-west direction. Divided into five aisles, it was paved with antique yellow and violet breccia; the facings were in marble of Luna; the ceiling of gilded bronze reposed on columns of granite. You even find the remains of five massive steps of *porta santa*, which elevated the monument upon a rich pedestal. The basilica survived the invasions of the barbarians and even the Vandals of Genseric; but the contests of the middle ages and the pious brutalities of the stupid and valorous Normans have buried in ruins a monument which, for Christians especially, must have been an object of veneration.

It was in the Ulpian Basilica that, in 312, Constantine, having assembled the notables of the empire, came and seated himself in the presbyterium, to proclaim his adjuration of polytheism in favour of the religion of Christ; it was on this day and at this spot that the prince closed the cycle of antiquity, opened the catacombs, and inaugurated the modern world. The Acts of St. Sylvester described many passages of the discourse in which, 'invoking truth against mischievous divisions,' and declaring that he ' put away superstitions born of ignorance and reared on unreason,' the emperor ordains that ' churches be opened to Christians, and that the priests of the temples and those of Christ enjoy the same privileges.' He himself undertakes to build a church in his Lateran palace.

The senators listened to the harangue in dull silence, for the patrician houses remained attached to the old worship. But along the aisles of the basilica pressed the Christian populace, now for the first time expanding in sunshine. When the emperor ceased speaking, 'there was as it were a long breath;' then the popular joy burst forth, and the cries of the multitude broke out ' for the space of nearly two hours.' They exalted the power of Christ and his glory, and then, the enthusiasm reaching almost to delirium, they declared to be foes of the emperor all who should not honour the God who had vanquished Maxentius; at last the populace, exasperated by the attitude of the senators, demanded the expulsion of the old priests and the proscription of all who continued to offer sacrifice. A massacre was imminent, when Constantine, again speaking, began to set forth the difference between the service of God and that of men : that the second is forced while the first is free. 'To be Christian,' he said, 'it is needful to desire to become one. To refuse admission to one who seeks it would be blameworthy; to impose it would be against equity; this is the rule of truth. Those who do not imitate us shall not lose our good graces; those who become Christians with us shall be our

TRAJAN'S COLUMN AND ULPIAN BASILICA.

friends.' Truly great on that day, Constantine had the tolerance of a sage, a rare virtue among neophytes; at one stroke he proclaimed the faith of Christ and freedom of conscience. To regain what he gave, not less than fifteen centuries have been needed.

It was without doubt in commemoration of the incident which took place here, that Sixtus V. placed the statue of St. Peter on the summit of the column of Trajan, to replace that of the emperor, which was carried off in 663 by that Constans II. who pillaged Rome. I do not think there exists any monument in the world more precious or more exquisite in its proportions than Trajan's Column, nor one that has rendered more capital service. It is of pure Carrara marble. The shaft is about ninety-seven feet high, by twelve of diameter at the base, and ten below the capital, which is Doric and composed of a single block; the structure consists of thirty-four distinct blocks, hollowed out and cut internally into a winding staircase. Along the outside, forming a spiral round the shaft, is a series of bas-reliefs, divided from one another by a narrow band which, running parallel to the inner staircase of a hundred and eighty-two steps, describes twenty-three circuits to reach the platform on which the statue is placed.

From the Ulpian Basilica, where he has just made the church free, let us follow Constantine to his Lateran house, where he founded the first cathedral. Built by Constantine in the enclosure of his palace, St. John Lateran is the metropolis of the Roman bishopric, as officially recognised by the emperors. St. Damasus was consecrated in the Lateran Basilica; it was there that since Sylvester I. the popes have taken possession of their see. At St. Peter of the Vatican the pope is the spiritual sovereign of the world; at St. John Lateran he is bishop; the basilica of St. John is the cathedral of Rome.

San Giovanni in Laterano is now little more than a place consecrated by great memories. The basilica of Constantine had lasted ten centuries, when, towards 1308, a fire destroyed the temple and palace. Clement V., who lived at Avignon, commenced the reconstruction, and carried it on a considerable way; then Urban V. and Alexander VI. continued and decorated it; Pius IV burdened the nave with its heavy gilded ceiling, and erected on the piazza the lateral façade with its two bell-towers, too far apart; Sixtus V. commissioned Fontana to add the portico, and Salimbeni to paint it. It was there that Nicholas Cordier placed the bronze statue of Henry IV., canon of St. John Lateran, like all the sovereigns of

France. Giacomo della Porta, under Clement VIII., rebuilt the transept; Borromini rebuilt the rest under Innocent X.; Clement XII. had the principal façade erected by Galilei, which provided a mean imitation of that of St. Peter's, and was, like that, surmounted by a regiment of statues. The style of the forerunners of Bernini presided over the work; as at the Vatican, it is a vast portico with the Porta Santa at

WELL OF THE SIXTH CENTURY, IN THE CLOISTER OF ST. JOHN.

the extremity, and five other entrances, of which the centre one, in bronze, is said to come from the Æmilian basilica : at the end of the gallery rises a colossal statue of Constantine, the only authentic likeness of that emperor.

Although St. John Lateran has been rebuilt at least three times, we are led to suppose that the fire of 1308, which destroyed the building of the fourth century, still spared the apse, or else that this apse had been re-erected before the end of the thirteenth ; for its vault is decorated with mosaics signed by Jacopo da Turrita, Fra Jacopo da Camerino, and executed in 1291 for Pope Nicholas IV. ; it was Gaddo Gaddi, they say, who finished them. In sentiment and style they are not very remote from art as it was practised in the Ile de France between 1200 and 1250 ; but here the design has more suppleness, and the colour has a sweet and tender brightness, which the mosaic workers of Venice two centuries later seldom surpassed.

If you are bent on finding some remains of the Lateran buildings

SANTA CROCE IN GERUSALEMME.

going back into respectable ages, you must seek them in the cloister. This monument of the thirteenth century, the arches of which surmounted by mosaics rest on small columns diversified by an ingenious fancy, this cloister is one of the most delicious erections in Rome or in the world. It can only be compared to that of St. Paul, belonging to the same epoch ; they both offer the variety of the buildings of the middle ages, made regular in harmony of outline by frequent resort to antique monuments. Under the arcades you see the massive seat of the old metropolis ; how many pontiffs have sat on this since the eighth century! They preserve here also a number of bas-reliefs

The Monuments.

earlier than the fourteenth, and notably, among other fragments of the old altar, a graceful carving, in which some small clerks blow with

PORTICO OF ST. JOHN LATERAN.

pipes on the pan of a censer. Let us also notice a marble statue of Boniface VIII. In the middle of this court, with some neglected plants growing around it, is a fine well of the sixth century.

264   *Rome.*

From St. John Lateran to Santa Croce, the fourth basilica of Rome, the distance is short. St. Helen, when she brought back from

PENITENTS ASCENDING THE HOLY STAIRCASE.

Jerusalem the Saviour's cross, built a church for it, which, being rebuilt by Benedict XIV. in 1743, with the exception of the apse, still betrays the inclination to imitate St. Peter's. But the bolder façade does not want grace; a pretty open campanile of the thirteenth century, a rustic chapel close by, masses of trees arranged among the buildings, make of the little church of Domenico Gregorini a series of landscapes.

One would not feel bound to visit it, if it had not preserved at the Tribuna of the high altar some large frescoes which represent the finding of the holy cross, the discovery of the three pieces of wood, the trials to which they were subjected, and the procession of St. Helen on her return to Jerusalem. These compositions are dramatic, still simple and already skilful: it is the apogee of the inspired school which goes immediately before Michelangelo and Raphael. This chapel is separated in two by a grating, which women cannot pass without incurring excommunication, while in the reserved space a chest is opened, in which they keep a very large fragment of the true cross, the only one whose authenticity can be guaranteed.

Let us return to the Piazzi del Laterano. Solitude and silence reign on the deserted plateau of St. John Lateran, and the grass grows on it; the obelisk of Thothmes, the greatest of known monoliths, turns round the piazza a shadow which from morning to night meets no creature. The street which, since the time of the Flavians, ascends from the Coliseum to the palace of Lateranus, becomes solitary as you draw near to the plateau; and when from a rather elevated point you view the few houses which are around you at a respectful distance, and the lower as they come nearest to the church, it seems as though they were prostrating themselves before their mother. On whichever side you turn, the sight and the mind are well repaid. From the ancient Porta Asinaria, by which Totila invaded Rome, to the Prænestine gate marked by a triumphal arch of Agrippa, the glacis descending in a gentle slope is bounded by the crenelated walls of Aurelian, in which the Amphitheatrum Castrense is incrusted, a ring whose collet is the basilica of St. Cross. On the other horizon, vague outlying grounds are surrounded by the Neronian and Claudian aqueducts connecting themselves with the walls, beyond which you discover the theatre of the earliest wars of the republic, spreading plains along which uncoil the old roads, recognisable by their tombs. The horizon is terminated by hills, and the ancient cities of Latium which decorate the pedestal of the Sabine Hills. To give perspective to these successive distances, you have curtains of dark trees, and nearer to you, in front of the Scala Santa, where the pilgrims climb on their knees the eight-and-twenty steps of the staircase of Pontius Pilate, the Triclinio, a fragment of the ancient refectory of the popes in the eighth century: Benedict XIV. added to it an apse to expose three mosaics of Leo III. on a golden ground. That in the middle represents the apostles girding themselves to go forth and preach to the nations; the two others, St. Sylvester and Constantine receiving from Christ's hands the Labarum and the keys; then St. Peter giving the pallium to Leo III. and the standard to Charles the Great; two portraits of the time, which are unique, and which survive in open air. Around you at this deserted extremity of the city, all is monumental, but without symmetry; all is celebrated and neglected.

SOPHOCLES.

The palace is only inhabited by the custodians. Sixtus V. had it rebuilt by Fontana on the foundations of the old edifice, which was burnt in the sixteenth century. The interior, a cloister with two stories, is damp, austere, and cold. As men could not live there, Gregory XVI. installed statues in it, and Pius IX. added an historical museum.

A few words, first, on the Gregorian collection, which occupy no less than fourteen apartments. Let us first note a bas-relief of Trajan with three other figures, a piece which comes from the old arch of that emperor, and has been taken from his Forum. No other likeness of Trajan has such delicacy or such truth of expression—the intellectual and benevolent physiognomy of a man who, understanding all, can pardon all.

The Gregorian museum possesses the finest draped statue I have seen: it represents a man of fine port, eloquent, sure of himself, accustomed to dazzle, practised in making his talents avail by the seductive authority of mien. Made to tell from head to foot by the clever negligence of the drapery, the figure is a thorough success, and the great Sophocles,—for it is he,—has taken with ease an imposed

CHRIST SYMBOLIZED IN ORPHEUS.

attitude which has become natural to him, and which completes the representation. Under the folds of the robe, which is half tightened round him, the body describes its lines in a harmonious curve, the head harmonizes perfectly with the attitude, the beard is curled with art, and the outlines are well balanced. It was near the old Anxur that they exhumed this masterpiece in the time of Gregory XVI.

But this Lateran Palace offers collections of a more curious kind in the galleries and in some chambers of the upper story, where they preserve the boxers and gladiators in mosaic that were taken from the Thermæ of Caracalla. These naked figures, stronger than nature, are likenesses with the names of the models; realistic works, if ever there were any, which give us vigour in all its ugliness, animal vigour stripped of all style.

Let us proceed to that portion of the museum which is an idea of Pius IX. The pontiff wished the house of Constantine and the first cloister of St. Sylvester to become a museum of Christian epigraphy and iconography. So, adding to the inscriptions the tombstones and sarcophagi got up every day in the course of the excavations, and to these elements joining the fac-similes of paintings that it was neither possible nor proper to take from the catacombs, Pius IX. formed so rich a collection, that all along the broad staircase of state, on the landings, in the chambers and galleries of the first story, the walls are entirely covered. This museum is a unique source of information as to the forms, the rites, the spirit, and the tendencies of dogma in those almost unknown ages.

At the first steps of the staircase you are stopped by a series of sarcophagi, in which bas-reliefs bring together the correlative symbols of the Old Testament and the New. One of the most complete is a large Constantinian vessel, of which the carvings placed over one another in pairs, and grouping several subjects in four divisions, reproduce the symbolism of our spiritual history. Man and his companion are represented as created not by the Father, but by the Trinity; Jesus draws from the side of Adam the first woman, the Father touches her brow, the Holy Spirit breathes a soul into her. The Son and the Holy Spirit are always beardless; the Father, after Olympian precedents, is also young, as Diespiter was. Then comes the First Fall, so represented as to banish every painful or humiliating idea: Christ gives to Adam and Eve the emblems of work: to him some ears of wheat, to her a sheep whose wool she is to spin. The second canto opens with the Incarnation of the Son; the magi come to adore; the Virgin is attended by two youths, the Holy Spirit and St. Joseph: the latter is constantly represented as young in the primitive monuments. In the next bas-relief Christ gives sight to the man born blind—symbol of the redemption. Then St. Peter denies his master: at his feet the cock crows; the second fall is a pendant to the first. Then the apostle repentant, and confessing the faith, follows pagans who drag him after them. Finally he becomes Moses, and explains the sense of the figures; it is he, Peter, who strikes the rock and makes the water gush forth, in which we see the troop of the faithful borne along; Moses and Peter play alternately the same part. In the centre of the sarcophagus are marked two unworked medallions; these tombs were prepared and carved beforehand, and only room was reserved for the portraits of the future purchasers.

The study of symbols teaches us to determine the Christian myths of those early times: we see religion completely formed at the end of the first century, in which paintings and sculptures are taken by choice either from the Gospel of St. John, a tardy and victorious reply to the scholars who thought it later than Eutychian; or from the allegorical picture of the reign of Nero, written by the same apostle at Patmos, and called the Apocalypse. Recent researches have shown equally

'A GROUP SLUMBERING OVER A CRADLE.'

plainly, contrary to the assertion of Mgr. Gerbet, that the first Christians did by no means abstain from personifying God the Father. For a long time they dissembled the mystery of the sacraments under emblems: the passage of the Red Sea meant baptism; the blind restored to sight, penitence; Jonas interprets the idea of resurrection. Adam, the first sinner, is always beautiful; Eve is often seated by the side of Mary, and in the hand of the first woman they place not one apple, but seven—the deadly sins. I noticed on frescoes of the first century, the Magian kings reduced to two, or raised to four; they wear Phrygian caps, and in these paintings the

Virgin is always pretty and elaborately draped. Certain subjects are represented by symbolical animals, on account of their crudity: thus, a sheep between two foxes on the edge of a fountain represents the chaste Susannah. So far as concerns usages and costumes, these drawings are invaluable. Besides the fac-similes, they have placed in the collection the remains of frescoes, from the era of the Cæsars down to the fifteenth century, fixed on canvas with much skill. A curiosity of the first rank is the seated statue of St. Hippolytus, bishop of Porto, a work of the third century discovered in the catacombs of St. Lawrence. The head is a restoration, but the monument furnishes us, engraved against the episcopal seat, with the Paschal calendar, which the prelate composed to refute the Quartodecimani, who obstinately persisted in celebrating Easter on the same day as the Jews.

The obelisk on the Piazza of St. John Lateran is, as I have said, the loftiest of the monoliths, and it is covered with curious hieroglyphics. Constantine brought it on board ship; he had it dragged to Rome, and set up in the Circus Maximus. Overthrown by the barbarians, it broke into three pieces, and the earth buried it; Sixtus V., who dug it up, had it fastened together again, and then erected it before his palace of Lateran.

CHAPTER XVII.

THE Colonna Palace is situated between the Corso and the Quirinal, on the slope of which the gardens extend, contiguous to the church of the Santi Apostoli; with that the buildings occupy one of the great sides of a long piazza, bounded on the north by the narrow Saporelli Palace, where died the last Stuart, nominally James III.

On account of certain analogies of style, the Colonna Palace presents a curious appearance to persons who have studied the decorations of our royal residences of the great age. It is not that the galleries are filled with paintings, but the selections are happy, the portraits of the family are of the highest value, and the Colonna Palace preserves pictures that are not to be found elsewhere. Such is the portrait in profile of a young man, by that Giovanni Santi, Raphael's father, of whom our biographers have not failed to make a mediocre painter, to enhance by so much the genius of the son. Unluckily, the works of Santi are very rare, but they are in general of a warm and vigorous colour for pictures of such exquisite finish: the Giovinetto of the Colonna Palace unites to the delicate physiognomy of a Francia the deep colouring of a Venetian.

As we were going away, Lorenzo Colonna, brother of Martin V., held us fixed under his glance: it is Master Holbein who places in your way this gentleman with tawny beard, mixed with the furs of a robe, and from whose features life shines tranquilly out. Contrary to what is customary, the search for the real does not in this portrait end in dryness; the painting is rich and powerful, and as the proportions are just, the colour assumes a deep brilliance. I have never seen one of Holbein's portraits comparable to this of Lorenzo Colonna.

Established in 1572, after the battle of Lepanto, to consecrate the glory of Marco Antonio Colonna, who commanded the Christian galleys against the Turks, the great gallery of this palace reminds one of that of St. Cloud, and still more of the gallery of mirrors at Versailles. The structure rests on pilasters in antique yellow; medallions and bas-reliefs have been disposed under each of the ten great windows, the intervals between them being occupied by panoplies of oriental arms; the frescoes tell the story of the Battle of Lepanto, along the arches of the ceiling. On a series of mirrors arranged down the hall, Mario de' Fiori has painted Cupids among the finest garlands that his pencil ever drew. Add to all this elegance and wealth a pavement of antique marbles; multiply in symmetrical proportions the furniture with its sweepingly turned lines, the giant consoles, of which the tables, of oriental breccia, are supported by Turks stooping and in fetters; Asiatic cabinets in ivory and lapis and ebony; count up the statues, the groups, the portraits, the cartoons; and you will have an idea of the vast gallery where, as at St. Cloud, the paintings like the portraits are arranged in the ornamentation. The more you look, the more convinced you are that Mansart drew his inspiration for the decoration of Versailles from the great hall of the Colonna Palace, and what increases the probability of this imitation is the timidity of the copy.

VIA DELLA PILOTTA.

The communication between the palace and its escarped gardens is by two or three bridges, each of one arch, thrown over a deep street, the Via della Pilotta, which runs round the foot of the hill, and on which the branches of the trees pour down festooned shadows. The palace, the ruins two thousand years old, the basins of green water, and this precipice changed into a cascade of flowers—all are in the very heart of the town, and in a very populous quarter.

Every one knows that the popes enclosed the most notable portion of the Quirinal between the walls of the vast palace, in which they have established a residence, if not for summer, at least for the semi-season, and also a residence for winter. But this erection of

FOUNTAIN OF THE PIAZZA MONTE CAVALLO.

Gregory XIII., designed by the Lombard, Flaminio Ponzio, finished under Sixtus V. and Clement VIII. by Fontana, enlarged by Carlo Maderno, completed by Fuga and Bernini, and restored under Pius VII. —the work of ten pontiffs, the Quirinal Palace has not had the honour of giving its name to the piazza which its principal façade decorates. In the middle of the piazza a jet of water plays in a basin of oriental granite; Pius VII. brought it thither from the Forum; above the basin stand in hard outline against the sky two athletic statues and two horses of marble, placed there by Sixtus V.; afterwards, Pius VI. subordinated the two groups, reducing them to serve as accessories to

T

a needle of red granite, once posted as sentinel before the Mausoleum

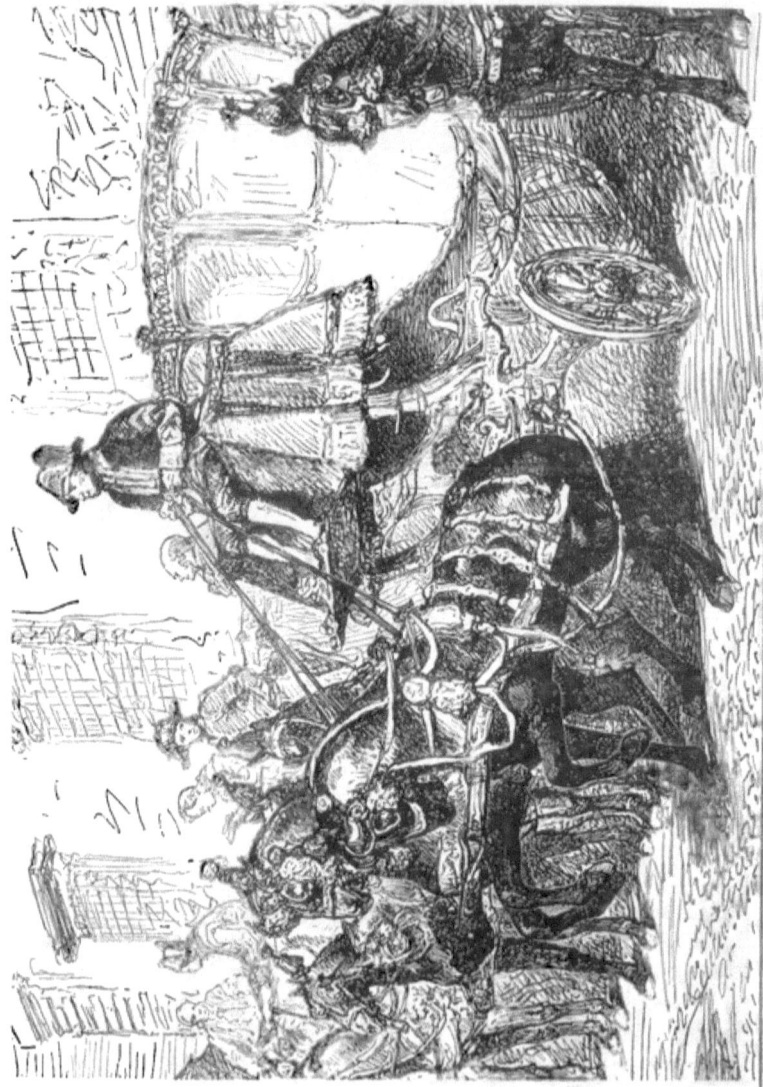

of Augustus. These fine figures, and still finer coursers—groups in which the Quirites amused themselves by recognising their old patrons, Castor and Pollux—these masterpieces attributed to Praxiteles and Phidias, chose the hill for pedestal, and renamed it. Unfortunately, they are cut in a porous marble which the damp blackens; placed too high, they only appear like a bare outline in the air; in another way the obelisk planted between the two disperses the interest, and this conflict of precious works adorning the Piazza Monte Cavallo produces a discordant effect.

Seen from the outside, the building is a fairly handsome barrack, soberly faced, with small architectural elegance. Ample staircases, an enormous court of cloistered appearance, the garden of peculiar arrangement—such is the aspect of the Quirinal.

The gardens of this great convent are turned into a royal residence, with their terraces, their statues, their fountains, their clipped avenues, their parterres cut into arabesques, their architectural arbours, and their flaunting kiosk which Fuga erected to be a buffet, in which the holy father in the midst of the landscapes of Battoni and Orizonte offers sherbet and coffee to the grandees of this world.

On certain days, the Quirinal, where grass grows and the spider weaves, sees the carriages and rich liveries of the prelates rolling up in front of its walls. This is when the palace transforms itself into an hotel for cardinals, and when, each evening, a motley populace of twenty nationalities, with eyes fixed on a large balcony, awaits the name of the master whom the conclave will give to themselves, to launch it on the echoes of the whole world.

The Via di Porta Pia, which continues that of the Quirinal, will take us to the Chartreuse of Sta. Maria degli Angeli. Buonarotti was over eighty when he took it into his head to plant in the rotunda of the Thermæ of Diocletian this church, which he had been entrusted to build by Pius IV. So, while he raised the floor of the temple twelve feet, he preserved the eight enormous monolithic columns of Egyptian granite which supported the entablature, and faced the bases with marble.

In the centre of the cloister with its hundred pillars of travertine, four cypresses, tossed by time and grown into irregular forms, which, Michelangelo planted, disguise the edge of the well like a tomb: the distant lines of the low galleries against a blue sky give to these sombre giants colossal dimensions The square of the court makes a kitchen garden, in which smile some Bengal roses, but nothing interferes with the silent poetry of an enclosure consecrated to meditation.

LA BARCACCIA AND THE STEPS OF LA TRINITA DEI MONTI.

Let us regain the street of the Quattro Fontane, and pass Capole

La Trinita dei Monti.

Case, to go as far as our church of the Trinita dei Monti, built on the Pincian in 1494 by Charles VIII. for the brethren of S. Francesco

HOUSE WHERE POUSSIN DIED.

de Paolo. It is a mediocre monument, but with a considerable appearance; to keep a favourable idea of it, confine yourself for a long time to looking at the outside, especially from the Piazza di Spagna, at the top of which it crowns a magnificent staircase.

On the Piazza di Spagna, in front of the College of the Propaganda, the nursery of missionaries for barbarous countries, rises the column of the Immacolata, which, since 1856, consecrates the dogmatic definition of the Immaculate Conception. They made use for this purpose of a shaft of Carystian marble, exhumed in 1778 from the Piazza Campo Marzio.

Everybody has ascended a hundred times, by its broad hollow with gentle steps, the slope leading from the piazza to which the palace of the Spanish ambassadors has given a name, to the Villa Medici and the Pincian Gardens. In proportion as you rise, you see the façade of the Trinita dei Monti lessen; it is cut in two by a little obelisk planted in front of the portico, where it tries to make itself big by the aid of a pedestal which is too long.

PERRON OF THE TRINITA.

On an angular pile by the steps of the church, two popes have displayed their arms; above they have placed an enormous capital taken from some temple of the third century; on this capital they have fastened a tombstone, and as no less has been done on the other side, this bit of bric-à-brac is an agreeable ornament to the space in which the Via Gregoriana and the Via Sistina come out, separated by the house with tetrastyle porch where Poussin

The Pincian Gardens.

died, ten steps from the house of Salvator Rosa, and nearly fronting that of Claude of Lorraine. These three sanctuaries guard the approach

ON THE TERRACE OF THE PINCIAN.

of the terrace, which ends at our academy of painting and at the Pincian Gardens. This park extends to the end of the hill, and descends on the Piazza del Popolo, which is so flaunting on the occasion of the festival of the Madonna, when, entering the city in gorgeous procession by the bridge of St. Angelo, the carriage of the sovereign pontiff, preceded by the cross-bearer on a caparisoned mule comes out of the Via di Ripetta on its way to Sta. Maria del Popolo.

The Trinita dei Monti and the old convent of the Minimes are occupied by the nuns of the Sacré Cœur; it is a fine establishment with most extensive grounds.

Nearly every morning I passed in front of the Trinita, on my way either to the Pincian for a view of the hills lighted up by the rising sun, or to the Villa Medici, at the approaches to which the artists find ready for them some damsels from the fields clad in rustic attire, the materials of local colouring for the use of the studios. There used often to plant herself a ravishing creature, that our students did their best to see with the eyes of Leonardo—La Pascuccia, whose wide black eyes and waving hair I have seen on many a canvas.

LA PASCUCCIA.

THE EMBLEMS OF JUSTICE (RAPHAEL'S STANZE).

CHAPTER XVIII.

LET us ascend the Pincian Hill. We will then enter the Villa Medici. Elevated on the hill of the gardens whence it dominates city and fields, the Villa, which you see from all sides, is masked by the two pavilions rising out above the trees, over a broad and clear façade. From the exterior side, which faces towards Rome, the building has a cold look; windows of tolerable simplicity and very spacious, a very high doorway crowned by a balcony—such is the unostentatious arrangement adopted in 1540 by Annibale Lippi when he erected the palace for the Cardinal Montepulciano. This soberness has been well conceived, especially if at the time they had the intention of making of the opposite side a gem of architecture enriched by a collection of bas-reliefs, the precious fragments of antique sculpture. This façade, with its portico sustained on splendid columns and watched by lions, is in vivid contrast with the other, of which the design has, without the slightest proof, been attributed to Michelangelo.

It is probable, for the rest, that the plan was modified when Cardinal Alessandro de Medici acquired possession of it, and gave it a name. He amused himself by decorating it in the few periods of leisure which he was allowed under Clement VIII. from the negotiations with which he was charged at the courts of various sovereigns, and among others at the court of the Béarnais, Henry IV. On the death of Aldobrandini, the cardinal having been chosen pope on the 1st of April, 1605, he took the name of Leo XI., and died only twenty-seven days after, leaving as many regrets as he had inspired hopes. The Cardinal de Medici commenced collections which under the Florentine sovereigns continued to enrich the villa on the Pincian: on the vase placed in front of the steps was once seen the Mercury of John of Bologna; a document recently published informs us that in 1671 the young Marquis of Seignelay admired in these gardens a Cleopatra, Ganymede, Marsyas, as well as Niobe with her fourteen

PORTICO OF THE VILLA MEDICI.

children. It was Cosmo III. who, towards the end of his interminable reign, despoiled the Roman villa for the benefit of his gallery of the Uffizi at Florence; the deserted husband of Margaret of Orleans died an octogenarian in 1723.

The most remarkable of the domestic apartments is the dining-room, adjoining a kitchen, whence issues that disturbing and too-familiar odour of such offices in lyceums and boarding-houses. This fine refectory is vaulted, and the arch has been divided into compartments, in which since 1811 the portraits of French laureates have been placed by their comrades; a brotherly idea, which too often suggests melancholy reflections, for how many are unknown among these laurelled

VILLA MEDICI (GARDEN FRONT).

heads! Independently of the bad taste that belongs to every period of fashion, two things struck me—how little common are passable portraits, and how rare on these young brows is the luminous halo of youth. One of the most extraordinary is Hector Berlioz, with high tufts of hair over the head of a cock, strangled in a cravat half a foot high. In the features of F. Halévy, nearly a child to look at, we have some trouble in recognising the amiable and saddened man, who bore with visible resignation the burden of his life. Ambrose Thomas (by Flandrin) and François Bazin are the models whom years have done least to alter; one of the masterpieces of the gallery is the profile of a musician painted by M. Henner. Among these likenesses, the epic laureates of 1812 and the romanticists of 1827 have, the one a sombre mien *à la* Curtis, the others Byronic expressions, which seem ridiculous to the more citizen-like realists of our own day. I may add that the establishment possesses a library, which is treated by the majority of these gentlemen with respectful consideration.

VIALE COPERTO, IN THE VILLA MEDICI.

Rome is the last city of our busy century in which abstinence from labour has kept its ancient dignity. Free from the thirst of amassing money, and from the desires of luxury, withdrawn by its indolent independence from the deterioration produced by manufactories,

Inspiration from Rome.

the Roman people, living in the open air in perfect freedom, have preserved their original beauty: they keep a proud air, imperious gestures, and the attitudes of sculpture. In no other country can you find such a collection of creatures worthy to furnish models in the highest style. Go a few furlongs away; the slopes that mirror in the Tiber their ruins and domes, the Sabine and Alban Hills, will revive all the inspirations of Claude and Poussin. Their historic landscapes, formed by the masters of the world, have preserved the balanced lines and grave aspects which, reminding us of far-off ages, make a way to the soul like some sounding harmony—

UNDER THE PORTICO.

that majesty of nature which in the language of art is expressed by the word *style*. In a word, this city, the ancestress of our civilizations, is the storehouse of the most numerous and the most perfect monuments of ancient and modern art alike. In later times the germs of the Renaissance, which had been developed in the neighbouring states, came and flourished in the capital of Martin Colonna, of Nicholas V., of Julius II., and of Leo X.; so that for all branches of art Rome is the vastest studio and the most complete museum that exists.

Assuredly it was here, and not elsewhere, that it was right to establish for sculptors, painters, and architects a centre of studies, a home for observation, where everything comes to take its just place and reach its own end.

If it had no other advantages than that of isolating in a spot where horizons expand and even silence is eloquent, a number of young men who at home would be made heavy by the triple prose of interests, examples, and dangerous pleasures, the Academy here would still be an advantage.

There is a grace which must leave in the understanding, the feelings, and consequently in the works, an ideal that is ineffaceable, in having lived for five years away from the commands of fashion and its purveyors, and having breathed the air with the marbles of Greece and the creations of Raphael and Michelangelo, who are there in their integrity; in having contemplated the beautiful under the horizons of Rome, and having absorbed the aroma of all its majesties; in having passed through the decisive phases of youth in the shade of the gardens where Armida is replaced by study, and where, as in the Elysium of the poets, you daily frequent, and almost hear speak, the great masters of the world by their own hearth.

ON THE TERRACE OF THE MEDICI GARDENS.

CHAPTER XIX.

IN the times when the Emperor Valerian was chastising the Christians at Rome, the pontifical see was filled by an old man who was a native of Athens, honoured under the name of St. Sixtus: he was put to death in 259, as his predecessor Stephen had been two years before. As he went to punishment, a young deacon followed close behind him, and cried to him with many tears, 'Will you go without your son? Shall I not help you more in this last sacrifice?' 'My son,' replied the old man, 'thou shalt rejoin me in three days.'

The deacon who thus invited martyrdom was called Laurentius. Sixtus II. intrusted to him the treasures of the church, and when he found himself being dragged to the prætorium, he bade him sell the sacred vessels and share the price of them among the poor. The bishop having been slain, the prefect enjoined on the deacon to hand these riches to the Ærarium, and Laurence having begged for some hours in which he might bring them together, reappeared with a crowd of mendicants in his train. 'Behold,' he said, 'the treasures of the children of Christ!'

Taking for a mockery these words which he could not rightly understand, the prefect commanded that the young Laurentius should be beaten with rods; then he had him stretched all bleeding over a gridiron heated red-hot by live coals. His courage and gentleness appeared so superhuman, that many people were converted to the Christian faith, seeing this execution, which took place on the 10th of August, the fourth day after the death of St. Sixtus, as he had foretold.

In the sixth century St. Laurence extra Muros, one of the patriarchal basilicas, was half buried; Pope Pelagius had it disimprisoned; making a centre of the apse, at the foot of which rest the remains of the deacon, he doubled the extent of the church by erecting aisle facing aisle. Towards 1216 Honorius III. simplified the temple,

288   *Rome.*

VIEW AT THE BACK OF THE CHOIR, SAN LORENZO.

which had two levels, by raising the presbyterium, of which the foundation was to a large extent filled up; the altar since then has been at a still greater height above the sepulchral vault. Pius IX.

BASILICA AND CONVENT OF SAN LORENZO FUORI LE MURA.

wished to exhume the whole: having completed the isolation of the church from the hill, he disengaged the eight fluted columns with

290 *Rome.*

TRANSEPT AND CONFESSIONAL OF SAN LORENZO.

Corinthian capitals of the Constantinian basilica, to which Pelagius

PULPIT OF THE GOSPEL, AT SAN LORENZO.

had added two pillars crowned with trophies and figures, and resting on bases adorned with rosettes and crosses. It is to Pope Honorius that we owe the fine mosaic which, on the arch of the vault, represents on one side St. Laurence and Pope Pelagius II. led before the Saviour by St. Peter, and on the other St. Paul between St. Stephen and St. Hippolytus, draped in white. The Christ is seated on the globe; Bethlehem and Jerusalem, his cradle and his tomb, are drawn at each end of this important composition. The pulpits, which Innocent III. had decorated with panels of red porphyry and green serpentine, are heightened in effect by settings of small mosaic. Rome possesses nothing in this kind which attains such charm of effect with so much simplicity. The choir having been freed by Pius IX. from the rubbish which supported it, they had to stay it on a colonnade, which upholds a ceiling of modern taste and out of harmony with the style of the church; this space isolates the tomb of St. Laurence, which you discern in shadow through a gilded grating. At the corners of the basilica they found doors walled up, which continued the aisles through the Catacombs.

The basilica, one of the five cathedrals of the pontifical Roman bishopric, possesses in the centre of its Presbyterium an antique and massive seat, which was decorated in 1254 with two graceful torse columns, was edged with fine mosaics, and was set in a facing of marble, with porphyry coffer-work framed with gems. We cannot omit to mention the ornamentation of a monument, on which so many centuries have left their traces. In fact the sculptured débris of palaces or temples, entablatures preserved from the primitive basilica, are supported on twelve antique columns of violet marble with Corinthian capitals. The upper gallery forms a square enclosure, resting on twelve other small columns with Ionic capitals, also fluted, and composed of a greenish granite from Egypt, the rarest in the world.

To close what concerns this church, let us not forget under its vast porch forty frescoes of the thirteenth century, consecrated to the legends of St. Laurence, St. Hippolytus, and that other saint who perished nine months after the Saviour—St. Stephen, the first martyr, and the second who prayed for his executioners. From the year 415, when the remains of Stephen were dug out from the field of Gamaliel, the Roman Deacon Laurence, and the Archdeacon of Jerusalem—St. Irenæus gives him this title—were gathered together under the altar of St. Laurence without the walls. The frescoes are extremely curious in point of movement and of costume, and for the usages which they reproduce; but they have been repainted with a heaviness which lessens their worth. After taking a last glance at

CLOISTER OF SAN LORENZO FUORI LE MURA.

the heraldic lions at the foot of the two pilasters of the doorways, and seen from the piazza the walls, with deep open cornice, of that house which, though so little striking without, is a magnificent temple within; after looking at the buildings of the Franciscans with their low cloister and sombre campanile, at St. Laurence on his pillar, at the cypresses of the cemetery—even then the interest of the place is not exhausted. There is a cloister which is very rarely visited. Its galleries have arches fully vaulted, narrow and low; their pillars, which are unlike one another, and are sometimes joined in pieces, adapt the gorge or cavetto which surmounts them to bevelled entablatures; three-lobed niches ornament the upper story, resting on a frieze in a romantic taste of a very accentuated kind. Earlier than the wonderful cloisters of St. Paul and St. John Lateran, this, which shows the same principle of Art in its beginnings, belongs to the eleventh century.

CONVENT OF ST. PUDENTIANA.

After returning to the city by a long rectilinear street, in which high walls hide the gardens of the Esquiline from you, and when you have crossed the piazza and passed the church of Santa Maria Maggiore, you observe at the corner of the Via Urbana a small church placed on a lower level of ground. St. Pudentiana is announced by a square bell-tower of brick, of solid and firm look, although on its four fronts it is opened by a triple row of three-lobed arches, supported by two columns. Each of these stories, adorned with small medallions of black marble, is finished by a cornice of round tiles, with modillions with projecting denticules; a double coping runs round the arches; a low roof surmounted by an iron cross crowns the whole, while tiny bits of vegetation mingle green veins with the tone of the brick. Such bell-towers are numerous at Rome; their form, derived from the antique style, ennobles in them a certain indefinable look of poverty and dilapidation.

The church is associated with the first patricians of Rome who professed Christianity; you still distinguish under the crypt the

ST. PRASSEDA AND ST. PUDENTIANA (CATACOMB OF PRISCILLA).

foundations of a palace of which Pius I. made an oratory in the year 154: this palace was that of a senatorial family, who are supposed under that pontiff to have given hospitality to St. Justin, as its ancestors had given to St. Peter.

Let us not be afraid of admitting as authorities the Acts of the Apostles, the **Epistles of St. Paul, the Acts** of St. Justin, the chronicles of Eusebius, **the works of Anastasius and** of **St.** Jerome, the Annals even of Baronius, **and the Bollandists,** who have compelled all to enter in. These writers follow for more than a century the family of the senator Punicus Pudens, who, with his mother Priscilla, had welcomed and protected St. Peter; the Acta have transmitted the memory of the children of this patrician, Pudentius and Sabinella; finally, that of the third generation represented by two brothers, Timothy and Novatus, and two girls, Prasseda, or Praxedes, and Pudentiana. Inscriptions confirm the witness of the sacred historians: the cemetery, underground, where, close to the Viminal, beyond the Salarian gate, Punicus Pudens and his wife were buried, has kept the name of Priscilla; St. Peter was represented there in the third century between the two daughters of Sabinella; in the eighth, Pascal I. discovered and brought to Rome the bodies of St. Prasseda and St. Pudentiana, the two hostesses of St. Justin: we still read in the catacombs of Priscilla the inscription of a Cornelia Pudentianeta, which attests the immense duration of this family burying-place.

DOOR OF ST. PUDENTIANA.

The Constantinian mosaic, of great size, executed in the tribune of the choir at the back of the high altar, and composed in honour of the family of Punicus Pudens, is something more than a document or a curiosity; it is a masterpiece of Christian antiquity. Giulio Romano must have loved this rare piece, which Poussin could never weary of contemplating and extolling. The composition is simple and well arranged in its symmetry: in the centre is seated Christ, draped in a toga of gold; to his right and left are placed St. Peter and St. Paul crowned, the one by St. Pudentiana, the other by her sister Prasseda; around these principal figures are grouped Pudens and his descendants, Pudentius, Novatus, Timothy, and Sabinella. The

MOSAIC OF ST. PUDENTIANA.

draperies of the Saviour are well distributed; the calm of the picture, the character and arrangement of the figures, are all alike remarkable.

It is the most ancient Christian picture that can be studied at Rome from the point of view of art.

In following to the bottom the Via Urbana which Urban VIII. had laid out, but which under the kings, as Livy tells us, was already called *clivus Urbius*, you fall into the quarter of the Suburra, which figures so often in the Roman annals. Let us turn our digression to advantage by going to the entrance of the Forum, in front of the choirs of St. Cosmus and St. Damianus, to look at mosaics nearly as important as those of St. Pudentiana, and which ought to find a place here. The church of St. Cosmus has enclosing it the colonnades and the sanctuary of an ancient temple. You will read everywhere that this temple was consecrated to Romulus and his brother; the truth is, that nobody knows to whom it was dedicated, and that probably from 526 to 530, when Felix IV. erected this little church, and gave it the pagan *cella* for vestibule, contemporaries knew no more than we do. This rotunda possesses an antique door of bronze, adapted to its primitive marbles.

CHURCH OF ST. COSMUS AND ST. DAMIANUS.

Placed upright on the summit of the arch, between St. Damianus and St. Cosmus, who are presented by St. Peter and St. Paul, the figure of the Saviour, blessing with his right hand, and with his left holding the Gospels, and clothed under an ample white mantle, with a purple dalmatic,—this figure with its nimbus possesses an incontestable majesty. St. Cosmus bears one of those crowns of flowers which covered the bread of oblation offered by the faithful—a usage perpetuated down to our own time. Distributed with great dignity, the draperies are well suited to the attitudes and forms; it is still somewhat antique art, but under another law. These mosaics can only be compared to those of St. Pudentiana, and to those which we shall soon see at Santa Maria Maggiore. Let us not forget that nine centuries afterwards, when he designed for the tapestries of Leo X. the cartoons of which seven originals are at Hampton Court, Raphael did not disdain for figure of the Saviour to copy, or almost copy, the Christ of St. Cosmus and St. Damianus.

Above the old theatre of Florus, and the piazza where the house of Propertius was, which Ovid and Tibullus used to visit, a few steps from the house of the Pudentii, and probably in their ground, were the Thermæ of Novatus, brother of Prasseda. Pius I. founded an oratory there, which Pascal I., in the eight century, erected into a church. Innocent III. ceded this temple to the monks of Vallombrosa, which is still very interesting, though it was *embellished* by St. Charles Borromeo, cardinal of St. Prasseda.

So far as restoration goes, saints are undoubtedly not so bold of hand as the other princes; for St. Prasseda has preserved a venerable and attractive air. Aisles divided by sixteen columns of granite, an altar-canopy supported on pillars of porphyry; a choir with two flights of steps of enormous blocks of *rosso antico*, the most valuable of stones, since it is no longer to be found—such are the materials which throw back into antiquity a Carlovingian temple all decked out with fragments of the pagan era. The great arch and the Tribune have mosaics also belonging to the ninth century, and curious from various points of view. While at St. Pudentiana the two sisters are crowning the apostles, here they are presented to Christ by the guests of the family, St. Peter and St. Paul.

This mosaic has a strange style about it; the taste and execution of it are of a wildness which proves that centuries elapsed between the composition of the almost classic work of St. Pudentiana and that of St. Prasseda.

Enriched with mosaics, mostly with a golden ground, curious in arrangement, adorned with exquisite splendour, this chapel is a perfect jewel-casket; the thirteenth century, completing it, was content to give it a certain fineness or delicacy which enhances the oriental character of the whole. On three sides the base of the wall

DOOR OF THE COLONNA CHAPEL, AT ST. PRASSEDA.

is faced with marbles of an amber shade; at the corners are raised on antique stylobates four granite pillars with gilded Corinthian capitals, and pedestals of four angels in mosaic, whose heads touch the top of the vault, which is occupied by a figure of Christ. The

SANTA MARIA MAGGIORE.

space is filled by several of the blessed, singularly apparelled; above the door are represented Sabinella, and St. Prasseda, St. Pudentiana, and St. Bridget; on the altar, between two columns of oriental alabaster, they have executed in mosaic a very incongruous Madonna.

With its crushed domes, its seventeenth and eighteenth century façades, its double porticos vaguely degenerate from St. Peter's, the patriarchal basilica of Santa Maria Maggiore would only announce a modern monument, if our countryman, Gregory XI., had not pre-

INTERIOR OF ST. PRASSEDA.

sented it with a great bell-tower of four stories, with a conical roof, which is the highest in Rome: that is not saying much. You see the tower from the two ends of the very long street which this church interrupts and divides,—the street which from Santa Croce to the Trinita dei Monti, touches the Esquiline, Viminal, and Pincian, going through populous regions and through deserts.

The "Crowning of the Virgin." 303

Santa Maria Maggiore is a great name: Peter the Venerable says that the basilica of Lateran apart, that of Liberius is the first (*major dignitate*) of the churches of Rome and of the world.

On the large hemicycle which goes round the Presbyterium, behind the master-altar, the Franciscan monk, Turrita or Torrita, with the suavity peculiar to a disciple of the Sienese school at the dawn of the prosperities of that republic, painted in an enormous medallion in a ground of starred blue, the " Crowning of the Virgin." The divine throne, a seat with two places, occupies the centre of this composition, in which the Christ is of a triumphant beauty. The remainder of the vault is equipped with saints on a gold ground, who are divided from the Virgin by two groups of angels, having above them and at the sides a sort of frame of intertwined branches, enamelled with flowers and animated by birds: nothing is richer or tenderer to the eye than the fair harmony of this decoration.

OFF TO THE CARNIVAL.

CHAPTER XX.

IT is on Shrove Tuesday that the diversions of a populace fallen into childhood, and collected together in a single street, reach the very frenzy of their gaiety. An hour before the Ave Maria, you ought to go through the Corso, from the Piazza del Popolo to the Piombino Palace, at the risk of being torn by Mænads. I do not know how the women with bouquets for sale succeed in moving between the close lines of carriages, or the dealers in *confetti* coming with fresh supplies for the trays which hang on the edges of the cars.

The Students of the Academy of France had organised a brake, hung with white, with escutcheons at the corners and gilded wheels: the enormous box was placed, like a nest, in a bed of leaves; the four horses had garlands of flowers for reins and harness. Clad in white, with African burnouses or flowered hoods on their heads, our young artists hurled such a profusion of bouquets, that they seemed to grow under their fingers. In the centre of the car, incense smoked in an antique tripod; at the back, behind a griffin, was a graceful little model, whom our gentlemen had daubed over into a negro. The Apollo of the Egyptians, Orus, carried a thyrsus on the front of the equipage.

The Carnival.

Four times while the carnival lasts, they end the day by a spectacle that it would seem impossible to improvise with a people gone mad with the glory of never obeying. The preparations are as curious as

PIAZZA DEL POPOLO.

Via del Babbuino.—S. Maria di Monte Santo.—Entry to the Corso.—S. Maria de' Miracoli.—Ripetta.

the representation itself. Towards half-past five, the soldiers have made the carriages pass round by the adjacent streets; there only remain foot-passengers on the Corso—a moving mosaic of hats and bonnets. Then the carabiniers, in files two broad, invading the middle of the street, divide the compact crowd in two; they heave it aside,

AWAITING THE ILLUMINATIONS. BY A. DE NEUVILLE.

so to say, on to the causeways, as snow is swept back on mountain roads. The centre is nearly empty, but unequally; the edge straggles over its border; so hardly is this first operation complete, before a

Clearing the Streets. 307

squadron of cavalry rushes forward at full gallop to finish the clearing

RACE OF THE BARBERI: THE START. BY H. REGNAULT.

of the street. After this double expedition the road is made, and the

308   *Rome.*

field swept clean.   Almost immediately, from the Piazza del Popolo,

GERMAN MASQUERADING: THE MARCH PAST.   BY H. REGNAULT.

where they are held back by cables that they not unfrequently break through, there are let loose on the Corso six Barbary steeds, wild and without any gear, without riders, or bits, or bridles,—free as in the desert. The mane plaited, with glowing eye and foaming mouth, they fly down this long narrow avenue, in which even the houses seem full of life and passion; they finish this straight course in the twinkling of an eye, terrified at the loud cries and shouts of the crowd at their side, and of the great quantity of people up at the windows. The swiftest are applauded and goaded on by an uproar that makes them rear, while the last are escorted by hissings and hootings. The cavalcade clears the space like some dark flash; behind it the throng resume possession of the street, which once more becomes choked up. At the outlet of the Piazza of Venice the *barberi* come rushing to the foot of the balcony where the Senator sits, who hands to the winner the prize of the race, as well as a great standard of precious stuff from ten to twelve mètres long. These are of woven silk and gold thread, of extreme magnificence, because the Israelites of Rome, bound ever since the Middle Ages to furnish this standard by way of feudal service, make it a point of honour to be generous.

As soon as the horses have vanished, madness resumes its course, until the hour when authority, by a monosyllable uttered by the cannon of St. Angelo suddenly restores the delirious city to its right mind. The confetti cease to rain down; the cries all stop; you see on the Corso only tranquil citizens making their way home.

The last evening of the carnival, the *barberi* gone and the night closed in, the carriages return to the Corso, where the masquerading pedestrians throng more thickly than ever. Small candles have been distributed, and around cars illuminated with torches, tapers, fireworks, every one holds up in the air his lighted *moccolino*. In the stands, balconies, windows, up to the roofs and inside the rooms, the *moccoli* are sparkling everywhere. To the prolonged shouts of the crowd have succeeded short and stifled laughs, little panting, breathless cries—slight and chirping noises of a most singular effect: a struggle has begun, which produces an indescribable animation, everybody trying to blow out the candle of his neighbour, and to keep his own alight—not only in the street, but also in all the houses.

If a man is too tall, or if he has got his *moccoletto* at the end of a long pole, they mount on his shoulders, or hang on to his arms, they pursue him with other poles, armed with bunches in the shape of extinguishers. On the cars, whose sides are scaled, the lights flicker and vacillate

310   *Rome.*

twenty times extinguished and twenty times rekindled. From the

THE GERMAN FESTIVAL: ENTERING THE GROTTOS. BY H. REGNAULT.

street you will see through the open windows of palaces, the lights moving rapidly on the ceilings, and madmen jumping about in continuation indoors of the exhilarating drama of the Corso; universal movement, and of a contagious fascination! I have seen princes, ambassadors, even prelates, battling in real delirium, and the noble beauties of Rome lost in the war of the streets, sacrifice, in order to extinguish tapers and resinous torches, their embroidered handkerchiefs, Indian shawls, and muffs of the finest furs.

Rome has other festivals like the carnival, but of German importation, and celebrates the 1st of May, a day of joy across the Rhine, where they still solemnise the new season. The masquerade which we are going to see was created by the artists of the German club, organised at the beginning of this century, when the Tedeschi borrowed from the French the custom of going forth to receive at the Ponte Molle the new recruits on their arrival at Rome.

The character of the fêtes recalls the Middle Ages, like every burlesque exhibition of pagan rites: it has its dignitaries, its militia, its corporations of musicians, of high priests, of cooks, of scullions, of poets, of masters of the ceremonies, and of Vetturini, who must all accept the office to which they are appointed, and dress themselves up in grotesque costumes. At daybreak the whole band goes out by the Porta Maggiore, and proceeds as far as the Terro de' Schiavi, a general meeting-place, whence the procession makes its way for the grottos of Cervara, seven miles from Rome, near Teverone. At the moment of departure, on a car festooned with garlands and drawn by four great oxen, whose ample horns have been gilded, appears the President, in the midst of his court of chamberlains, of madmen, and poets: he passes his countrymen in review, makes them a solemn and grotesque discourse. As at the Feast of Unreason, asses furnish a heroic mount to the heroes of the masquerade, they are harnessed in toys from Nuremberg; their riders are clad in garments which make them look like good-men of the woods.

The tumult of crowds at last awakens the desire of silence and repose. The carnival prepares you by striking contrast for the spectacles of the Villa Albani Castelbarco. The porticoes and their statues, the verdant terraces, the masses of tropical trees rising in clumps out of a foreground of flowered beds, stand out with a firm harmony against the rosy distance and the azure of the Sabine hills. The silvery snows in the sky make a wonderful frame for the lemon-trees, the pine, the laurel of the poets, the cypress, and the palms of the desert, bringing to the city of the apostles a reminiscence of Jordan.

The constructions of the villa, bedizened in the Greek manner of the last century, were designed with a view to a museum of antiquities, and made worthy of a family, originally from Epirus, who,

TERRACES AND PORTICO AT THE VILLA ALBANI.

after the wars of Skanderbeg, quitted the glades of Pindus for Italy. Winckelmann, a skilful renderer of the ideas of the learned Cardinal Alexander Albani, purified the idea of the nephew of Clement XI.;

the illustrious archæologist realised theories, which with the French only produced the school of David and the antiquity of Thermidor.

Among the marbles of the Villa Albani you will notice a number

GARDENS OF THE VILLA ALBANI.

of mutilated copies of statues of renown, and many pieces of the later ages; you will also come upon an astonishing profusion of pieces of the rarest quality, and of monuments which you do not find elsewhere.

CHAPTER XXI.

THE galleries are the principal attraction of the Palazzo Borghese, where artists and the public are admitted to copy, as freely as in any other museum, the masterpieces which have been so long in collecting; twelve salons (the whole ground-floor) are filled with panels and canvases. One of the principal merits of this collection is that, better than any other, it makes us acquainted with the school of Ferrara, not in its primitive masters like Galassi or Cosimo Tura, but in the disciples and granddisciples of Francia and Lorenzo Costa, in that pleiad where, round Dosso-Dossi and Garofalo, gravitate artists like Mazzolino, Francis and Jerome Cotignola, Ercole Grandi, Scarcellino, Ricci, Girolamo da Scarpi, down to the Bonona, who was such an imitator of the Caracci. It may even be remarked that the chiefs of the school figure more extensively here than their satellites: Benvenuto Tisi, called Garofalo, is represented by a Holy Family, and by the Marriage at Cana, a small but precious reproduction of a great picture that is lost; by the Resurrection of Lazarus, painted for the church of St. Francis at Ferrara; by a Madonna between St. Joseph and St. Michael; by the Descent from the Cross, so justly famous, which opposes to the same subject treated by Raphael in his youth the rivalry of an inspiration drawn from his third manner by a disciple of genius. Both pictures are in the Borghese Gallery. Let us also mention the Adoration of the Magi, by Mazzoline of Ferrara, the rival of Tisi; and the Circe of Dosso-Dossi, one of the rare masters among the Ferrarese; the colouring is almost Venetian.

The Cæsar Borgia, counted among the Raphaels, about which there has been most talk, is a very remarkable figure, strangely arranged: but nothing proves that it represents the nephew of Alexander VI., while everything shows that it is not by Raphael; the absence of certain supplenesses and the uniformity of tone would make one

presume rather that this portrait was painted by a skilful artist after
an ancient engraving. The neighbouring portrait, a Cardinal,
belongs to Raphael; but you are reduced to a guess about this, under
the retouchings with which they have plastered it over. There is no
necessity to think oneself obliged to take for masterpieces of Leonard
or Francia all the works of the old school of Milan and that of
Ferrara, in these galleries. However, the Borghese Palace possesses
one pearl of Francesco Francia, which may serve for a touchstone;
that is the small kneeling and ecstatic figure of St. Stephen, a clear
painting of a supreme *finesse*, and of a feeling that is almost beyond
this world; round this picture everything grows pale and heavy, and
seems effaced.

If, reader, we had to visit this gallery together, we should go

NUPTIALS OF ALEXANDER AND ROXANA.

straight to the Danaë of Correggio, and we should look at it for long
in every possible light. Then come the Caracci, Guido Reni, Carlo
Dolci, and the Paduan with his Venus at her Toilet, and Albano
with his Seasons. Here is the only profane picture of Federigo
Barocci—Æneas carrying away his Father. The movements and
the heads possess grace; but what a singular notion for an ascetic, to
seek the sensual and redundant manner of Correggio! A picture to
rejoice Jordaens or Goya is the Holy Family of that Caravaggio
who compromised with such adroit cynicism the name of Michelangelo. What a hectorer of a painter! Yet a leonine tread, after
all, bringing out of the canvas a splendid relief and fleshliness of
scandalous opulence.

The Nuptials of Alexander and Roxana, forming two subjects in which allegory and emblems of gallantry come in as in the time of Gessner, show us points of Moreau the younger, of Boucher, or of Lancret, raised to the dignity of the beautiful. What an absence of primness and affectation in this heroic pastoral, and yet how the artist has dissembled his vigour under a grace in which nothing is enervated!

The Borghese Palace possesses, besides some pieces of merit, two gems which neither the amateur nor the historian can despise. One is the portrait of Maria de' Medici, by Van Dyck, very delicate in physiognomy, very expressive, and remarkable for the differences which it offers in point of expression and character, as compared with the more common interpretation of Rubens. The other is one of the finest Holbeins, and the best preserved that I have seen; it represents, in full light and facing you, a person clothed in furs and with a bonnet on his head. The notice tells us that the original is unknown; in reality it is the portrait of the Emperor Maximilian, while still only archduke and before he wore a beard.

Since we have gone through the Borghese galleries, let us finish the afternoon at their villa, so as to appreciate the collections of the family as a whole. The important church of Santa Maria del Popolo will be passed on the way. The uncle of Julius II. had it rebuilt in the fifteenth century by the Florentine Bacio Pintelli, who invited, for the embellishment of his work, the great artists of his country, at the very time when they had their best inspirations.

At the threshold you are attracted to the first chapel to the right, which was established by the family of Sixtus IV., as is proved by the Rovere arms, that rooted oak which was so good a symbol for Pope Julius. Pinturicchio, by some luminous frescoes, lighted the angles of the vaults and the tympana, where he drew some anecdotes from the life of St. Jerome, who reappears in the altar-piece, representing one of those cradles where the Madonna kneels with the saints, to adore the child-god whom she has brought. The subject lends itself to subtle interpretations of physiognomy, for it is necessary to render at once the protection of maternal sentiment and the respect commanded by divinity. In the circumference of the altar the artist has lighted up one of those landscapes which every one has dreamed of, and which the mystic painters discovered in the horizons of the future life. In the midst of these splendours rise the tomb of Cardinal Christopher della Rovere, by a Florentine of the good time, Rossellini perhaps; the perfections of this sculpture remind one of

Santa Maria del Popolo. 317

the famous mausoleum of San Miniato. You will find Pinturicchio again in the third chapel, the whole of which he decorated for Sixtus IV.; it was here that he surpassed himself in the picture of

PIAZZA AND PORTO DEL POPOLO—CHURCH OF SANTA MARIA.

the Assumption, near the bronze statue of a sleeping bishop, which Pollajuolo would not disavow. Pinturicchio in the following chapel has given for guardians to two fine Florentine monuments, the

Fathers of the Latin Church. Finally, he painted in the vault of the choir at the back of the high altar the Coronation of the Virgin,

TOMB OF WILLIAM ROCCA (SACRISTY OF SANTA MARIA DEL POPOLO).

surrounded by compartments ornamented with pale lightness, containing the four Evangelists and four Fathers, as well as the Sibyls stooping. Pinturicchio shows himself the immediate forerunner of Raphael; the charm of his figures, the ordering of the compositions,

FLORENTINE STATUES, BAS-RELIEF OF THE PISANS (CORRIDOR OF THE SACRISTY).

all make one think of the Vatican. As we have seen, this church is important for the work of a great master nearly unknown elsewhere and whom we shall find again, less brilliant and less pure than here, at the Sistine and in the apartments of Alexander VI.

It is in the choir of Santa Maria del Popolo that there rise to right and left, up to the vault, the two finest Florentine tombs that Rome possesses; Julius II. had them executed by Andrea Contucci for the Cardinals Basso and Ascanio Sforza. In the second, the statues of the Virtues, and especially of Force, are splendid pieces. The arrangement of the compositions, their delicacy which is never dry, their opulence which remains sober, that sumptuosity which remains grave, and so much grandeur without emphasis—all contribute to recommend these monuments. We ought not to forget the windows of Peter and Claude of Marsillac, and not of Marseilles, as so many critics have written it. They were Dominicans from Limoges, whom Leo X. summoned to paint the glass of the Vatican, an art in which the French were without a rival in the Middle Ages. Of all the works that these masters executed at Rome, where they acquired such reputation, there only remains these—a Life of the Virgin; John della Rovere had them designed by Pinturicchio. Carlo Maratti, and Caracci, and Contucci, who restored with tact a portion of the frescoes of the Perugian master, also made their mark at Santa Maria del Popolo. We will neglect them, to make our way into the chapel of the Chigi, who unluckily re-handled and modernised this church.

The Chigi were bankers of Julius II. As is usual with financiers arrived at the plenitude of fortune, these, in the decoration of their chapel, strove to eclipse the powers they had ransomed; they wished that Raphael should design them a statue, and they had it executed by Lorenzetto: it is Jonas, gracefully seated on his whale. Lorenzetto made for pendant an Isaiah, whom Jonas depreciates by the comparison. The painter of Urbino designed the whole chapel; its cupola, its mosaic, cartoons for the frieze, as well as for the altar-piece (Birth of the Virgin, intrusted to Sebastian del Piombo, and too meanly completed by Salviati). In the last chapel let us not omit, besides two Florentine monuments, one of which was erected between 1501 and 1507 for a Cardinal Pallavicini, who, having so fine a shrine prepared for himself, wished to enjoy it before being closed fast in it—let us not omit to recall that among the flags of the pavement are set some figures from tombs of the fourteenth century, the well-preserved remains of the earlier church—a frequent and always praiseworthy usage.

The Statues.

These hints would give a very inadequate idea of the importance of Santa Maria del Popolo, if we did not add those which are wanting everywhere, namely—the mention of three other Florentine tombs of the fifteenth century, very admirable, and one of them, that of William Rocca, Archbishop of Palermo, may be attributed to Benedetto da Maiano: they were remounted in the sacristy, when they cut the ancient cloister to consolidate the terraces of the Pincian. Finally, in the corridor of this sacristy, where you will find in an *ex voto* three statues of 1497, there is over a door a bas-relief belonging to a school that is rarely represented at Rome. It is a sculpture of the Pisans—the Crowning of the Virgin. The piece is remarkable; you already feel in it the approach of Giotto.

BERNINI'S DAPHNE.

The enormous number of the statues assembled in the Palace of the Villa Borghese occasions a lively astonishment, when we learn the origin of so rich a gallery. When, after his marriage with Pauline Bonaparte, Prince Camillo Borghese, *invited* by his brother-in-law to sell his collection, had seen it depart for the Louvre, where it constitutes the museum of antiquities, he was seized in presence of his depopulated galleries with a very natural regret; then he had all his

Y

estates thoroughly explored, and they gave him, like the sowing of Cadmus, a second crop of men in marble, yet more abundant than the

FOUNTAIN IN THE BORGHESE GARDENS.

first; such is the source of the present collection. What treasures must be hidden in a soil out of which, without leaving your own property, you extract a quarry of statues!

Bernini's Works

In the saloon of Hercules, the statue of the hero in female draperies is remarkable enough, but the great sarcophagus representing his labours is still more so. Winckelmann has described its lid, on which are figured the Amazons going to the succour of Troy. The small triangular altar is more ancient; it goes back to the school of Ægina. And let us not forget the Daphne, whom the laurel already wraps in its bark, and whose fingers are growing out into branches; it is the only antique statue that represents her during her transformation. In the gallery is a line of clever modern busts of the emperors,

THE BORGHESE VENUS.

of red porphyry, with draperies of alabaster, placed on pedestals of African granite. Let us note a splendid urn of porphyry, and an exquisite bronze representing Nero as a child.

On the upper story are grouped three interesting works of Bernini's youth. Æneas carrying away his Father is a rather cold group, without great elevation, but in which the legs are very fine and the execution consummately skilful; the artist was fifteen when he worked with this authority. David with his Sling is a portrait of Bernini at twenty; his Daphne pursued by Apollo, struggling in the arms of the god, and crying out while undergoing transformation, is a work of just renown—a vivid piece, executed with great force and knowledge in its minutest parts, and which must have shed the halo of masters round a brow of only eighteen springs.

Bernini, who is very well represented in this palace, executed a magnificent bust of Cardinal Scipio Borghese, who built the house. Among so many marvels, in the number of which the Borghese Gladiator figures, purely modern art is introduced by Canova, thanks to the beauty of his most celebrated model. It is here that the Princess Pauline lends to Venus—made young once more—forms made for the marble. Among the remarkable works of Bernini must also be reckoned the fountain in the Borghese gardens.

PORTICO OF OCTAVIA.

CHAPTER XXII.

THE road to Tivoli leaves Rome by a gate constructed by Sixtus V. in the aqueduct of the Marcian, Tepulan, and Julian waters, at the time when this pontiff supported his Felice aqueduct on walls successively restored by Octavianus, Titus, and Caracalla. Under this arch of solid structure retreated in perspective the trees of an avenue all radiant with fresh verdure: they half veiled the battlements of the city and of the Tiburtine gate.

At Tivoli the Sabine hills open out in a horse-shoe: the old town, founded, they say, more than four centuries before Rome, by refugees from Argos, occupies the southern extremity of the semicircle, and looks to the north, which contributes to the freshness of the site.

A number of old houses, and hilly streets with shops which have nothing in them; substructures on every side; old postern-gates where the aloe blossoms in the crevices of the wall; a chattering populace; long alleys, low rooms whence in the evening issues the sound of rhythmic songs, with the tabor; cascades on every side, even under the eaves of a crest in which the houses, piled one over the other, seem to be on the point of being launched into the abyss; below terraces the sheer rock; finally on the side of this cavernous arch, a stream shot forth in three leaps with frightful uproar—all this is Tivoli.

On the rocks above the falls are the circular Greek Temple of Hercules, as well as the little square Temple of the Sibyl, both standing on the edge of the precipice. Nothing is more charming on these denuded rocks than the rotunda, which is earlier than Tiberius, with its Corinthian fluted columns supporting an entablature, adorned with festoons and bucrania. Its execution is of extreme delicacy, and we have the contrast between rugged creation and the refinements of art. It was under the foundation of the temple that, five-and-forty years ago, the great cascade of the Arno still poured its waters; an inundation came, which carried away the upper sluice and unchained such a deluge over the town, thus perched on the brim of an abyss, that the swollen torrent swept away a whole cluster of houses.

In order to save the ancient houses and buildings, it was necessary

RAVINE: TEMPLE OF HERCULES, CALLED OF THE SIBYL.

to turn this terrible scourge aside, and by digging a covered channel for the Arno in the heart of Monte Catillo, to open another outlet for the stream, which now falls more to the left. But only the main sheet of water goes down here: the town being placed as it were over a sieve, from all sides of the hill and over an enormous breadth the waters make their escape from the town, like columns from a besieged

A STREET AT TIVOLI.

town making a furious sortie. They form little cascades in a carpet of thick verdure, and it is only at the opening of the valley that, after this dispersion over half a league of fall, the army of waters proceeds to reconstitute itself compactly in the channel of the Teverone. To heighten the splendour of this long spectacle, each point of elevation is crowned with a monument of the Renaissance or of antiquity: there is the convent which has replaced the house of Catullus; there is the pretended villa of Mæcenas, a vast block of ruins which were the great Temple of Hercules; there are the green campaniles of the house of Ferrara, the highest cypresses in the world; farther on are the much-contested villa of Horace, and the incontestable fortress of the Varus who let his legions be massacred.

"SOME PECORARI LIKE CLEPHTS." BY H. REGNAULT.

As soon as you arrive up here, you want to see and embrace all; and as from this little hotel of the Sibyl, where so many travellers have come to perch themselves, the eye wanders over the exordium of the drama, you only pass through the house to plunge immediately, with or without a guide, into a sort of perpendicular labyrinth. The descent to the cascade by an intertwining pathway is one of the most entertaining, so much has the work of ages cut and slashed the rocks and complicated the vegetation of this brilliant cascade. Galleries, niches, grottoes, porches, have been worked in the tufa, which is all honeycombed with pigeon-holes, with black pigeons flying in and out. Helping the work of men, the waters have fashioned aqueducts; they have excavated, and then petrified, tree-trunks in which rivulets make their way. Alpine plants wed with those of Greece: the acanthus with the erodium, the myrtle with the cyclamen.

The inspiration of antiquity and of the palace of Armida erected by Tasso, lends a strange charm to the villa of the Cardinal Hippolytus d'Este, uncle of the Eleonora whose beauty was so fatal to the poor Torquato. With its grottoes of mosaic where the water drips in sounding drops, its pieces of green water where the lotus languishes, its theatrical magnificence and its neglect, this deserted and lordless fairyland produces the impression of a palace of romance and adventure.

Between Tivoli and the Villa Adriana, at the head of the plain in the last recess of the mountain, you could recover a host of subjects worked by Claude and Van Blömen, and nearly all the grounds of Poussin; the younger schools, beginning with Joseph Vernet, have all illustrated this district. We made our way down into it the next day, by the slope opposite the cascatelle which you see on your left, as, from the winding glades through which you pass you watch the many changes in the outlines of Tivoli, crowned by loftier crests.

When Adrian on his return from Syria which he had governed, from Athens where he had been archon, from the wild regions of Britain and Armorica which he had explored as a traveller, from Judæa which he had held subject, from Asia Minor and Egypt which he had studied as an archæologist—when this crowned patron of all tourists, wearied with the toils of empire and travel, wanted to instal his souvenirs, he laid out as gardens some leagues of a country that was varied with many dells and slopes. To find, as in an album of souvenirs, what had charmed him in his journeys over the face of the world, he bade his architects reproduce the Academy, the Lyceum, the Prytaneium, the Pœcile of Athens; the Temple of Serapis at Canopus, a theatre at Corinth, and the Pyramids of Giseh. He even had Tartarus executed just as Homer had described it, "*etiam Inferos finxit*," says Spartianus; and the Elysian fields as Virgil dreamed them. Thanks to the topography of the district and its richness, he succeeded, by excavating green basins and transplanting mountains, in creating a second time the wonder of Thessaly—that Vale of Tempe, where the river Peneus under its mighty trees hid from Olympus the pranks of Pan, unveiled by Ovid.

It was from the Villa Adriana that the collection of philosophers

assembled at the Vatican came; hence came the Medicean Venus, the
Antinous, a set of Egyptian statues, a menagerie of animals in marble,
the four pillars in porphyry of the Ciborium of Santa Maria Maggiore
and its thirty-eight Ionic columns of cipollino polished like ivory.
The Faun in antique red of the Capitol, and the Adonis of the Villa
Albani, have slumbered amid these thickets.

By the reign of Caracalla, this sublime madness of Adrian was only
a storeroom; after Totila, who besieged Tivoli, the villa became a
quarry. Its gardens, in turn abandoned and restored to cultivation,
owe to these changes of fortune an aspect of wildness, which raises
them to the majesty of true nature: its trees are enormous; but under
the meadow-lands you divine substructures, and vaulted abysses open
in the turf.

REMAINS OF THE VILLA ADRIANA.

CHAPTER XXIII.

NO one, that I know of, has ever verified the statement that the Vatican contains eleven thousand rooms, and if it is true, no pontiff has visited them: what is certain is that among the buildings of this assemblage of palaces belonging to all ages, and where Bramante, Raphael, Pirro Ligorio, Fontana, Maderno, Bernini, and so many others have worked, they count up twenty courts, and that to move among them they had to construct two hundred and eight staircases.

The Vatican museums form so vast a labyrinth that, before involving ourselves in them, it would be better to prelude by the Libreria Vaticana. A broad nave, ending in the middle of a long transverse gallery—such is the place that Sixtus V. had arranged by Domenico Fontana for the manuscripts of the pontifical library, leading out of the Borgian apartments, where since 1840 they have arranged a considerable portion of the printed books, now reaching far over 100,000. What raises the Vatican Libreria above other collections is the value and number of its manuscripts; of these they reckon now 27,000, some of which go back to the fifth century. All ages and all peoples of Europe and Asia have furnished their contingent to this treasure. It is to be regretted that, to furnish us with striking points of comparison, Pliny did not transmit the numerical inventory of the first library of Rome, founded for his contemporaries by Asinius Pollio, who placed in it the statue of Varro, while that writer was still living.

The establishment is of ideal magnificence; all is arranged so as to give a festival to the eyes. While in places like the Bodleian at Oxford, and still more in the typographical cemetery in the British Museum, the people who write, as well as the people who read, are overwhelmed by the sight of the great mass of books which they will never be able to know, which prove to you the vanity of composing more, and which are piled up over your head in endless walls; at the

VATICAN LIBRARY.

Vatican, on the contrary, you do not see a single volume. It is under cover of a multitude of shut and gilded presses, illuminated by

THE THRONE-ROOM AT THE VATICAN.

fresh colouring, a really magical decoration, that to the nine thousand manuscripts of Nicholas V. are added the collection of the learned

Fulvio Orsini, who in his childhood begged alms, and who has left a splendid cabinet; that of the Benedictines of Bobbio, so rich in palimpsests; that of the Castle of Heidelberg, stripped by Maximilian of Bavaria, chief of the Catholic league; the substance of the Libreria of the Dukes of Urbino, collected by Guid' Ubaldo of Montefeltro, and increased by the Della Rovere; the fine books of Christina of Sweden; the library of the Ottoboni, commenced by the old Pope Alexander VIII., who, pressed in his old age to enrich his kinsmen, gave for reason, "*Son' gia le venti-tre e mezzo;*" the Capponi collection, bequeathed in 1746 by the Marquis Alexander, who, in his quality of *Foriere maggiore*, was charged with organising the Capitoline Museum for Clement XII., and who enriched the Kircher collection with so fine a bequest; the complex cabinet of the Cardinal Zelada, another librarian; finally, the Greek manuscripts of the convent of Grotta Ferrata, and those of Cardinal Maï, acquired by Pius IX. There are eighteen Slav manuscripts, ten from China, twenty-two from India, thirteen from Armenia; two from the old land of the Iberians; eighty in Coptic, and one from Samaria; seventy-one from Æthiopia; five hundred and ninety of Hebrew origin, and four hundred and fifty-nine of Syrian; sixty-four from Turkey, seven hundred and eighty-seven from Arabia, and sixty-five from Persia, illustrated with fine miniatures.

The Gallery of Pictures, transferred in 1857 from the Borgian apartments to the top of the Vatican Loggie, passes for a wonder, because it is composed of hardly forty works, which are signed with the greatest names. Pius VII., who instituted it, placed there, in 1816, the pictures which were restored to Italy by France after the robberies of the first empire, and since that time the pontiffs have slightly enriched this museum, which owes more than one gem to the munificence of Pius IX.

One of the most remarkable pictures is the "Coronation of the Virgin," which Raphael executed in 1502 for the Benedictines of Perugia. It is a Perugino without leanness, with the same simplicity ennobled by an instinct of style; the taste of Raphael discloses itself with unconscious originality; you will recognise higher aspirations in it than in the work of Perugino. Still the "Virgin on the Throne," by the latter, surrounded by four Saints at prayer, is more clearly a master-work: we have a more perfect conviction that the artist has given complete expression to his whole idea. It is the apogee of the art which preceded the Dioscuri of the Renaissance, and perhaps

Perugino's masterpiece, containing exquisite figures, powerful in colouring, on a fine horizon with cleverly sketched buildings. He painted it for the Commune Hall of his native town. France, who

PORTA ANGELICA—PONTIFICAL RESIDENCE IN THE VATICAN.

carried it off, did not care to keep it: it was one of those unappreciated gems, with which the Thermidorian school reproached Bonaparte for loading his baggage-waggons.

Out of the forty-two pictures of this gallery, the Louvre received, and then gave back, one-and-twenty. But the works that were taken away from the pontifical states at the time of the victories of the French were not restored by the popes to the cities or to the establishments which had lost them: the convents and basilicas of Rome, the cities of Perugia, Pesaro, Foligno, even the sanctuary of Loretto, remained stripped for the benefit of the Vatican: is not this abuse of sovereignty rather like the excesses of victory? Let us also observe that the paintings which in 1797 gave rise to these spoliations by the French were by preference academic works due to Guercino, Valentin, Nicholas Poussin, Guido Reni, Andrew Sacchi; to the Bolognese, or the Romans, or the French who followed them. "The Virgin and St. Thomas" of Reni is one of the most mediocre pieces you can look at; yet it was dragged from Pesaro to Paris, and the Italians took it back with honour from Paris to the Vatican, instead of restoring it to Pesaro, so much did the name of Guido dazzle the people! As it may be curious to draw up in connection with the Pinacotheca the list of compulsory restitutions by the French after 1815, we will remind the reader that, out of twenty-one pictures taken back from Paris, Fra Angelico, Poussin, Valentin, Guercino, Michelangelo of Caravaggio, Giulio Romano, associated with Penni, called Il Fattore, figured each of them for one subject; Baroccio, Andrew Sacchi, Guido, each furnished two; Perugino three; Raphael five, among them that famous "Transfiguration" which occupies a room apart, facing the "Communion of St. Jerome" by Domenichino, a cardinal piece which the French had also to restore, and which, owing to a tradition of admiration, caused more bitter regrets to amateurs fifty years since than the sacrifice of all the rest of the gallery.

It remains to us to speak of the "St. Jerome" and the "Transfiguration," which face one another from each side of a vast casement, leaving in the background at the bottom of the room a picture which the fine world looks at far less—the Madonna of Foligno.

The "Transfiguration" of Raphael is assuredly a fine picture, although the author has emancipated himself in it from unity of action, which is lauded as a general thesis by the classic admirers of this master; they have had to admit the double vision of a poem in the clouds and a drama with its peripeteia on the earth. Jesus, transformed in the azure between Moses and Elias, the mystic figures of the apostles, the kneeling bodies of St. Laurence and St. Julian, the patrons of Cardinal Julius de Medici who was destined to become

Clement VII.—the whole of this scene of Tabor goes back further even than the youth of Raphael, up to the primitive Florentine traditions; only the prestige of an extremely ennobled style and design has prevented the filiation from being striking. This evangelical legend of the Transfiguration Raphael took as a theme before the first door of Ghiberti, and Ghiberti himself found the arrangement in Giotto.

From the time when Raphael Mengs classified this above all the works of the Sanzio, even to the day when Quatremère de Quincey proclaimed it the finest picture in the world, such doctrines must have exercised over taste an influence which explains the common infatuation for the Communion of St. Jerome. That was, as has been often enough repeated, the only picture fit to be compared with the Transfiguration. What a lesson for Raphael, if only it had not been posthumous! Nicholas Poussin, who placed on the same line two painters above all others, Raphael and Domenichino, considered the St. Jerome as one of the finest pictures in Rome. If we preserve independence and candour enough to shake off imperious prejudices, we shall recognise that the composition of the St. Jerome, too sensibly inspired by Augustin Caracci, is cold. Its principal charm is derived from a background of admirable landscape, under a sky on which hover some tolerably stiff angels.

It is time to penetrate into the numerous galleries consecrated to the masterpieces of antique art. This long journey we will begin with the primitive ages. It is to Gregory XVI. that the Vatican owes two collections, which take us back even beyond historic times to the origin of the arts in the farthest east and old Latium. The Pope Capellari was a Venetian; the establishment of the Egyptian museum, and the erection of an Etruscan museum, express the ideas of an artist and a scholar. Let us first make our way through the Egyptian galleries.

After getting together the elements of this colossal collection, the judicious Gregory XVI. undertook the task of separating, so as to make them the object of an instructive study, the Egyptian pasticci that fashion or caprice produced under the emperors, and particularly Adrian. The colossal marble Antinoüs, the last-born of the demigods of sculpture, is the capital piece of this section of the museum; it was found in the Villa Adriana. Like all the Antinoüses, this is executed with a feminine exquisiteness of rounded and velvety outlines. It is a figure cut by a Greek, under the hieratic arrange-

z

ment of the sacred royalties of Egypt, and in the attitude of a Roman: this threefold character is clearly indicated. The Nile, an enormous recumbent figure, is equally allied to Greek art.

After having seen among the Egyptians the remains of an art earlier than our written traditions, it is well to go and compare it on the spot with that of the Etruscans, of whose history we are ignorant. To pass from one study to the other, and from the first museum to the second, the eyes receive a very stirring distraction in the quarters of the Vatican Greece which you have to go through. It is impossible to help stopping in a certain hall which forms a vestibule, and which, being open on several sides, with a splendid staircase in three flights for ascending to the galleries, forms a centre in a very labyrinth of wonders of which you have vague glimpses.

This, through which we are passing, is called the Hall of the Greek Cross; an architectural gem. The mosaic in the middle, the red granites, the columns of coralline breccia and green porphyry which support the arched vaulting and lateral entablatures of the marble steps; those bas-reliefs set to right and left of the central archway; the vase of green granite which serves on the architrave as a point for the perspectives of the upper vault; the simplicity of a frieze in which lilies, stars, and eagles mix, and that Boreas of the storm,—pieces detached from the new arms of the good Pope Braschi; the sphinxes which guard the stairs, and that happy arrangement which allows three stories of splendours to be embraced under different lights; the animation, the modest richness, the delight one has in visiting at home, in an abode prepared for them, the gods and heroes of Attica—all this seductive harmony and peaceful movement affect one with a fulness of contentment so rare, that there results a lively intuition of the superiority of classic works when brought to such a point of perfection. This sanctuary, where you are surprised not to meet Alcibiades and Phryne, forms part of the charming constructions which Pius VI. intrusted to Camporese and Simonetti, two artists of high worth, and yet which no biography has thought it worth while to name. The great doorway of the hall is set up in Sienese granite; its two shafts, supporting Egyptian colossi serving as caryatides, rise under an entablature that bears vases of red granite; an entrance of severe beauty, brightened by a bas-relief which occupies the centre. You see those glorious profiles moving and ever renewed, as slowly, and with eyes drawn away on all sides at once, you ascend the steps leading to the Etruscan museum, the second creation of Pope Gregory XVI. This collection struck me as more curious than the other, for it was newer to me.

Researches having exhumed small objects, which belonged to usual life, in such numbers that this gallery is for the Etruscans, and perhaps Sabellians as well, what the Pompeian museum at Naples is for the Romans, we are in a position to characterise so many different works by establishing certain distinctions among them. I observed that in the domestic carvings, such as bas-reliefs, small bronzes, terra cotta, funeral monuments, the sentiment of the ideally or conventionally beautiful is, just as among the peoples of the west during the Middle Ages, subordinate to animation of expression; while in the decoration of ceramic works appears a certain idea of heroic form made slighter, it is true, by the wish to put the subjects on the stage in a clear and definite action. To bring out these characteristics by means of contrasts, they have exhibited Greek vases by the side of Etruscan vases with white grounds, which are the most ancient—two distinct sources that were long confounded together. The potiche of the Education of Bacchus, the great tazze or pateræ of the Argonautic series, are like our paintings and statues of the Roman period, but possessing more elegance; a superiority of taste that seems to be inherent in the Ausonian soil.

CHAPTER XXIV.

N paying homage to the persevering liberality which has endowed the universe with its most magnificent museum, we cannot help pointing out to the recognition and gratitude of nations four sovereigns of our age, who to crown so great a work surmounted many obstacles. These missionaries of art are Pius VI., Pius VII., Gregory XVI., and Pius IX. We should add Clement XIV., if by beginning the Clementine collection Pope Ganganelli had done more than yield to the impulse of his treasurer-general, Cardinal Braschi, who was shortly to become Pius VI.

You penetrate into this labyrinth by a long vaulted avenue, which Bramante built, and where Pius VII. organised the lapidary museum. At the bottom of the perspective you perceive a distant grating; it cuts the wide corridor in two; it is the barrier which limits this suburb. Tombstones and sarcophagi are drawn up in a double row along the preliminary alley, whose walls are a mosaic of inscriptions; just as, to come to Rome, you follow the Appian Way all lined with tombs, so you get into the Vatican city by a road of sepulchres. These monuments succeed one another over a length of nearly six hundred feet; all is classed by kinds, centuries, creeds, purposes. On one side extend, in rows over one another, family epitaphs; then friends, consular personages, patricians of imperial lineage; finally people belonging to the different trades. In front of this inlaying of marbles, set in the right wall, are arranged between the windows the sarcophagi as well as the inscriptions of new-born Christianity, pages taken from the Catacombs and written in Latin or Greek; sometimes in a hybrid tongue and illustrated by symbolical designs. These inscriptions are usually short but expressive; in presence of them we still perceive the ardent anguish of beings, turned to air these eighteen centuries past.

The first gallery of the Chiaramonti museum, organised by Pius VII., contains nearly eight hundred works of art; the heroic

THE CHIARAMONTI GALLERY.

figures, the tombs with their masks, the portraits, the gods accommodated to Latin rites, all tell you the ideal history of Rome, but written in Greek; not one work has come forth from the soil; the works of elegance and beauty are tribute paid to the conquering race by the vanquished of Athens and Argos; the sons of Homer formed to poetry, but they could never raise to sculpture, the soldiers who had to subdue a world. The Romans were masters only in architecture; it belonged to the legislators of property to teach nations the art of construction.

To approach all the marbles in these galleries would be to paraphrase a catalogue, so I shall do no more than mention what remain in my memory. The first is a bust of Julius Cæsar, the head draped as high pontiff on the point of sacrificing. Cæsar is represented in the last years of his life; his face, seamed and furrowed, betrays a supreme lassitude, the dry expression of a man who has exhausted everything. No word would convey the contemptuous majesty which, on this luminous and ruined head, unites with a mixture of nobility, pedantry, and moral desolation. How is it that they have not made a model of the masterpiece which transmits to us so profound a revelation? Further on, the fine sarcophagus of Junius Evhodus and his wife, found in the excavations at Ostia, represents the legend of Alcestis, copied from older bas-reliefs. This romance of conjugal love traced on the marble is a homage of Evhodus "to his very dear and very blessed wife, Metilia Acte." These people, who had little dread of death, prepared tombs most tastefully adorned, and gallantly offered like a madrigal to the loved object. Close by is a magnificent urn, where you see the grapes being trampled in a vat, and above, Bacchus seated with Ariadne—a work of the time of the Antonines. The collosal bust of the Pallas taken from old Laurentum would be worth a description. The Athlete in Repose, which the waves of the sea had rolled to the port of Antium, where it was found, is a figure of peculiar elegance; the bas-relief of Azzia Agela presents us, as surprised in the practice of the habits of domestic life, the deceased seated on a triclinium before her worktable. Near a colossal head of Octavianus, represented young, is a statue of his successor at the opening of his reign; Tiberius is seated, clothed in the chlamys, knotted over the shoulder, and crowned with oak-leaves; he holds with one hand a long sceptre, while the other rests on the Parazonium. This statue, found at Veii, is splendid; the aristocratic beauty of the features, the kindly animation which shines in the expression, gives to the head a fascination that throws suspicion on the veracity of Tacitus. The unique bust of Julia, the daughter of Augustus, was exhumed, under Pius IX., at Ostia, in the same place as the youthful Augustus in Parian marble, the most delicate likeness of the first of the emperors.

Let us be on our guard against incarnating the supple spirit of Cicero in that big, good-natured face, which we see in plaster in our French museums and provincial schools. The real Marcus Tullius, conformable to the authentic Greek medal published by Father St. Clement, is that lean head with meagre cheeks, with penetrating and caustic expression : a strangely living figure, whose expressive lines Themis and Apollo seem to have hollowed together. The great man has not on his nose the traditional mole ; for he was called Cicero like his father and like his brother Quintus, and not because he had a wart like a vetch on his face. The true bust of the Chiaramonti museum is numbered 423; and there is no cast of it.

A curious statue, the unique portrait of a Cæsar whose medals are most rare, is that of Diadumenianus, the son of Macrinus, whom Heliogabalus's soldiers massacred at the age of sixteen. Ælius Lampridius describes to what a degree the army was dazzled, when for the first time it saw this youth appearing in the imperial vestments, "*siderius et cœlestis.*" The colours of life play in his cheeks ; the sculptor has warmed the marble by investing it with certain effects of painting. Here, close by his side, is another Tiberius, of Pentelican marble, still very young, half naked, with drapery treated by a very skilful hand ; the latter, more real, has an air of astonishment almost of brutishness; the man of Capreæ seems to show himself. The head of Antoninus Pius (505) is of a fine character. The Cato (510), an empty face with hanging lower lip, is apocryphal. The colossal bust of Isis, "queen of the elements," as Apuleius says, a perfect

SARCOPHAGUS OF THE BACCHANTES (see p. 352).

THE BRACCIO NUOVO.

testimony of the emigration of this worship among the Greeks in the time of the Ptolemies, is of Pentelican marble. Near the draped bust of Annius Verus in his infancy (559), there is another, the free execution of which, stripped of every mere school process, deserves a glance; they suppose it to be Domitius Ænobarbus, the happy sire of Nero. Let us observe also a grand statue of an emperor, whom his decapitation makes anonymous, and between whose shoulders, in accordance with a too frequent practice, they have planted the head of Claudius. Although it has no longer arms or head, the statue numbered 638 has forms of such heteroclite beauty, that everybody fancies he sees an androgynous representation; the set of the drapery assigns it to a fine epoch of Grecian art. Treated with greater fancy and a purity which is not any less, the Ganymede carried away by an Eagle is a piece of irresistible effect; the wings of the metamorphosed Jupiter form a little pavilion over the head of the tearful *giovinetto*: "they often asked from the sculptor Leucares," Pliny tells us, "the reproduction of so successful a statue." It was near the mole of Cæcilia Metella that they discovered the bust of 698, bearing the name of Cicero: it is only mentioned here to prevent confusion with the real likeness mentioned above. Against the panel before this, the important sarcophagus of Nonius, in marble from Luna, deserves mention, though it is mediocre from the artistic point of view, and contemporary with Caracalla. These Nonii were a family of freedmen, grown rich in the oil trade, and having on the road to Ostia their villa and sepulchral mole. Between the pilasters of the sarcophagus they have cut a *mola asinaria*; but here the ass is replaced by a mare. The bas-relief represents the implements used in squeezing the olives; the hollow vessel for collecting the liquid, the *quartarius* and *sextarius* for measuring it, the pierced trowel for keeping back the kernels and the pulp, panniers and baskets —everything connected with such a business.

The Braccio Nuovo was built for a museum. The architect was aware that he would have forty-three very important statues to put in relief. So he divided the length of his gallery into twenty-eight niches, and the apse into fifteen, and he was thus able to set the statues in a series of arches; then before the pilasters which separate them he placed a row of as many busts on pillars of red granite. At the intersections of the arches are other busts supported on consoles; between the frieze and the keys of the arches bas-reliefs are set; an entablature with very projecting modillions serves as base for vaults, ornamented with coffer-work cut hollow into the stone, vaults supported by twelve Corinthian columns of the finest cipollino. Each of the

AUGUSTUS (BRACCIO NUOVO).

doors has its pediment resting on precious colums; the light falls amply distributed upon charming mosaic pavements; in the middle of the gallery rises a Greek vase of black basalt on a pedestal of red granite. Thus the gallery is constructed for what furnishes it, and the statues only form a natural decoration.

One of the important pieces of this gallery, the statue of Augustus, found several years ago at the villa of Livia, has replaced, in consequence of the munificence of Pius IX., the Antinoüs with the attributes of Vertumnus, which had been restored by the pupils of Canova. The Augustus is one of the good statues of the Vatican.

In one of the niches people admire the statue of Modesty, a large figure with a diadem on its head, whence a long veil falls back over the peplum, which covers a robe of heavier stuff with majestic folds. These three different draperies arranged over one another are admirably wrought; but we should only give a reserved acceptance to the hand, which is heavy, and to the head, which is only tolerably noble in its pose: both are modern; the head has been composed from medals, with a superior appreciation of antique art. Two very singular statues fronting one another, the one of Titus, the other of his daughter Julia, often stopped me by their pitiless reality. The son of Vespasian is short, squat, thick-set, with a good-humoured and sensual face; he wears big winter shoes; his figure and shape are particularly individual; you would recognise him from among a thousand, by back or side, as if you had lived in intimacy with him. A hive of honey is carved at his feet, the panegyric of a delicate symbolism. Fleshly, short, stout, like her father, Julia is of a masculine ugliness, cynically portrayed. The Faun of the gardens of Lucullus belongs to a pure art, and would be a gem if it had not been so much restored; the Euripides is an authentic likeness of a simple work, old, therefore, and of the best style; the Demosthenes, in a natural and collected position, with rather thin arms, a developed neck, a deep eye, a laborious brow, a lip on which eloquence is stamped, is the figure of a thinker and a master of expression. Here, truly, is the orator of the Olynthiacs, and not that athletic and shorn, mask portrait of some good liver which for so many years has been passed off in our schools of design for a famous Greek.

What a contrast with the true figure, so expressionless and morose, of an Athlete, a supple and vigorous frame, in which people consent to recognise the pure reproduction of a statue of Lysippus, that which the murmurs of the people forced Tiberius to restore to the Thermæ of Agrippa!

348 Rome.

THE PIO-CLEMENTINE MUSEUM.

There is plenty of character and spirit in the face of Antonius:

the man here seems above his part; the mouth especially has a slightly mocking delicacy which expresses a versatile intelligence, almost one of our own time, and, what is so unexpected, the madman who lost the empire of the world to follow Cleopatra has an air which is rather profoundly vicious than sensual. What a contrast with the face of Lepidus,—the head of a bird, with a toneless eye, a soft brow, a retreating chin which throws out an inert mouth; he is too like the part he played. A fine and curious statue is the Nile, half recumbent and surrounded by sixteen nurslings at play about his big body, and trying to climb up on to it; they represent the ascending

THE NILE (BRACCIO NUOVO).

degrees of the fertilising overflow of the stream, which to give a prosperous year has to mount sixteen cubits. The sixteenth seems to be coming to life out of a basket of fruits. The base represents ichneumons, plants, oxen, ibises, and even hippopotamuses. It was under Leo X. that near the Minerva, where Serapis had her temple, they exhumed this splendid piece. Let us still mention for their rarity the statues of Lucius Verus, of very studied finish; of Domitian, who recalls so closely the fraternal personages of Titus and Julia; and a superb bust of Luna marble representing Philip the Father, the predecessor of Decius—a very fine likeness for the time. You also pass a statue of Claudius, in which they have only had an arm to re-make, and on the features of which is plainly stamped the credulity of the husband of Messalina.

This is, as everybody will understand, only a feeble sketch of the hundred and thirty-six works of art among the Braccio Nuovo; among which, it is well to remark, between the bas-reliefs, a Marriage Scene, the Triumph of Marcus Aurelius, and that of Titus, in which you see better than in the arch of the Via Sacra, the ordering of the procession, the spoils of the Temple, those of the conquered, and the retinue of Israelitish prisoners. The very mosaics of the pavement are important, especially that representing the Travels of Ulysses, whose vessel, having just doubled the rock of Scylla, traverses the waves where they hear the song of the Sirens.

DEMOSTHENES (BRACCIO NUOVO).

As on your way to the Pio-Clementine Museum you pass a second time before the statues of the long Chiaramonti Gallery, these monuments, in their rather bare locality, after the splendours of the Braccio Nuovo, seem to be no more than the plebs of the Vatican city; but the return to this avenue is an inappreciable preparation for the crescendo effect, which will again quicken the attention by a series of surprises. One flight of stairs takes you to the great museum, where by a singular contrast you only meet at first a labyrinth of small chambers, sanctuaries each preserving its patron divinity. Clement XIII. and Clement XIV. began to unite together the collections formed by their predecessors from Julius II. downwards; but Pius VI. is the true founder of the Pio-Clementine Museum; he constructed seven large cabinets or galleries; his excavations and acquisitions enriched it with nearly fifteen hundred statues. The public approach the Belvedere by a square vestibule. In the middle of it is the Torso of the Belvedere, a colossal fragment of herculean stature in Greek marble. In the time of Alexander VI., when this marble was found near the theatre of Pompeius, models contemporary with Pericles were rarer than they are now. This possesses great value; for its author, Apollonius, son of Nestor of Athens, has affixed his name to it. And it made a revolution in art; Michelangelo studied it to such a degree that he was wont to call himself pupil of the Torso. In the round vestibule which comes next is a fragment of a statue with some remarkable drapery, a document which Raphael analysed; and a fine statue of a woman seated.

The next cabinet, containing the inscription of L. Mummius, the conqueror of Corinth, and a colossal bust of Trajan, is dedicated to Meleager, the ideal of beauty in the time of Canova. This celebrated figure, in which the hero rests on his lance between his dog and the head of the Calydonian boar, unites in a rare degree those qualities of elegance which began, nearly a century ago, to mark that lower kind of beauty which is sometimes called distinction.

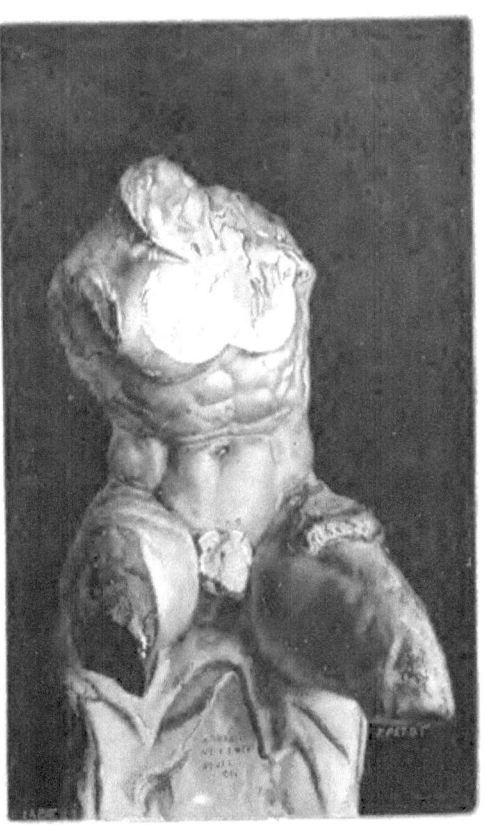

TORSO OF THE BELVEDERE.

We now come to the Octagonal Court, of which you would convey a more just idea by calling it a square, with portions cut out. Under the arches are placed separately, in a series of cabinets, so as to be seen without distraction, some pieces that are known to the whole world. Under this portico is the great sarcophagus found against St. Peter's, in digging the foundation of the sacristy, and which represents, in an exquisite design, a Dance of Bacchantes (see p. 343). Turning to the right, is a Sacellum dedicated to Canova, in the presence of the Perseus and the Pugilists. If Canova sometimes gives us his inspiration somewhat chilled, we cannot deny its power. The Perseus reveals rare gifts; but besides that the pose recalls with a less expressive accent the bronze of Cellini under the loggia of the Orcagna at Florence; the limbs have not the same bounding suppleness; the free, exquisite—one might almost say tender, limbs of the marble of Canova fall in the elaborate search for the distinguished.

THE PERSEUS OF CANOVA.

Before the great figure of marble, lustrous as an onyx, of the Apollo of the Belvedere, unexpected sensations awaited us. As it appeared to us in all its luminousness, against the greenish grey ground of the cabinet which it occupies alone, you are dazzled at the real incarnation of the god —*Deus, ecce Deus!* And suddenly an idea presents itself,—the copies are not faithful; people do not know it. Seized in a moment by an effort of supreme happiness, the pose has something more determinate, the expression of the face justifies it more formally, than in the multiplied reproductions in plaster. The head has nothing collected or cold; it is associated in every muscle with the power of the eye, of the lips, of the swelling nostrils; the glitter of the polish renders it moist and quivering. Whether the Apollo of the Belvedere is a Greek marble or marble of Luna, whether it has been copied from a bronze or not, these are secondary questions; the criticisms of the restorations of Montorsoli, seem to me mere puerilities. Found near the sea at Antium, and acquired by the Cardinal della Rovere, who first of all placed it in his palace adjoining the SS. Apostoli, the Apollo with which Julius II. crowned the Vatican is one of its most ancient conquests. It would have exercised a more prompt influence on art but for Michelangelo, who, under the charm of the Torso and some fragments (for he did not see the Parthenon), made the aberrations of the second Grecian epoch prevail over those of the third, which was less wide, but more seductive for the contemporaries of Canova.

Three Rhodian sculptors, Agesander, Polydorus, Athenodorus, have left no less renowned a group, occupying a separate division, and which was found in 1506 in the ruins of the palace of Titus, in the spot where Pliny had described it; this is the Laocoön. The effect of the original marble is so superior to that of the representations that we are led to consider them all as derived from copies, and not from a cast. In replacing a missing arm, Giovan Angelo Montorsoli has extended it, while, from certain signs left in the hair, it is

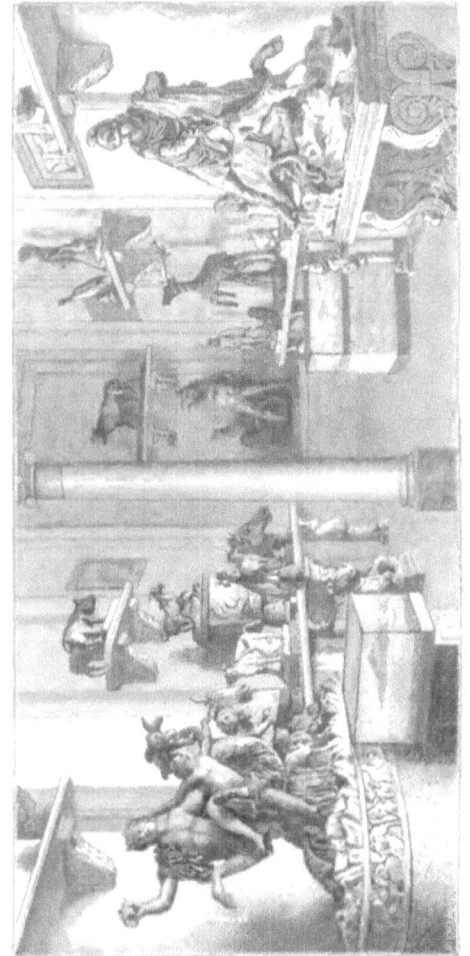

HALL OF THE ANIMALS (PIO-CLEMENTINE MUSEUM).

presumed that this arm was convulsively folded back behind the head with an expression of desperate grief. Others attribute this arm to Bacio Bandinelli; it would be difficult for me to explain without periphrases why I think it more modern. Pliny, who supposed the group to be cut in a single block (the sutures not then being visible), describes the Laocoön as *opus omnibus statuariæ artis præponendum*, and Michelangelo called it a miracle of art.

Round the five chapels, whose patrons we have now celebrated, you meet many monuments which ought to be examined at leisure, such as the bas-reliefs and sarcophagi, in which the usages of the life

ANTIQUE GROUP (HALL OF THE ANIMALS.)

and rites of pre-Christian faiths are described. Some historical figures diversify the curiosities of which the court is the centre; I remember a Venus-mater, with her Bambino, a likeness of the wife of Alexander Severus, at the foot of which is written that this statue was offered to their ancient mistress by her two freedmen, Sallustia and Elpidia.

In the cabinet of Mercury, a bas-relief on which they have cut an Egyptian procession in a primitive taste, struck me as remarkable for simplicity and ingenuous grace. Let me also mention the panel of an ancient tomb (60) on which, between likenesses and genii, you discover through a half-open door the interior perspective of a temple; and the bas-relief of the Sacrifice to Mithra, on the cornice of which we read, *Soli invicto deo;* and the Roman lady as Bacchante, lying with graceful abandonment on the sepulchre where she sleeps so heavily; and the large bas-relief (81) representing a Sacred Procession, with lictors, and likenesses of consuls and pontifices; and the Ossuary, in the form of a house, which held the remains of Quintus Vitellius; and the elegant sarcophagus of the Nereids . . . . . To be equitable one ought either to mention all, or to refer to nothing; but when the memory is full, this is not easy.

The Hall of the Animals was begun by Pius VI., and established by his successor. This collection has been cleverly arranged by Francesco Franzoni, whose numerous restorations are generally supple and well conceived : Franzoni, one of the celebrities of modern sculpture, a name well known in Rome, is absent from all our biographies, miscalled universal, which ignore equally a good half of the masters of the Florentine school. In the Attack on a Young Stag we find a peculiar

MENANDER (PIO-CLEMENTINE GALLERY).

species of hound, of a spring and muscular power excellently rendered, and with rare beauty; the type is less flat-nosed than ours; the ears are cropped as we crop them now. At the side is the Combat between a Bear and a Bull. The two Greyhounds, of which one playfully bites the ear of the other, are the Apollo and Venus among greyhounds: you would say as much of the Hunting-Dogs, of the Whelp putting out its paw, of the Setter of violet brecchia, of a Bull of the same marble, of the Cows, of the Running Greyhound, and many other subjects. Horses are rare, but in the midst of this marble menagerie an important place is given to grotesques and to animals for food; the pleasures of the table flourished at the beginning of the empire. There are ducks, cocks and hens, quails, a goose whose pose is a masterpiece of observation; a lobster in green Carrara marble which cheats you into thinking it real; water-fowl, a hare, a bustard; a turkey, the merit of which can only be fully appreciated by people who have had to contend with this humoursome beauty and its gobbling anger. Among the burlesques one must not leave out a toad in antique red; nor the rats and crabs of green porphyry, and the scorpions; nor the lynx, and some curious storks quaintly represented. In the Group of Mithras, where a bleeding bull has his blood licked up by a dog stretching to reach the wound, the accord of the style with reality is surprising. In composing the Rape of Europa, the artist has skilfully made the divinity of Zeus radiant on the head of the bull. Hercules drags away the Nemean lion, which is dead enough, and whose slackened limbs possess a surprising reality. I should omit the Commodus on horseback in hunting-dress, if it had not inspired Bernini with his equestrian figure of Constantine under the portico of St. Peter's: this landmark will help to find, close by, the group of the eagle with its brood of eaglets, huddled together like the voracious dynasty of the pelican. It is a work of astonishing vigour. The Panther of veined alabaster, with its stripes given by the marble, is a gem; but the recumbent Tiger in Egyptian granite, coarsely modelled in surfaces in so stubborn a material, is still more remarkable. The Lion in grey marble, larger than life, with a calf's head between its claws, is curious in point of execution; the body, of superlative polish, has a fleshy solidity that is exaggerated, to give lightness and crispness to the mane, which is very abundant, and is still left shaggy and heavy. There are the head of a cow and the head of an ass crowned with ivy, which are models; the second, in grey marble, seems a depository of the soul common to the whole race of nags. And what charming groups! The small Goat bitten by an asp, the Stork defending against two serpents a frightened she-goat and a kid at suck; the Sow with her litter, superb in mass, with much character extracted from a simple hint; the Pelican holding her young in her open sides, the Chained Cerberus carried away by Hercules . . . . . one ought really to refer to all.

Two personages seated at the end of the Pio-Clementine Gallery attracted me so, that, to rejoin them the more rapidly, I neglected plenty of other wonders on my way. The one to the right is Posidippus, and the other Menander. The statue of Posidippus, simply wrought, in harmony with the familiar ease of the attitude, is clad in a tunic, and with the pallium thrown over the left shoulder. The poet, a true academic head, wrinkled with age, but subtle and pensive, holds a roll between his fingers, which have rings on them.

Menander is robust and younger; in fact, he scarcely lived beyond fifty years. It is by his resemblance to the likeness in the famous bas-relief of the Farnesina that Quirinio Visconti recognised this prince of Greek comic authors, who most likely lived before Posidippus. The attitude has more movement; the poet in repose, with his left arm resting on the round back of the seat, his head inclined as for study of what is passing before him, has the conformation of a man of alertness, with the roundly caustic expression of an observer wearied of the scenes of the world.

THE ARIADNE (PIO-CLEMENTINE GALLERY).

Turning back after thus saluting the master of Plautus, we come upon an Apollo Citharædus, in whom *cognoscenti* claim to recognise Nero—a more than doubtful assertion. There follow the Wounded Adonis, as beautiful and as stupid as he ought to be; the Bacchus lying down, of great repute, because it has become defaced, which gives it a false air of the grand epoch, and rescues it from dryness;

the Opelius Macrinus, the unique statue of an emperor of whom the medals are rare, an interesting monument of the art of the third century, when the science of interpretation was yielding to the mechanical imitation of nature. Treasures are buried on all sides in Rome; the enormous Bath of oriental alabaster was recently found in the middle of the Piazza SS. Apostoli, in repairing a water-conduit. Nearly opposite, beside Æsculapius, is Hygeia, the goddess of health; a friend whom you find passing fair the moment she leaves you, the statuary regretted her perhaps, for he has made her adorable. This figure, which must belong to about the same time as the Danaid of Præneste, is far from equalling the Faun leaning on the trunk of a tree, which was discovered in the Marsh of Ancona, and is a copy from Praxiteles; the original, mutilated and reduced to a torso, was found in the excavations on the Palatine. Finally, under an arch between columns of antique yellow flanked by candelabra of marble, with figures worth describing, is lying that celebrated figure of Ariadne deserted, which an ophidian bracelet caused people to take for Cleopatra, when Julius II. had this masterpiece placed in the Belvedere. The tunic half undone, the sorrowful features, the veil falling from the head, the tumbled folds of the drapery—all indicate the prostration which follows violent anguish. The sarcophagus of the struggling Giants whom we see changing into hydras—the pedestal of this noble piece—is of an inferior and later school.

These galleries are so rich in likenesses, that they present images of royal children hardly mentioned in history, such as Annius Verus, a son of Marcus Aurelius, who was proclaimed Cæsar at the age of three, and who died three years afterwards. When you have visited the Capitol and the Vatican, you know the great people of the Roman empire more distinctly than our own kings and heroes anterior to Henry VIII.

CHAPTER XXV.

To go through the great Italian gardens that were planned in the fifteenth and sixteenth centuries is to acquire an idea of the paradises realised by proconsuls, and discovered later by the ascetics in their mystic dreams. The Eden of the successors of St. Peter and Julius II. is a poetic solitude. On three sides the perspectives extend by views over the distant country, and the foreground composed of architecture like rock-work, of marbles and clipped foliage, prepares happy contrasts with the thickets, the brambles, the scorched hills; next with the violet undulations, and sometimes the snows that lie beyond. The valley is divided into compartments; limited by terraces, the squares where low plantations make figures of rosettes, are framed by walls, tapestried with orange-trees cut into hedges, in which the gold of fruits and the perfumed alabaster of the blossoms give animation to the foliage. Shut in by partitions of box and laurel, high as groves of oak, the avenues cross and recross one another, half veiled by those shades which call the night and prepare for mystery. Here and there antique tombs give colour to dreams, and statues, now and again standing out in the hedges, give you a start.

You thus advance from surprise to surprise, hesitating which way to go; for at each outlet you feel yourself drawn away, as far as the Loggia, a miniature villa which was constructed by that lucky namesake of the Medici, who owed their patronage to his name, and who, to justify so ambitious a relationship, instituted seminaries, founded the Vatican painting establishment, and directed Pirro Ligorio, his architect, by the traditions of the reigns of Leo X. and Clement VII. This construction, the most irregular of works in taste and style, gives a happy idea of the caprices and jovial humour of Pius IV. In truth, never have the debauches of architecture dreamed since by our painters of gay merrymakings exceeded the amusing simplicity of this *chinoiserie* which was inspired by Giovanni da Udine. Terraces, open galleries, cabinets of painting, marbles and rock-work, bas-reliefs and festoons of verdure, baths and boudoirs, basins and fountains, are all mixed in premeditated confusion; unforeseen effects are renewed at every step; the mosaic and the quaint delicacies of the statuary are further enlivened by the pencil of Baroccio, Zucchari, and Santi di Tito.

I proceeded to the end of the Gallery of Maps, the farthest of the halls of the second story. Between the thirty which on one side, as on the other, give light to this long perspective, Gregory XIII., the reformer of the calendar, had painted in colours enormous maps of the provinces of Italy. By his order, the gallery was furnished with marble benches and a double row of Hermes, antique busts resting on high pedestals. Simply paved, this chamber has for vault a many-coloured paradise of medallions, of coffer-work, or trophies of stucco framing paintings, where projecting pediments are peopled with statuettes flitting under the arches, and representing Loves or Angels, according to the disposition of the spectator. I traversed rapidly the Gallery of Maps, and I did the same with that of Tapestries. You are astonished to find even under the roofs, above the Chiaramonti Museum, new aisles as high and as rich in columns, archways, precious marbles, and splendidly decorated vaults. Paved with polished marble, in which the pedestals of four porphyry columns are reflected, the Galeria degli Arazzi is of more sober ornamentation; it was only finished under Pius VIII.: all interest is invited by these famous tapestries which Leo X., for the decoration of the Sixtine chapel, had executed from designs furnished by Raphael. They are fourteen in number, but they only attribute eleven to the master himself, the same number as the cartoons. I had seen the seven of them which are at Hampton Court. The Tapestries are more finished, and of a richer shade of colour, and they do honour to the Flemish workmen, for they have worked without heaviness, from simple hints; but then in these hints what freedom, what brightness! Below the principal subjects, which offer scenes taken from the Gospels, are arranged between the borders, almost as a sort of predella, other subjects, borrowed from the history of the Medici.

As I had a long way to go, I can only mention in passing the most remarkable pieces in the Gallery of the Candelabra, such as the Great Bowl in which Silenus and the Fauns make the vintage,—a work of a fine style; the wounded Phrygian Soldier, a piece of a later age, but of extreme vigour; the small Vase of brown Egyptian granite; the Ceres with fine draperies in Parian marble; the Bowl in which horses and dolphins carry Neptune; the Cup of red oriental granite streaked like Spanish beans; and that which has such pretty handles, composed of adders twisted into masks (it is of superfine porphyry, dark green on light green, with marblings). These gems are on altars of marble

GALLERY OF THE CANDELABRA.

and jasper, covered with inscriptions. On another vase, in the shape of a mortar, are sketched emblems mixed with animals; you could not believe the degree to which, among so many objects of classic execution, the differences in process are numerous and extraordinary. The Mortar round which Bacchantes dance in a ring, as well as its cylindrical base, in which cities and provinces figure, is a model of grace and lightness. If one allowed oneself to be fascinated by the splendour of certain gems, such as a Goblet, a Vase in semi-transparent alabaster, streaked with concentric zones, and two other Vases of rose-coloured alabaster, veined with the tenderest shades, one would run the risk of passing inattentively the splendid sarcophagus which serves as a support for them, of which the bas-reliefs are very remarkable.

As I left the Hall of the Candelabra, and went by the magnificent staircase of Simonetti, I entered the circular hall of the Biga, so called because Pius VI. had placed in the centre a chariot with two horses, a Biga of marble, which long served in the church of St. Mark

THE BIGA.

for a cathedra. Entrusted with the restoration of this Greek car, the pole of which ending in a ram's head had been preserved, Franzoni fitted wheels that are somewhat heavy, he made a new head for the fine galloping courser, of which Prince Borghese had made a present to the holy father, he created a second horse, and the monument was re-established. To plant a head in the antique style on an admirable equestrian torso is no vulgar merit, and this restoration is a masterpiece of the kind; only the ornamentation of the car, composed of foliage flowing among rosettes, and mingled with wheat-ears, was of inimitable workmanship. The whole seemed so wonderful to

Pius VI. that, to instal the Biga, he had this rotunda constructed by Camporese, with a cupola imitated from the Pantheon, resting on a marble cornice, supported by eight fluted columns with Corinthian capitals. Besides the famous chariot, the hall of the Biga contains some pieces of value: an Indian Bacchus of the second century, a bearded figure with long plaited hair, clad in a sleeved tunic, with

CASINO OF PIUS IX.

sandals;—the small sarcophagi with the races of the circus drawn on them: interesting pieces, for the one comes from the catacomb of St. Sebastian, while the other, which was found in the same vineyard as the tomb of the Scipios, is of rare delicacy. Let us also recall the Apollo Citharædus, and the Discobolos of Pentelican marble, found on the Appian Way, a celebrated statue, so correct as to have acquired a didactic value. Still, notwithstanding its irreproachable proportions, how inferior it seems to the reproduction of the Discobolos of Myron, placed close by! The admirably posed figure of a young athlete hurling the discus shows a nature at once full of spring and strength; the arms and chest modelled broadly with simplicity, the secret of

[EXIT FROM THE PONTIFICAL GARDEN.

which was too soon forgotten, recall the great epoch symbolized by the name of Phidias. The artist who drew his inspiration from the bronze of Myron, has written on the base, at the foot of which is a strigil: ΜΥΡΩΝ ΕΠΟΙΕΙ. The huntress Diana, with a quiver on her shoulder and a dog by her side, is thrown into a kind of movement, and displays a face which reminds us of the gallant figures of the youth of Louis XIV.; but what a model of grace and execution!

The Round Hall is the splendid and striking restoration of an antique saloon. You would suppose yourself there to be in the galleries of Mæcenas, of Verres, of Cicero, or of Titus, and you may

THE ROUND HALL.

analyse the causes of this illusion. To create the Round Hall, that great and venerable friend of the arts whom we call Pius VI. proceeded like the contemporaries of Augustus; he disposed the casket for gems he had collected beforehand, instead of doing as we do, who build a box without thinking beforehand of the contents. The pontiff Braschi possessed eight fine colossal figures, ten busts, an enormous vase of red porphyry, and the mosaic pavement of an ancient rotunda. So he placed a cupola upon ten fluted pilasters of Carrara marble; between each of them they made an arched niche, to hold the great statues on pedestals of Greek marble; before each pilaster were placed the busts on brackets of red porphyry; the mosaic of Otricoli, where Medusa is encircled by the Combat by the Lapithæ and Centaurs, and where Tritons move with Nymphs and Chimæras, was again made the pavement of an antique hall; finally, the basin of red porphyry, forty-one feet in circumference, found in the Thermæ of Diocletian, was installed in the middle of the hall erected to contain it. In this rich arrangement all is justified, all contributes to a certain harmony, all is homogeneous and seems to belong to one and the same age.

Whilst visiting these halls in the garden the light had changed its zone; the already purpling rays of evening were falling on to the western slopes of the Vatican, and the shadows of the trees spread over the flower-beds. Far as I could see, not a soul was visible; the statues, like vain spectres, only brought me into irritating mistakes; the air was stifling and dumb; the nests were silent.

Around is no noise; in the air from time to time the clear ring of some convent bell. But to complete my tour through the gardens, to which I should never surely return, I ascended the path which had fascinated me, and turned towards the sacred groves of the spot. A few glimpses and openings allow you to follow the oblique course of the Tiber through the Campagna; sarcophagi bequeathed by the earliest Christian ages disclosing themselves among the brambles, you decipher Cæsarean inscriptions under the ivy; Diana, the nymphs, Sylvanus, the god Pan, shine out from the masses; they are at home, and have no look of shivering in their exile, as in our northern regions.

CHAPTER XXVI.

IN the year of grace 1511, on All Saints' Day, Julius II. offered to the admiration of his court the three first frescoes of Raphael in the chamber of the Segnatura, as well as the still unfinished paintings with which Michelangelo, since May 8, 1508, had been decorating the vault of the Sixtine Chapel. Nothing had been seen hitherto comparable to these masterpieces, which have never been surpassed in subsequent times; so their appearance assigns a precise date to the culminating point of the Renaissance.

Projects, which had nothing ambitious about them, prepared these considerable results. In coming to the Holy See, Pope Julius felt a repugnance to inhabit apartments that had been defiled by the Borgia family, and he had others made ready on the upper story; then he wished, in memory of his uncle, Sixtus IV., to decorate the ceiling of the chapel which this pontiff built. With the clear-sightedness of a man of taste and authority, he entrusted the apartments to Raphael of Urbino, who had been presented to him by Bramante, and, while fully appreciating Sanzio, he required that the vast spaces of the Sixtine vault should be taken by Buonarotti, who would fain have declined, who had never tried fresco, and to whom it was necessary to give lessons as to a scholar, before he executed as his first essay the finest page that any master has ever traced.

For this enormous work Bramante recommended Michelangelo; Michelangelo recommended Raphael. Julius II. held to his point; he fell into such fury, that Buonarotti had to yield. A novice as a painter, he, who was covered with glory as a sculptor, was thirty-four years old; Raphael was only five-and-twenty. Both had drunk of the Dantean spring, both had received the religious and liberal tempering which, under the influence of Savonarola, warmed the last inspirations of the school of Umbria; finally, the eldest and most energetic had not yet exercised any ascendancy over the other.

THE IGNUDI (VAULT OF THE SIXTINE CHAPEL).

The first time I crossed the threshold of the Sixtine Chapel, the lower part of the church, which only is accessible to the public, was crowded with people, because the sovereign pontiff was to assist at mass; cardinals, secular and regular, robed in grey or red, furred in ermine, occupied the benches of the sacred college, divided from the faithful by a high balustrade. I was struck with the simplicity of the building: a high long hall reduced to the four walls, without architectural ornaments, with rectangular windows pierced over the frieze. To the right, a tribune half grated, with trellis-work for the choristers; at the bottom a very simple altar with four steps in front, covered with a carpet; to the right of this altar, which has only six tapers, separated from the great piece of the Last Judgment by the mantle of a narrow baldachin, a raised seat for the pope; that is the Sixtine Chapel. It has no other decorations but the paintings with which it is entirely covered, up to a height of some fifteen feet above the ground. It was to furnish the lower part that Leo X. commissioned Raphael to execute on subjects of Holy Scripture the series of compositions, of which the artist painted between 1515 and 1518 eleven cartoons, to be executed in tapestry at Arras.

Antonio of San Gallo constructed the Pauline Chapel for Pope Paul III., who had it decorated with large frescoes: Buonarotti, become indistinguishable, falls into full accord with Zuccarri and with Lorenzo Sabbatini of Bologna. Let us hasten to remark as an extenuating circumstance, that the two frescoes of the author of the Pensieroso, ill preserved and copiously restored, have been much compromised; but there are plain remains of the composition, the idea, the design of the general outline. That which represents the Conversion of St. Paul on the road to Damascus is coldly academic; the Saint, in a coldly forced attitude, only represents a pose inflicted on a model; Vasari would have been less slack, and he could not have been harsher. In the Crucifixion of St. Peter, placed opposite, the apostle, executed with his head downwards, raises it already suffused with blood, by a convulsive effort which contributes to the *anatomic sonata*, and gives it a skilful and most horrible grimace for theme. We should attribute to a pupil of Bronzini the no less morbid representation of St. Paul, who in the other picture seems thrown over on his side, blind and stupefied, while his horse takes to flight, and his companions stand round him in terror. Postures, muscles, torsoes, instructive qualities, forms sanctioned by convention, yes; but soul, sentiment, inspiration,—seek for these! You discover in the sky a Choir of Angels, crossed by the Christ launched against his crushed foe. God plunges from the clouds head foremost, like a sunbeam or a rock; this has been borrowed by Tintoretto in his Miracle of St. Mark.

Between the services, which are not very frequent, the paraphernalia of worship do not encumber the wide Presbyterium of the chapel; this vast oblong hall, with painters at work in it, puts on the appearance of a studio. The steps by which you mount to the altar, the lateral steps which raise the stalls of the choir, are covered with a green carpet, which on Sundays brings out so effectively the long trains of the purple mantles, and which on the open days offers relief to eyes that are fatigued by the mass of paintings. Let us not forget that besides those of the ceiling and of the friezes, and the Last Judgment, the nave is divided into twelve large frescoes, divided from one another by settings that simulate pilasters, and are enhanced by arabesques matching the golden chandeliers. The neighbourhood of Michelangelo does cruel wrong to these works, which are really interesting and considerable; for they were executed here between 1475 and 1500, under Sixtus IV., Innocent VIII., and Alexander VI., and are due to the coryphæi of the most brilliant epoch of the Precursors.

The six frescoes on the left are consecrated to passages from Exodus and Deuteronomy; those on the right are taken from the narratives of the Gospel.

Near the altar a picture of Perugino, the Baptism of Christ on the banks of the Jordan, a work executed in conjunction with Andrew of Assisi, and in which the amusement of a picturesque landscape weakens the interest of the personages, answers to the Journey of Moses and Zipporah to strive against Pharaoh. It is the moment when the prophet sees himself menaced on his road by an angel who is turned aside by the daughter of Jethro, a symbolical figure of the Virgin interceding. The emblem has been seized with a rare sentiment by Luca Signorelli, the favourite pupil of Piero della Francesca, that conquest of Perugino, which Michelangelo, who loved the artist, could not entirely recover. The work has a charm; it is superior to the piece by Perugino; the Angel seen from behind, the placid Moses, Zipporah, the landscape, all is fed with Florentine ambrosia. The most eminent of the pupils of Filippo Lippi, Sandro Botticelli, whom Sixtus IV. set over the undertaking of this decoration, has grouped in one frame, Moses slaying an Egyptian,—Watering the Flocks of Jethro,—Putting to Flight the Midianite Herdsmen,—and Coming to the Burning Bush. Opposite the same painter has placed Christ tempted by Satan; a subject admirably arranged, peopled with graceful figures, and faces of life-like serenity.

Farther off, Jesus calls to him Peter and Andrew, as Moses had called Aaron and the chiefs of the tribes who followed him out of Egypt through the waters of the Red Sea; a parallel recalled in two splendid frescoes. Cosimo Rosselli executed one, which is too rich in details; the first master of Michelangelo, Domenico Ghirlandajo, who, in the apse of Santa Maria Novella, reproduced so curiously, in his Life of the Virgin, the usages and fine society of the fifteenth century, executed the other. The scene passes on the banks of a river which retreats in perspective, marked by monuments and slopes; a poetical point of view, in the foreground of which are the truly religious figures of Christ and the two apostles who are to follow him. To the Adoration of the Golden Calf, episode of the presentation of the tables of the law, Rosselli has opposed the Sermon on the Mount, in which the landscape, which is charming, is supposed to have been painted by Piero di Cosimo. A number of figures arranged with grace, an action well rendered—such are the salient merits of this picture, in which one cannot forget peculiarly likeable and truthful groups of attentive women. Peter Perugino, taking his revenge, is superior to Botticelli representing Korah, Dathan, and Abiram, where the last mystic of the Umbrian school seems to add size to its qualities, to represent the Christ handing the keys to St. Peter: never has this master shown himself so simple and so noble. The composition has a monumental character, enhanced as it is in the background by two triumphal arches of fine architecture, between which we recognise the polygonal temple that in his Spozalizzio at Milan, Raphael could not have copied there, as is said; for at the time when this artist painted it he had not come to Rome. Both of

JULIUS II.

them, Perugino first, then Sanzio, borrowed this monument of fancy from a charming bas-relief of Orcagna on the tabernacle of Or' San-Micaële, which bas-relief presents, besides, the Marriage of the Virgin, exactly as Raphael reproduced it a hundred and twelve years after Orcagna's death. I do not know whether I ought to claim the priority in an observation which I never read anywhere.

To the Promulgation of the Ancient Law, followed by the Death of Moses, by Signorelli, answer in the evangelical chronicles the Institution of the Eucharist and the Passion of Christ. To put himself in harmony with the outcome of Mosaic history, Cosimo Rosselli was careful to show us, beyond an open loggia behind the Cœna, the distant drama of the Garden of Olives, and the lines of the cross on the horizon. The principal subject is admirable for gravity and contained emotion; Judas seems to me to have all the air of some usurer. In spite of the Flemish retouchings of the sixteenth century, described by Taja, this fresco is extremely fine: Luca Signorelli and Sandro Botticelli seem to me to occupy the first rank in this interesting exhibition, the last ray of the fair days of Florence and Umbria. For the rest, Michelangelo, while extinguishing the torch of the first, even here pays him homage by numerous borrowings from the Last Judgment of Orvieto. These two precursors ended in obscurity, especially Botticelli, who, after having shone with a livelier brilliance, was reduced to get the bread of his old years by a subterfuge. They received him at the Hospital of Santa Maria Nuova of Florence where he deposited large chests of great weight and well-sealed, while he promised his inheritance to this house of refuge, which procured him interested attention down to the end of his days. On the death of the painter in 1515, they opened the chests, and found in them only stones,

THE PROPHET JOEL (CEILING OF THE SIXTINE).

The Ceiling. 373

And now let us stretch ourselves out on the green carpet of the cardinals; let us make a cushion of a footstool, and, like Jacob, let us gaze upon the heaven opening. To subject to a certain order the figures which he designed to create, to obtain the means of varying their proportions and multiplying their number without introducing confusion, to diversify the surfaces by depths, and to graduate the interest, Michelangelo provided as ground for the ensemble of the work an architectural deception, which makes air and distances intervene in this enormous field, peopled with episodes united in a capacious symmetry. He simulated on the border vertical pilasters, adorned with bas-reliefs, as well as an entablature on which appears to rest a vaulting, divided into arches producing a series of central medallions, forming nine deep openings. In consequence of these arrangements, and by the help of a linear decoration, clear in tone, and thrown out by projections of shadow, the artist has transformed into a storied vault what is really only a ceiling.

DELPHIC SIBYL (CEILING OF THE SIXTINE).

On the sides between the windows, the Prophets and the Sibyls, strange impersonations, truly antique types of a theogony and an art that are new, seem in continuation of the friezes to bear the sky of the vault on their heads, and raise it still higher. There have never been called to the service of a deception such magnificent creations as these figures, so full of life, so solemn, so tormented in spirit as the holy books describe them, and redeeming their incoherence by simplicity of execution, by the suppression of every trivial ornament, by the truth of the draperies in all their magnificent amplitude. Genii and emblematical figures of a dainty kind accompany and harmonise these colossi of beauty—yes, of beauty; the term includes the charm which is accessible even to the vulgar, and which subsequently Michelangelo disdained for the exaggerations of force. The Erythræan Sibyl, whose head is attached with admirable skill, has a profile of exquisite purity; in pose gracefully contrived to bring out exquisite arms, the Delphic Sibyl is not only very fine, but extremely attractive and charming in her vague and dreamy expression. These legendary Pythonesses are absent-looking, and as if unconscious; they listen with amazement to what the divine Spirit forces them to announce, without being able to understand it.

I am particularly struck by the extraordinary aspect of the Prophets; one seems to have always dreamt of them as this. Their images disclose persons of another faith, of another race, than those of Greece; as robust, but tormented in spirit and consumed by study. Their powerful heads, whose beauty is wholly intellectual, a source of expression and of diversity unknown among the Greeks, have the air of discovering the decrees of the future, or to succumb to the fatigues of inner toils; it seems as if the breath of God had burnt them! The dogmatic epopee of the Bible, fixed in the youthful memories of Michelangelo by the paraphrases of Savonarola, is illustrated here with the impetuosity of a Dantean poet, with the gravity of a Christian who believes his legend.

Sovereign authority is so inherent in the giant of the Renaissance, that, by an involuntary transposition, the spirit incarnates it, so to speak, in all his impersonations of supreme power. It has been said that he has depicted himself in the likeness of Julius II.; people think they come upon him also in the stricken and inspired heads of the Prophets; in his Moses we hear him breathe; and the Father of the creation is more than ever Michelangelo. He too has *created*, without a reminiscence of pagan antiquity, and created in perfection, the Man and the Woman, prototypes unknown until then. As for the Father, "*principium et fons*," it is Michelangelo who has dreamed the least commonplace image of the Being who reproduced himself in us, to launch it, either across the chaos which the resistless will is dispersing, or on the waters over which it moves like the breath of a spirit, or in the clouds, where it kindles the stars; three frescoes as strange as they are sublime.

God, in fact, draws from the slime, as a reflection of himself, the First Man, whom we see on an inclined plane, as on the edge of a planet, starting into life, placid, wondering, naked on the naked earth. Force, elegance, and subtle harmony of form have produced nothing in painting which is comparable to this; the innocent, expressive head, in which thought has just dawned, in which instinctive gratitude is the prelude to adoration, is of a touching inspiration, and so it is modern and Christian. The pose of Adam, half recumbent, resting on one elbow and the other arm stretched out towards God, the attitude which from the right shoulder to the foot gives a nobly balanced outline, is admirable; and wrapped in a dark flying drapery, upheld by a group of angels crowding into this conch of drapery as into a nest, God the Father, Olympian and smiling, hovers in the air; approaching our planet without touching it, he extends his arm towards the extended arm of his creature, and with the index touching the index of the first man, he has just imparted to him the vital fluid, and

THE CREATION OF MAN (FROM THE ROOF OF THE SIXTINE).

brought to life within him that spark of light which is the soul. There is here a quite new idea, which seems as if it had been inspired by modern sciences—the transmission of life by the electric contact of two fingers which meet. The group of seraphim surrounding the Father of the universe, while it adds to the charming figures of the composition, enhances the majesty of God and the gravity of his presence. The Creation of the Woman who, born of the side of the slumbering Adam, throws herself forward towards the Creator, sooner awake, readier to present herself, than the Man, also reveals to us beauties that have no rivals. God eyes her pensively, severely, without illusion; nothing can be more imposing than the sibylline majesty of that draped figure, who reads the future and foresees the annals of the world down to Calvary.

It is for the next subject, the Fall of Man and his expulsion from Eden, that the author has reserved, so far as the woman goes, all the philtres of the fountain of beauty. Once engaged in the perilous work of her sex, Eve will become wholly resistless; stooping in a posture which shows her charms at the best, at the foot of the tree to which her companion already stretches out his hand, she turns towards the serpent, with an androgynous body coiled round the

THE CREATION OF WOMAN (FROM THE ROOF OF THE SIXTINE).

trunk, eyes which try their power, while the treasures of her bosom are directed on the side of Adam. Thus the presentation of the first woman is double in some sort; God created the mother of human creatures, splendid for fecundity; the Serpent transforms her, and produces the Siren. Michelangelo has made her so lovely, that Raphael, to preserve the recollection, came and copied her with his own hand; Lawrence acquired this drawing, which I have seen at Oxford.

In many of these compositions, Buonarotti has drawn his inspiration from a master little known among us; but he was great, for he

The Fall of Man.

possessed in germ the style of Michelangelo, and he lived nearly a century before him. There is some analogy between the two careers: Jacopo della Quercia (of Siena), for whose works people contended, was harassed and oppressed by two towns which tore him from one another, just as Buonarotti was by Pope Julius and the Medici. It was in 1506 and 1507, fifteen months before undertaking the roof of the Sixtine, that Michelangelo saw the bas-reliefs which frame the portal of San Petronio of Bologna. This shows the empire of tradition, and in no way lessens the glory of Buonarotti; it would be otherwise if he had remained inferior: it is thus that the Eve of the

THE FALL OF MAN (FROM THE ROOF OF THE SIXTINE).

Barberini Palace, inspired by the first fresco of the Sixtine, adds nothing to the renown of Domenichino.

The Sacrifice of Noah, the Deluge, the Drunkenness of Noah, complete the incomparable series. This last subject is striking by a mixture of grace and gravity which, considering the scope, possesses a fitness that is really full of distinction. On the pendentives of these feigned vaultings, one would remark quite as much, if they were of more important dimensions, a dozen other subjects, among which we will content ourselves with calling attention to the Brazen Serpent, in which we cannot behold without emotion a dying woman stretching forth her arms; then Judith, after her expedition, dexterously arranging, in a basket balanced on the head of her attendant, the head of Holofernes. The heroic criminal is seen from behind; you expect her to turn round, such skill has the painter shown in making you suppose that she must be of a triumphal beauty.

But why dissertation, when homage is so much more becoming! Let us conclude by noting an impression that every one has felt. On the days when you have visited the Sixtine, it is impossible to take any interest in other works until the next day; even statuary seems gloomy and stiffened. No painter subjugates you with such absolute tyranny, and nothing could show better than such a proof the sovereignty of that baptized Phidias who was Michelangelo.

The upper story of the southern portion of the Vatican is devoted to Raphael and his auxiliaries. The rooms or Stanze are the in-

POETRY.

differently distributed and uninhabitable apartments, which Julius II. disposed above the Borgia quarters; the Loggie, commenced by Bramante, are surmounted by galleries constructed, from 1415 onwards, by Raphael, and decorated by that artist, assisted by his school. Before halting at the Loggie, let us enter a sort of antechamber, so justly called the Hall of the Chiaroscuri, and bend our steps towards a narrow door always kept shut, but which an attendant will open for us: it takes you to a small chapel which many strangers miss, and in which we shall see the oldest Florentine frescoes that the Vatican has preserved. How this oratory, which was finished by Nicholas V., escaped the demolitions of Julius II., who swept away from these apartments the paintings of Luca Signorelli and Perugino, save one for which Sanzio interceded,—how Leo X., Clement VII., and after them the partisans of the decline, failed to substitute for the work of the Beato Angelico some pompous mediocrities of Lauretti,—we cannot possibly tell.

This chapel was begun by Fra Angelico under Eugenius IV.

Another pontiff, Nicholas V., the true founder of the Vatican magnificences came and passed long hours in this boudoir for prayer, by the side of Fra Angelico, his old companion of the Dominicans of Florence. While the monk let his brushes work, they discussed pro-

THEOLOGY.

jects for rebuilding St. Peter's, for organising the Vatican library, for concentrating in Rome the intellectual forces of the West.

Six of the frescoes are devoted to the life of St. Stephen, the five others to St. Laurence. Fra Angelico, in the legend of St. Laurence and in that of St. Stephen, has presented Sixtus II. and St. Peter under the likeness of his friend and benefactor, Thomas of Sarzana (Nicholas V.). The Consecration of the two deacons bequeathes to our eyes true likenesses of the pope who celebrated the great jubilee of 1450. A dreamy, delicate, and mystic head; the small, mild, penetrating eye; a small, rather sarcastic mouth, under a big nose, which is so long as to end by becoming pointed—this is the strangest of sympathetic figures.

From the point of view of ideas, if not of processes, this chapel is on the straight road which starts from Gentile da Fabriano and Masaccio, and ends with Raphael.

From this chapel we return to the Loggia.

It was a perilous task to undertake after Michelangelo to illustrate the Bible, and especially to reproduce the creation of the world. Raphael had the art of being great with scanty dimensions; his compositions, while lofty in style, yet preserve the familiar poetry of the legendary narratives. The first acts of the creation, those in which Jehovah struggles with matter, bear comparison with the Sixtine.

It is a fit moment for recalling, for people who have not yet seen Rome, that this dismantled ruin, described as Camera della Segnatura, because once two pontifical tribunes (designated by this word, which means the record of a process) held their sittings in it, has on its walls the Dispute on the Holy Sacrament, placed before the Schools of Athens, as well as Jurisprudence opposite to the Parnassus, and that the four medallions so often engraved, Theology, Philosophy, Poetry, and Justice, adorn in this same room a vault in which the artist has placed subjects from Scripture by way of pendentives. So this Tribune of Raphael contains the most august wonders of his imagination and his pencil.

The subject is the Poem of the Soul. To its overtures correspond the notion of divine things, and then that of natural things (*causarum cognitio*)—the lot of philosophy, which knows better whence they come than whither they go. Hence arise the sentiment of right, and in the ideal order the sentiment of beauty, the correlative of virtue,—art and poetry. These are the four summaries that Raphael has inscribed on the vault under the emblems figured in the medallions Philosophy looks far off; she holds two volumes—one concerning morality, the other the study of external phenomena. Calm, with closed eyes, Justice has a diadem of iron, the metal of force and not of cupidity. Poetry or inspiration (*numine afflatur*) is only spirit and light: the eye is keen, the lips are parted to speak, the face is radiant. Laurels are intertwined in the hair; a lyre to the left and a book to the right symbolise inspiration and study. Indifferent to terrestrial objects, austere and chaste, Theology points with her finger to the Trinity below; she holds only a thick black volume—the Gospels.

In face of the dogma which sums up all, Raphael has described the intellectual labours of the ancient world in search of truths. But the Word had not descended; man being far from the heavens, the light is not so bright : such designed inequality of light gives to the schools of Athens a solid depth, which depends as much on the will of the painter, as on the tendencies of this or that fellow-worker. It is a just and philosophic idea, borrowed perhaps from our mediæval glass and the Byzantine frescoes, that of classing among the precursors, in regard to the saints, Aristotle, by whom logic has come to us, and who, with authoritative hand, points to the earth which his doctrine has subjected ; then Plato, with inspired gestures showing the heavens, whose problem he has dimly discerned. They are surrounded by the

THE FIRST SIN (LA SEGNATURA).

divers schools, but the pagan world is grouped around them. The procession of Aristotle is numerous ; the spiritualistic Plato has fewer followers. In the camp of Aristotle they are more speculative : Euclid, and Archimedes under the features of Bramante, with compass in his hand, are surrounded by their disciples, and are at work at geometry. One of these scholars, seated to the right of Archimedes, is Frederick II., Duke of Mantua, brother-in-law of a nephew of Julius II. Zoroaster unravels the system of the world ; Ptolemy marks out its geography ; every one is at work or else is discussing ; but the pagan prototype of the ascetics, Diogenes, who has just thrown away his basin, turns his back on the schools, and by his indifference demonstrates the nullity of systems. Close by there declare themselves, vague Negation, personified by Arcesilas (the symbol of uncertainty is turned in one direction and looks in another); then Doubt, under the impassive and contemptuous figure of Pyrrho; he watches a disciple repeating with the ardour of conviction the doctrines of Aristotle.

Among the precursors and the faithful of the Platonist company, are Empedocles, Epicharmus, and Pythagoras, with Theologus and Theano, with Anaxagoras and Archytas near them; then the sombre Heraclitus near Æschines, and Socrates, who perceived unity; he is standing and instructing his pupils. Close on their track, approach, after Alcibiades and Xenophon, the young Duke of Urbino della Rovere, and Raphael himself, just opposite Perugino; it was behind Zoroaster that Vasari pointed them out; finally, a good number of those dreamers who, by inspiration, touched the divine intuition, deceiving themselves like Hippias, placed quite at the bottom, or who, though unwearied seekers, found nothing but void and melancholy. A tall young man in a white mantle fringed with gold represents Francis Maria della Rovere, Duke of Urbino by the adoption of Guid' Ubaldo. The classic Aristotle has on his side, in a niche of the façade, Minerva, the wise goddess of constituted bodies; behind Plato is Apollo the inspirer. Among the grisailles of the lower portion figures the Siege of Syracuse, in reference to Archimedes, and in honour of the martyrs of the scientific ideal.

The blameless enforcement of right, the sentiment of perfect equity, seemed to Raphael so far above human passions, that the attributes of jurisprudence present themselves alone, without any historic personage. A head with two faces, Jurisprudence, serene, and with an expression of mildness and clemency, with her young profile looks into the mirror (see p. 281). In her breast is fixed in a medallion the winged head of a Gorgon. Moderation offers her a bridle, and Penetration his torch. The past instructs her: she looks behind her with the profile of an old man. Protecting Force, armed with a green branch, which would be an olive if *la Rovere* did not mean an oak, and seated on a lion, completes this exquisite and noble group, which, for a wonder, Audran has not made too dull: people may form a tolerably just idea of it at the French School of Fine Arts, in an excellent copy by Paul Baudry. The neighbouring compartment is shared between the civil law and the common law: on one side Justinian hands the Digest to Tribonian:

on the other, Gregory IX. receives the Decretals, under the features of Julius II., who is attended—priceless likenesses—by two cardinals destined to be his successors, Giovanni de' Medici, still young, who is to be Leo X., and Alexander Farnese, who will become Paul III. Near them, a third prelate represents the Cardinal del Monte. It is in the background of this fresco that chance has executed by Raphael's hand a striking likeness of Napoleon I. The authenticity of these pictures has been discussed: they are the master's; only, having been more damaged than the others by the Tedeschi of the Constable, they have been more restored than was necessary. In the grisailles of the plinth, which pursue the idea in its development, and which were executed by Polydore of Caravaggio, aided by Maturino the Florentine, Moses and Solon promulgate their laws.

What shall we say, finally, of that glorification of poetry, which collects on one Parnassus, to honour the Italy of Petrarch and Dante, all the great poets under the patronage of the Muses and the presidency of Apollo? Consecrated to the revival of ancient literature, this piece breathes all the enthusiasm of the sublime years which opened the sixteenth century. Placed opposite to a blonde and tender picture, the Parnassus has a very firm tone, with amber lights to bring out the adorable figures with which Raphael endows the ten Muses, including Sappho among them. Under this name, the master sketched the profile of one of the intelligences of his time, the courtesan Imperia, to whom the casuists pardoned much because she loved the beautiful much. Dying young and bewept by the greatest men, the idol of Augustin Chigi, Imperia, worthy of the time of Pericles, made herself the muse of the friendship which encourages and sustains. A purer celebrity, Vittoria Colonna,—sprung through her mother from the Montefeltro family, who of their palace at Urbino had made another Parnassus,—Vittoria is drawn sitting, sceptre in hand, at the feet of Apollo. This profile, which in the medals rivals antique cameos, is easily recognisable; in immortalising this heavenly creature, Raphael rewarded her beforehand for the devotion with which she was soon to surround Michelangelo; a holy flame, which was the consolation and stay and last joy of the noble old man!

To show to what a degree Raphael was a colourist, it would be enough to isolate one of the corner panels; that, for instance, in which the figures of Poetry and Philosophy, divided by small camaieux, surmount the masterpiece, of such purity of design, in which the First Fault is represented. The gilded field of the sky, coloured by a delicate chequer imitating mosaic, plays with the ground of verdure, whence stands out with rosy freshness the young and supple body of the first woman: the arabesques of the frame, in which the pearl-grey and the blue are harmonised by the golds accented by flame-colour, isolate and bring out this wonderful gem. The finest of the four medallions from the point of view of colour is Philosophy.

The ceiling of the Sixtine Chapel, and the Camera della Segnatura, offer a synthesis of modern art raised to the intelligence of ancient art; this is my reason for closing the exploration of Rome by the study of these two monuments.

THE END.

PRINTED BY J. S. VIRTUE AND CO., LIMITED, CITY ROAD, LONDON.

www.ingramcontent.com/pod-product-compliance
Lightning Source LLC
Chambersburg PA
CBHW030428300426
44112CB00009B/908